MODERN BRITISH PLAYWRITING: 2000 – 2009

VOICES, DOCUMENTS, NEW INTERPRETATIONS

Dan Rebellato is Professor of Contemporary Theatre and head of the Drama and Theatre department at Royal Holloway University of London, UK. He is the author of *Theatre & Globalization* (2009) and *1956 and All That* (1999), *The Suspect Culture Book* (2013) and co-editor with Maria Delgado of *Contemporary European Theatre Directors* (2010). He is on the editorial board of *Contemporary Theatre Review* and is a contributing editor for *New Theatre Quarterly*. He is also a playwright, and his work (plays and translations/adaptations) has been performed on stage and radio in Britain, Europe and America.

In the same series from Bloomsbury Methuen Drama:

MODERN BRITISH PLAYWRITING: THE 1950s
by David Pattie
Includes detailed studies of works by T. S. Eliot, Terence Rattigan, John Osborne and Arnold Wesker

MODERN BRITISH PLAYWRITING: THE 1960s
by Steve Nicholson
Includes detailed studies of works by John Arden, Edward Bond, Harold Pinter and Alan Ayckbourn

MODERN BRITISH PLAYWRITING: THE 1970s
by Chris Megson
Includes detailed studies of works by Caryl Churchill, David Edgar, Howard Brenton and David Hare

MODERN BRITISH PLAYWRITING: THE 1980s
by Jane Milling
Includes detailed studies of works by Howard Barker, David Lane, Sarah Daniels and Timberlake Wertenbaker

MODERN BRITISH PLAYWRITING: THE 1990s
by Aleks Sierz
Includes detailed studies of works by Philip Ridley, Sarah Kane, Anthony Neilson and Mark Ravenhill

MODERN BRITISH PLAYWRITING: 2000 – 2009

VOICES, DOCUMENTS, NEW INTERPRETATIONS

Edited by Dan Rebellato

Series Editors: Richard Boon and Philip Roberts

B L O O M S B U R Y
LONDON • NEW DELHI • NEW YORK • SYDNEY

BLACKBURN COLLEGE
LIBRARY

Acc. No. BB56642
Class No. UCL 822.9209 REB
Date 23.01.14

Bloomsbury Methuen Drama
An imprint of Bloomsbury Publishing Plc

50 Bedford Square	1385 Broadway
London	New York
WC1B 3DP	NY 10018
UK	USA

www.bloomsbury.com

Bloomsbury is a registered trademark of Bloomsbury Publishing Plc

First published 2013

© Dan Rebellato, Jacqueline Bolton, Michael Pearce, Nadine Holdsworth,
Lynette Goddard, Andrew Haydon, 2013

All extracts in chapter 3 Documents are copyright the respective authors.

All rights reserved. No part of this publication may be reproduced or
transmitted in any form or by any means, electronic or mechanical,
including photocopying, recording, or any information storage or
retrieval system, without prior permission in writing from the publishers.

Dan Rebellato, Jacqueline Bolton, Michael Pearce, Nadine Holdsworth and
Lynette Goddard have asserted their rights under the Copyright, Designs
and Patents Act, 1988, to be identified as authors of this work.

The moral right of Andrew Haydon to be identified as the author of
chapter 1 has been asserted.

No responsibility for loss caused to any individual or organization acting
on or refraining from action as a result of the material in this publication
can be accepted by Bloomsbury or the authors.

British Library Cataloguing-in-Publication Data
A catalogue record for this book is available from the British Library.

ISBN: HB: 978-1-4081-8199-7
PB: 978-1-4081-2956-2
ePub: 978-1-4081-7787-7
ePDF: 978-1-4081-2958-6

Library of Congress Cataloging-in-Publication Data
A catalog record for this book is available from the Library of Congress.

Typeset by Newgen Imaging Systems Pvt, Ltd, Chennai, India
Printed and bound in India

CONTENTS

GENERAL PREFACE

This book is one of a series of six volumes which seek to characterize the nature of modern British playwriting from the 1950s to the end of the first decade of this new century. The work of these six decades is comparable in its range, experimentation and achievement only to the drama of the Elizabethan and Jacobean dramatists. The series chronicles its flowering and development.

Each volume addresses the work of four representative dramatists (five in the *2000s* volume) by focusing on key works and by placing that work in a detailed contextual account of the theatrical, social, political and cultural climate of the era.

The series revisits each decade from the perspective of the twenty-first century. We recognize that there is an inevitable danger of imposing a spurious neatness on its subject. So while each book focuses squarely on the particular decade and its representative authors, we have been careful to ensure that some account is given of relevant material from earlier years and, where relevant, of subsequent developments. And while the intentions and organization of each volume are essentially the same, we have also allowed for flexibility, the better to allow both for the particular demands of the subject and the particular approach of our author/editors.

It is also the case, of course, that differences of historical perspective across the series influence the nature of the books. For student readers, the difference at its most extreme is between a present they daily inhabit and feel they know intimately and a decade (the 1950s) in which their parents or even grandparents might have been born; between a time of seemingly unlimited consumer choice and one which began with post-war food rationing still in place. Further, a playwright who began work in the late 1960s (David Hare, say) has a far bigger body of work and associated scholarship than one whose emergence has come within the last decade or so (debbie tucker green, for example). A glance at the

Bibliographies for the earliest and latest volumes quickly reveals huge differences in the range of secondary material available to our authors and to our readers. This inevitably means that the later volumes allow a greater space to their contributing essayists for original research and scholarship, but we have also actively encouraged revisionist perspectives – new looks – on the 'older guard' in earlier books.

So while each book can and does stand alone, the series as a whole offers as coherent and comprehensive a view of the whole era as possible.

Throughout, we have had in mind two chief objectives. We have made accessible information and ideas that will enable today's students of theatre to acquaint themselves with the nature of the world inhabited by the playwrights of the last 60 years; and we offer new, original and often surprising perspectives on both established and developing dramatists.

Richard Boon and Philip Roberts
Series Editors
September 2011

Richard Boon is Emeritus Professor of Drama at the University of Hull, UK.

Philip Roberts is Emeritus Professor of Drama and Theatre Studies at the University of Leeds, UK.

Acknowledgements

Thanks are due to all the contributors to this book for their rigour and timeliness and to Tim Crouch, David Greig, Simon Stephens and Roy Williams who so generously gave me access to unpublished works. Particular thanks go to Jacqueline Bolton for putting together Simon Stephens's unpublished material and to Andrew Haydon for stepping in to provide a punchy survey of the decade. I am very grateful to Richard Boon and Philip Roberts for the invitation to contribute to this series and to Mark Dudgeon for guiding it on its way – thanks, in particular, for not insisting that this volume be called 'The Noughties'. My colleagues and students at Royal Holloway have informed my thinking about the theatre of this period and I find it almost impossible to separate my thought from theirs.

For me the best thing about this fascinating decade was meeting Lilla, who has been there through this book's evolution, and to whom I gratefully dedicate it.

INTRODUCTION
LIVING IN THE 2000s

1. Domestic life

What things cost

	2000	2010	% increase
A pint of milk	34p	44p	29
A litre of petrol	77p	112p	45
A first-class stamp	27p	41p	52
A colour TV licence	£104	£145	39
Average West End theatre ticket	£28.84 (2001)	£45.12	56
How much computer memory you can buy for £100	20GBs	1TB	5000
Average salary	£18,939	£26,510	40
Average house price	c.£80,000	c.£165,000	106
Inflation across the decade			30

What we bought
DVD box sets, iPods and iPod docks, iPhones, iPads, smartphones, Nintendo DS, Sony PSP, Xbox, PS2, Wii, flatscreen TVs, HD TVs, e-books, scooters, wi-fi broadband, hybrid cars, GPS systems, Guitar Hero, World of Warcraft, The Sims, Grand Theft Auto, Ugg Boots, Crocs, aviator shades, skinny jeans, digital cameras and camcorders, Bratz Dolls, moleskine notebooks, netbooks, Big Mouth Billy Bass, Activia yoghurt and music by James Blunt, Dido, Amy Winehouse, Leona Lewis and Coldplay.

What we didn't pay for
Google, newspapers, movies, music, Skype, Facebook, Twitter, MySpace, LinkedIn, Tumblr, Wordpress . . .

Family life

Marriage continues its 30-year decline. The post-war peak in the marriage rate was 1972, which saw 425,241 marriages. By 2010, this figure has almost halved to 232,990. However, to that figure we might add the 40,000 civil partnerships conducted after December 2005. The number of cohabiting couples increases sharply from 2.1 million in 2001 to 2.9 million ten years later.

The divorce rate, meanwhile, is also gradually decreasing from its peak in 1994, which saw 14.2 divorces per 1,000 of population, to 10.5 per 1,000 in 2009, the lowest figure since 1977.

Although in October 2007 a report by Population Action International finds that Britain had the highest rate of teenage pregnancy in Europe, these figures are slowly declining through the decade from 42.7 conceptions per 1,000 girls aged 15–17 in 2001 to 38.3 in 2009. The number of single-parent families grew steadily from 1.7 million in 2001 to just under 2 million in 2010. In 2010 half a million more people are living alone than the 7 million in 2001.

Language in the 2000s

The ubiquity of internet use creates acres of new vocabulary; a new generation of **digital natives** would **ego-surf**, **google**, **blog** and **podcast**. The best might be **citizen journalists** and **netizens**, but they might also be **lurkers**, **trolls**, **cybersquatters** or **cyberbullies**, conducting **flame-wars**, **pwning** or **rickrolling** you or **phishing** for your personal details. They might use **tablets**, **avatars**, **apps**, **wikis** and **web 2.0**, would participate in the **blogosphere**, **crowdsourcing** ideas and watching **tweets** and **status updates** go **viral**. They ♥ their **smartphones**, especially the **Crackberry**, sometimes to the neglect of their friends ☹.

Elsewhere you might meet **fanboys**, **chuggers**, **free range kids**, **yummy mummies** and **milfs**, **metrosexuals**, a **bridezilla**, a **hoodie** or **chav** with an **ASBO** or a **WAG** with a **trout pout**. You might have a lot of **bling** or be **fugly**, **drop the f-bomb**, go **glamping**, play **buzzword bingo**, **rock up** for a **flash mob** or get involved in a **bromance**. Words and phrases from popular culture as always make their way into ordinary speech and people would ask **'am I bovvered?'**, describe someone as **'the only gay (or anything else) in the village'**, and note that someone or something **'does exactly what it says on the tin'**.

Simples! It is reported that **slebs** sometimes referred to non-celebrities as **'muggles'.** The point where something goes into decline after losing sight of its original idea is referred to as **jumping the shark** (after an episode of 1970s sitcom *Happy Days* involving an improbable shark jump) but after an eccentric appearance of the Oprah Winfrey show where Tom Cruise 'athletically' expressed his love for Katie Holmes this could also be called **jumping the couch.**

Typical comic word-formations come from adding prefixes and suffixes like **-fest** (boozefest), **-tastic** (glamtastic), or **uber-** (uber-expensive). New slang terms include **bred** (mates), **bare** (a lot), **buff** (sexy), **dope** or **sick** (cool), **butters** (ugly), **safe** (hello), **jokes** (funny), **brap!** (gunshot). During the decade **'pants'** disappears as a word for 'bad', to be replaced by **'gay'.** A new word of approval for anything unusual is **'random'.**

Politics produced its own vocabulary: the **war on terror** gave us **shock and awe, axis of evil, extraordinary rendition, WMD, regime change, homeland security, freedom fries, sexing up, dodgy dossier;** UK domestic politics produces **the third way, big tent politics, joined-up thinking, the big society, dog-whistle politics, Blairistas** and **Cameroons, non-doms, flipping** and the policy idea to **hug a hoodie.** Environmental politics gives us **carbon footprint** and **greenwashing.** US satirist Stephen Colbert describes George W Bush's slippery rhetoric as **'truthiness'.**

Smoking continues its slow decline, marginally aided by the introduction of a smoking ban in public places that came into force in July 2007. The long-term trend is very marked, however, with numbers of smokers almost halving between 1980 and 2009.

Not unconnected with this trend, life expectancy continues to rise through the decade, passing the 80-year mark for women.

2. Society

Work

Until the credit crunch of 2008 (see p. 31), Britain in the first decade of the twentieth century is a pretty prosperous place. Average salaries outstrip inflation across the decade, house prices double and unemployment goes from 1.7 million in January 2000 to below 1.4 million in September 2004, the lowest rate since the 1970s.

3

As the credit crunch begins to hit, this pattern is thrown into reverse, unemployment reaching 2.47 million in September 2009 (it would go even higher as the recession settled in).

What jobs are we doing? According to the Office of National Statistics, by the end of 2010, 82.6 per cent jobs were in the service sector and only 8.1 per cent in manufacturing. This confirms the long-term trend away from manufacturing and towards services – in 1970 the service sector accounted for 53 per cent of the UK economy, compared to around 75 per cent 40 years later.

Crime

The decade sees the paradoxical pattern of crime rates falling, particularly for violent crimes, yet a widespread perception that the crime rate is increasing. This may be connected to a number of high-profile murders, particularly of children and old people, and disproportionate media coverage of race-related criminality.

Corporate scandals

In 2002, several major US corporations collapse amid accusations of serious fraud. The most high profile is the energy company Enron, which had been named 'America's most innovative company' by *Fortune* magazine for six years in succession; after the company files for bankruptcy in December 2001, it becomes clear that its financial strength is an illusion produced by accounting practices that hide its enormous losses. The company's Chairman Kenneth Lay and CEO [Chief Executive Officer] Jeffrey Skilling are put on trial in January 2004 and are both found guilty four months later. The scandal also brings down the major accounting firm Arthur Andersen, which is shown to have failed in its responsibility to accurately audit Enron's accounts, and is guilty of shredding documents in advance of the judicial investigation. The Enron scandal is quickly followed by the collapse of telecommunications company WorldCom, where accounting irregularities are estimated to have inflated the true value of its assets by $11 billion. The company's CEO, Bernard Ebbers, is sentenced to 25 years in prison for his part in the affair. In late summer 2002, the CEO L Dennis Kozlowski and CFO [Chief Financial Officer] Mark Swartz of Tyco International are revealed to have stolen and defrauded over $150 million from the company,

4

using Tyco funds to buy and furnish Kozlowski's apartment, including a notorious $6,000 shower curtain. In the same year, similar accounting fraud and insider trading are discovered at Global Crossing, Qwest, Kmart, Adelphia Communications and ImClone Systems, whose subsequent trial for fraud sent domestic goddess Martha Stewart to prison for five months. The revelations of corporate fraud and personal greed, alongside President Bush's reluctance to act decisively, raise significant doubts about capitalism, reinforced six years later as the credit crunch hit.

The decade begins with the conviction of Dr Harold Shipman, a family GP, believed to be responsible for more than 250 killings. (When he hangs himself in prison in August 2007, the *Sun* reports the news under the headline 'Ship Ship Hooray'.) But it is crimes against children that receive most coverage. In July 2000, eight-year old Sarah Payne is abducted and murdered by registered sex offender Roy Whiting in West Sussex. In March 2002, 13-year-old Milly Dowler is kidnapped and murdered by serial killer Levi Bellfield. In August that year, in Soham, Cambridgeshire, school caretaker Ian Huntley, seemingly without motive, lures ten-year-olds Holly Wells and Jessica Chapman into his home and kills them. Perhaps the most high-profile disappearance of the decade comes in May 2007, when Madeleine McCann, aged three, disappears from her parents' holiday home in the Algarve and at the time of writing has still not been found.

Dreadful though these events are, they seem to exert a peculiar grip on the tabloid press, which stops at nothing in pursuit of the story. In the aftermath of Sarah Payne's murder, the *News of the World* decides to 'name and shame' convicted sex offenders by printing their photographs and locations in its pages. The vigilante mentality this unleashes includes an infamous episode in August 2001 when Dr Yvette Cloete has her home vandalized by a mob unaware of the difference between a paedophile and a paediatrician. In 2011, as part of the Leveson Inquiry, an investigation into the behaviour of the press, it is alleged that journalists 'hacked' Milly Dowler's phone, deleting messages, thus giving her parents false hope that she is still alive. The testimony of Madeleine McCann's parents to Leveson is a devastating story of bullying, intrusion and harassment by the press.

These crimes remain, for all their horror, domestic. The 2000s also sees criminality on a global scale. The early part of the decade sees a series of Corporate scandals (see p. 4) that produce devastating financial collapses, but even those are dwarfed by the greed and negligence that lead to the global economic downturn of 2008. The decade also sees the establishment of the International Criminal Court to try crimes against humanity, genocide and war crimes. Some argued that the invasion of Iraq is itself a war crime and call for the arrest of the political leaders that masterminded it.

Others would point to perhaps the most horrifyingly spectacular single act of criminality of the decade, perhaps of the century: 9/11.

9/11

On the morning on 11 September 2001, a group of 19 young men hijack four passenger jets. At 8.46 am, American Airlines Flight 11 is deliberately piloted into the North Tower of the World Trade Centre in lower Manhattan. At 9.03 am, when the second plane, United Airlines Flight 175, strikes the South Tower, the United States realizes it is under attack. Half an hour later, American Airlines Flight 77 is flown into the Pentagon in Virginia. A little after 10.00 am, United Airline Flight 93, possibly headed for the White House, is brought down by its own passengers in a field in Pennsylvania. The fires burning in the Twin Towers weaken its steel structure and half an hour apart, both towers collapse. 2,996 people are killed in the attacks. Osama bin Laden, founder of militant jihadist group al-Qaeda, claims responsibility for the attacks, citing US policy towards Israel, the presence of US troops in Saudi Arabia and sanctions against Iraq. 9/11, as it would come to be known, dominates global politics for the decade, leading to the so-called War on Terror and a number of retaliatory terrorist attacks around the world.

Terrorism

The 2000s sees an intensification of global terrorism, much of it associated with jihadist groups like al-Qaeda, Jemaah Islamiyah or

Abu Sayyaf, which believe that Western global hegemony needs to be resisted in the name of Islam. What is distinctive about this new wave of jihadist terrorism is its use of suicide bombers and its mass targeting of civilians. However, in Afghanistan and Iraq, al-Qaeda and other groups use these methods to support the insurgency against occupying Western forces.

2000 *Oct* USS Cole bombed while being refuelled in Aden, Yemen (17 dead).

2001 *Sep* 9/11 attacks on United States (see box p. 6)

2002 *Oct* Bali Bombings: attacks on nightclubs in the tourist district of Bali (202 dead)

2003 *Nov* Istanbul bombings: attacks on two synagogues and the British Consulate (61 dead)

2004 *Feb* SuperFerry 14 Bombing: a ferry setting out from Manila explodes (116 dead)

    Mar Madrid bombing: ten bombs on four commuter trains kill 191 people and cause 1,800 casualties

    Mar Ashura Massacre: Iraq, coordinated attacks including rocket launches and suicide bombings (178 dead)

2005 *Jul* 7/7: London bombings on public transport (see box below)

2006 *Nov* Sadr City Bombings: coordinated attacks (215 dead)

2007 *Apr* Baghdad Bombings: coordinated attacks (198 dead)

    Aug Qahtaniya and Jazeera, in Iraq: coordinated suicide bombing attacks on Yazidi (Kurdish minority) communities (796 dead)

2008 *Nov* Mumbai attacks. Eleven coordinated and simultaneous attacks kill 164

7/7

On the morning of 7 July 2005, four jihadist terrorists detonate bombs on the London Underground and one on a double-decker bus, killing 56 and injuring 700. Three of the bombers come from Leeds and one from Buckinghamshire. In a videotaped message discovered after the attacks, the seniormost of the four men, Mohammad Siddique Khan, claims that the attacks were in response to the British government's attacks on Muslims in Afghanistan and Iraq, and its support for the United States and Israel.

A fortnight later, there is a copycat attack, with three bombs on the Underground and one on a bus, but the detonators fail and the bombers are all arrested by the end of the month. In June 2007, two car bombs are discovered and defused before they can go off, and almost simultaneously a Jeep, loaded with explosives, is driven through the walls of Glasgow Airport; the impact detonates some of the gas canisters and the two would-be terrorists flee, on fire, from the jeep where they are apprehended by baggage handler John Smeaton, who explains, 'I thought, "Glasgow doesn't accept this. This is Glasgow; we'll set aboot ye"', and becomes a national hero.

Not all terrorism in the period is associated with jihadist groups. In Russia, an ongoing struggle for independence by Chechen militants – more nationalist than religious – sees civilians targeted in the early part of the decade with bombings on a commuter train in December 2003, on the Moscow Metro in February 2004, and on two domestic passenger aircraft in August that year. In October 2002, three armed groups storm a Moscow theatre holding its audience captive and in September 2004 other separatist militants hold 1,100 children and teachers hostage in a school in Beslan, North Ossetia. 700 people die in these actions. More mysterious are the anonymous letters containing Anthrax sent to journalists and politicians in the United States in the immediate aftermath of 9/11, in which five are killed. A year later, over three weeks in October 2002, a sniper kills ten people in and around Washington DC before being apprehended. The motive for these killings has never been satisfactorily explained.

Sexual politics

The 2000s are mixed for feminism. The pay gap between men and women slowly continues to narrow, though by the end of the decade it is still calculated at 20.2 per cent. Women continue to make inroads to the top jobs in business, politics and culture. In 2007, there are eight women in Tony Blair's Cabinet, and Gordon Brown appoints Jacqui

Smith the first woman Home Secretary in UK history. However, a BBC survey in 2011 finds that while women make up 36.5 per cent of Head Teachers and public appointments, in other fields, like the military and the senior judiciary, figures are very much lower. Only 16 per cent of board members of FTSE-100 companies are women.

In addition, Ariel Levy argues in *Female Chauvinist Pigs* (2005) that some of the gains in dignity and independence made by women in the 1970s and 1980s are now in reverse. In particular, there is a hypersexualization of women in popular culture – perhaps well characterized by The Pussycat Dolls and the resurgence of burlesque and pole dancing as supposedly liberating activities for women – which filters down to street fashions and behaviour. Carmine Sarracino and Kevin Scott in *The Porning of America* (2008) note how images and attitudes from hardcore pornography have flooded into the mainstream, where making a sex tape or dressing like a porn star has become, to some extent, normalized.

For lesbians and gay men, the decade sees a major breakthrough in the passing of the Civil Partnership Act in December 2005 after which, for the first time, same-sex couples can have their relationships legally recognized in a civil ceremony. By the early 2010s, both the British Prime Minister and the US President have expressed sympathy for the idea of legalizing gay marriage itself.

In 2000 the ban of homosexuals serving in the armed forces is lifted and Section 28 of the Local Government Act 1988 (which restricted Local Authorities from supporting homosexuality) is repealed in Scotland (2003 in the rest of the United Kingdom). In 2001, the age of consent for homosexuals is reduced to 16, the same as for heterosexuals. In 2005, equal rights of adoption and in 2008 equal rights to fertility treatment are established between gay and straight people and the Equality Act (Sexual Orientation) Regulations of 2007 prohibits any discrimination in the offering of goods and services.

Some of these laws are tested in the courts. In 2007, Andrew McClintock, a magistrate, goes to an employment tribunal claiming religious discrimination because his Christian beliefs apparently do not permit him to place children for adoption with gay couples and he has been forced to resign. In 2008, Peter and Hazel Bull refuse, on religious grounds, to allow a gay couple to stay in their Cornwall hotel and are taken to court. In both cases, the Courts uphold the laws against discrimination.

Homophobia has not disappeared though. In 1999 neo-Nazi David Copeland bombs The Admiral Duncan, a gay pub in London, as part of his far-right terrorist campaign. Through the decade there is a series of homophobic murders including those of Jody Dobrowski, Michael Causer and Ian Baynham.

Race and politics

Race continues to be a faultline in British culture. It takes nearly 19 years after the murder of black teenager Stephen Lawrence in 1993, to find the racist perpetrators of the crime guilty. The police's failure to investigate the crime properly, indeed the institutional racism of the police, continues to rumble through the decade. In 2012, the Institute of Race Relations names 96 racist murders since that of Stephen Lawrence, 61 of them in the 2000s.

Racial tensions are heightened after the terrorist violence of 9/11 and the London Bombings of July 2005 and the Islamic communities in Britain increasingly find themselves subject to hostile commentary and attacks. Tensions between Black British and British-Asian groups spill over into violence in a race riot in Birmingham in October 2005. Particular anxiety focuses on the body- and face-covering *burqa* and *niqab*; government minister Jack Straw in October 2006 expresses discomfort at talking to women whose face he cannot see. Debates about the veil muddily mix concerns about separatism and integration, women's rights and anxieties about terrorism. Straw's (relatively mild) remarks are taken up by right-wing newspapers like the *Daily Express* who campaign for the veil to be banned.

The far right is quick to exploit tensions over Islam in Britain. The fascist British National Party is sharply criticized for using an image of the London Bombings on an election leaflet with the words 'Maybe now it's time to start listening to the BNP'. They emerge from the 2006 local elections with 49 councillors nationally which rises to 55 in 2008. In the 2009 elections to the European Parliament, the BNP wins 2 seats. This is the high point of their electoral success and influence and, controversially, their leader Nick Griffin is invited to appear on BBC's *Question Time* in October. His performance is not impressive and in the next two years, the party is torn apart by internal conflicts and in the 2012 local elections it will be virtually wiped out.

In August 2009, the English Defence League (EDL) is formed, a mixture of far-right activists and football hooligans, who claim their only ambition is to resist the influence of Islam in Britain. Their demonstrations, though not large, are marked by intimidation, vandalism and violence. Their attempts to present themselves as reasonable and moderate are undermined by the relevation that the Norwegian neo-Nazi mass-murderer Anders Behring Breivik met and was influenced by the leadership of the EDL.

Environment

In February 2007, the Intergovernmental Panel on Climate Change concludes that the case for global warming being caused by human activity is 'unequivocal'. In September 2007, scientists are shocked to discover how quickly the Arctic ice cap is disappearing – far more quickly than any previous models have predicted. The decline in sea ice will mean a rise in sea levels and represents a significant threat to several low-lying territories around the world. Other likely symptoms of global warming include the heatwave that sweeps Europe in August 2003 and leads to 35,000 deaths and Hurricane Katrina which devastates New Orleans in August 2005.

There is a good deal of public attention to the threat of environmental catastrophe. Former US Vice-President Al Gore's documentary *An Inconvenient Truth* (2006) is a surprise box-office hit around the world. A well-meaning series of rock concerts, Live Earth, in July 2007, attempts to publicize the need for environmental action, though the event itself is estimated to have a carbon footprint of around 75,000 tonnes. Novels like Cormac McCarthy's *The Road* (2006) and Margaret Atwood's *The Year of the Flood* (2009) depict the consequences of global ecological catastrophe in unsparing terms.

Frustratingly, there does not seem to be the political will to do anything about it. The Kyoto Protocol of 1997, which committed its signatories to significant reductions in greenhouse gases is signed by

191 states, though not the world's biggest producer of carbon emissions, the United States. In June 2007 leaders at the G8 summit release a communiqué announcing their 'aim to at least halve CO_2 emissions by 2050'. Many criticize the vague figure, the long timescale, and the fact that the commitment was not binding. Bizarrely, the United Nations (UN) Climate Change Conference of 2009 recognizes the need to act urgently to limit global warming but offers no binding commitments to do anything. The 2009 European Union (EU) Energy Directive commits the United Kingdom to generate 15 per cent of its energy from renewable sources by 2020 and the 2009 Budget sharply increases funding for wind farms; however, less than 5 per cent of UK energy is from renewable sources by the end of the decade.

Carbon fuels continue to be at the heart of the Western way of life and governments are wary of meddling, even in the face of potential catastrophe (and the Deepwater Horizon oil spill in April 2010 is a reminder of the oil industry's immediate capacity for disaster). A loose coalition of right-wingers, suspicious of government intervention, and Big Oil, wanting to protect its financial interests, successfully confuses public opinion. A leak of emails from the University of East Anglia's Climate Research Unit is exploited by climate-change sceptics to suggest that scientists had been hiding or manipulating data. Although these claims are found to be baseless, a BBC poll in February 2010 finds that only 26 per cent of British adults believe that global warming is the result of human activity, a sharp contrast to the near unanimity of the scientific community.

3. Culture

Music

More than any individual band or singer, the most important influence on music in the 2000s is its means of distribution. The development of the MP3 encoding format means that music is suddenly very portable and very shareable. Websites like Napster, Limewire and Pirate Bay begin to post MP3 files of songs that can be downloaded quickly, without cost or loss of quality. In January 2001, Apple releases iTunes, a convenient way to download and store legal downloads on a computer, and, in November that year, releases the first-generation iPod, making it possible to carry your entire music collection with you. In February 2010, the ten-billionth track is downloaded from iTunes (which, you will be delighted to know, was 'Guess Things Happen That Way' by Johnny Cash).

This has several effects: first, it represents a major challenge to the music industry, which sees a substantial loss of earnings from piracy; however, their attempts to sue file-sharers are widely regarded as heavy-handed and largely ineffective. Touring becomes a more reliable source of income than recording, a shift symbolized most directly in October 2007, when Madonna signs a new $120 million contract not with a record label but with a concert promoter, Live Nation. On the other hand, it becomes possible to make music cheaply and easily with home software like Audacity (2000) or Apple's GarageBand (2004) and upload it within seconds for listeners worldwide, bypassing record labels. Sites like YouTube and MySpace are also new ways for singers and bands to find a public.

In the 2000s, music's encoding as digital object has some effects within the music itself. Electronica of various kinds becomes mainstream, from the ambient wizardry of Iceland's Sigur Rós to the global reach of Lady Gaga. Music as a digital form is apparent in the music itself; Cher's 1998 hit 'Believe' had used Auto-Tune technology to create a prominent electronic vocal effect and auto-tune is a dominant sound in the 2000s, ranging from Daft Punk's 'One More Time' (2000) to Rihanna's 'Disturbia' (2008). Music as digital object has other effects too: the track can be disassembled and re-assembled very easily. Remixes and sampling date back at least to the 1970s, but the 2000s sees the emergence of the 'mashup' as a musical form, in which two or more songs are fused together to create a radical new juxtaposition. The most celebrated example is Grey Mouse's *The Grey Album* which wittily combines Jay-Z's *The Black Album* (2003) with The Beatles' *White Album* (1968), but also notable is Dean Gray's *American Edit* (2005) which prolifically and joyfully mashes up every song on Green Day's *American Idiot* (2004) with a range of samples from Queen's 'Bohemian Rhapsody' (1975) to the *Doctor Who* theme (1963).

Mashups go mainstream with The Sugababes's 'Freak Like Me' (2002) which mixed Adina Howard's 1995 hit with a massive sample from Gary Numan's 'Are "Friends" Electric?' (1979) and Madonna's 'Hung Up' (2005) which builds itself around a huge slice of ABBA's 'Gimme! Gimme! Gimme! A Man After Midnight' (1979).

Since listeners can download songs in isolation, the decade sees a cultural shift away from the album to the individual track. This and the greater availability of free music mean wider and more promiscuous music tastes. As a result, perhaps, the first decade of the twenty-first century is a time of extraordinary variety in music, not dominated by any one genre. The decade sees waves of interest in Emo, Skate, Nu Metal, Dubstep and Nu Folk. In 2003, 1980s hair-metal even has a brief comeback with the success of The Darkness's 'I Believe in a Thing Called Love'. British indie, in the form of bands like Bloc Party, The Editors, Keane, Snow Patrol, is a continuing presence but the energy of BritPop seems exhausted and the much-touted Next Big Things of British indie – Franz Ferdinand, The Arctic Monkeys, The Libertines – never quite manage to achieve the unifying national profile of a band like Oasis in the 1990s. Only Coldplay, purveyors of stately anthemic rock, go from indie to global success.

Undoubtedly the characteristic sound of the decade is Urban: a loose genre incorporating Hip-Hop, dance music and R&B, marked by American artists like Rihanna, Beyoncé, Alicia Keys and Usher. UK Hip-Hop is vigorously renewed by the development of Grime in the early part of the decade, marked by deep basslines, complex rhythms and lyrics that turn away from the gangsta and bling of US Hip-Hop to darker, more authentically British experiences. Wiley, Dizzee Rascal and Lady Sovereign are the first to come to public attention, but by the end of the decade it appears as if this music, too, has been almost entirely commercialized. The Streets, a band name that disguised the multi-instrumentalist Mike Skinner, produce several Hip-Hop/Garage albums of unusual complexity and wit.

Five of the ten top-selling singles of the decade are produced by reality TV shows, like *Pop Idol*, *Popstars* and *X Factor* and the deft move of these shows is to realize that ten weeks of promotion is almost guaranteed to produce huge record sales, even if most of the careers of these 'stars' are short-lived. Two exceptions came in 2002: Will Young who wins *Pop Idol* and Girls Aloud who win *Popstars The Rivals*. Both go on to forge respectable careers; Girls Aloud's distinctive pop-mash-up style is created by Xenomania, a production team of genius, who create some of the most inventive and memorable pop music of the decade, including Girls Aloud's 'Wake Me Up' (2004) and 'Biology' (2005), Sugababes' 'Round Round' (2002) and 'Hole in the Head' (2003), Frank's 'I'm Not Shy' (2006), and albums for Franz Ferdinand and The Pet Shop Boys. Indeed, unless the rock snobs prevail, maybe the 2000s will be seen as a golden age of chart pop, with inventive and uplifting singles taking us right through the decade from All Saints' 'Pure Shores' (2000) and Kylie Minogue's 'Can't Get You Out of My Head' (2001) to Beyoncé's 'Single Ladies (Put A Ring On It)' (2008) and Lady Gaga's 'Bad Romance' (2009).

Books

The best-selling novels of the 2000s are the seven Harry Potter books by J. K. Rowling (1997–2007) which together sell close to 450 million copies. The best-selling single book is Dan Brown's *The Da Vinci Code* (2003), believed to have sold 80 million copies by 2009. Stieg Larsson's 'Millennium' trilogy – *The Girl with the Dragon Tattoo* (2005), *The Girl Who Played with Fire* (2006) and *The Girl Who Kicked the Hornet's Nest* (2007) – is ubiquitous at the end of the decade.

> 'The [Harry] Potter books in general are a prolonged argument for tolerance, a prolonged plea for an end to bigotry, and I think it's one of the reasons that some people don't like the books, but I think that it's a very healthy message to pass on to younger people that you should question authority and you should not assume that the establishment or the press tells you all of the truth'.
>
> J. K. Rowling, 2009

A surprise literary fashion is the 'misery memoir', autobiographical accounts of surviving traumatic experiences, particularly abuse. The genre grows large enough through the decade to get its own section in bookshops, sometimes called 'Tragic Life Stories', sometimes 'Painful Lives'. Estimated in 2008 to amount to 9 per cent of the UK book market and typified by titles like *Please, Daddy, No* by Stuart Howarth and *Don't Tell Mummy* by Toni Maguire (both 2006), the genre begins to fall into disrepute as doubts circulate about the authenticity of books like Misha Defonseca's *Surviving with Wolves* (1997), James Frey's *A Million Little Pieces* (2003) or Kathy O'Beirne's *Don't Ever Tell* (2006).

The British literary novel continues to be stylish, elegantly written, if sometimes, formally, rather conservative. Highlights of the decade include Ian McEwen's *Atonement* (2001), Zadie Smith's *White Teeth* (2000), Sarah Waters's *Fingersmith* (2002), Monica Ali's *Brick Lane* (2003), Zoe Heller's *Notes on a Scandal* (2003), Alan Hollinghurst's *The Line of Beauty* (2004), Kazuo Ishiguro's *Never Let Me Go* (2005) and Hilary Mantel's *Wolf Hall* (2009). Several novels attempt to address our post-9/11 world, including Iain Banks's *Dead Air* (2002), Ian McEwen with *Saturday* (2005), Mohsin Hamid's *The Reluctant Fundamentalist* (2007), Nadeem Aslam's *The Wasted Vigil* (2008) and Sebastian Faulks' *A Week in September* (2009).

Popular non-fiction include Malcolm Gladwell's *The Tipping Point* (2000), Lynn Truss' *Eats, Shoots & Leaves* (2003), Steven Levitt and Stephen Dubner's *Freakonomics* (2005) and Richard Dawkins' *The God Delusion* (2006).

Fashion in the 2000s

The key British fashion designer of the decade is Alexander McQueen, but the barriers between street and the catwalk break down with ranges by Karl Lagerfeld, Stella McCartney and Roland Mouret in high street stores.

The main looks of the decade are skinny jeans, shorts with tights, hipster jeans, cargo pants, long shirts and big belts, *enormous* handbags, ugg boots and ankle boots. The mid-decade boho look sees peasant skirts, ethnic prints and even ponchos becoming fashionable. Roland Mouret's Galaxy dress in 2006 brings flattering glamour back to women's style. Male fashion also adopt the skinny jeans, vintage clothing, aviator shades and, briefly, beards.

Technology begins to transform the book-reading experience. The online retailer Amazon opened its UK website in October 1998 and by the end of the decade is selling almost one in four books in the United Kingdom, threatening the survival of many independent bookshops. With the launch of its Kindle e-book reader in 2007 (as well as the Sony Reader in 2006), e-books begin to grow in popularity. In July 2010, Amazon announces that e-books are outselling hardbacks for the first time. Websites like Project Gutenberg and Google Books make out-of-print books digitally available for no cost.

Movies

The movie industry is hit by new kinds of online piracy in the 2000s, though Hollywood continued to score enormous box office hits with massive franchises like *Lord of the Rings* trilogy (2001–3), the Harry Potter movies (2001–11), the Bourne saga (2002–) and the *Pirates of the Caribbean* series (2003–). Digital technology continues to find its way onto the screen in the new kinds of animation associated with the Pixar film studio which produce astonishingly inventive children's movies such as *Monsters, Inc.* (2001), *Finding Nemo* (2003), *The Incredibles* (2004), *Ratatouille* (2007), *WALL-E* (2008) and *Up* (2009); elsewhere the use of CGI is very widespread, particularly in the biggest box-office hit of the decade, James Cameron's *Avatar* (2009); often CGI is a painterly device that expresses the power of the film-makers imagination – but at other times, as in the ludicrous *2012* (2009), it only exposes its lack. The IMAX format offering movies of much greater resolution and projection size establishes a firm presence through the decade. At its end, there is a revival of interest in 3D cinema.

'We live in a time where we have a man who's sending us to war for fictitious reasons . . . Shame on you, Mr Bush, shame on you'.

Michael Moore's speech accepting the Best Documentary Oscar for *Bowling for Columbine*.

A trailer for *Spider-man* (2002) features the villains' helicopter being caught in a web hung between the Twin Towers and after 9/11 it was swiftly withdrawn; nonetheless, it's hard not to feel that the success of superhero movies in the decade – *X-Men* (2000), *Spider-man* (2002), *Daredevil* (2003), *Batman Begins* and *Fantastic Four* (2005), *Superman Returns* (2006), *Iron Man*, *The Incredible Hulk* and *The Dark Knight* (2008) – owes something to a desire for American self-assertion after the shock of 2001. 'With great power,' muses Peter Parker at the end of *Spider-man*, 'comes great responsibility' before twirling around the American flag.

Elsewhere, the movies more directly address the events of 9/11 and everything that followed: *11'09"01* (2002), *At Five in the Afternoon* (2003), *Fahrenheit 9/11* (2004), *Jarhead* (2005), *World Trade Centre* and *United 93* (2006), *In the Valley of Elah* (2007), *The Hurt Locker* (2008), *The Messenger* (2009), *Four Lions* and *Green Zone* (2010). *Man on Wire* (2008) is a documentary about Philippe Petit's illegal tightrope-walk between the Twin Towers in 1974 and is an elliptical take on 9/11.

British cinema careers between escapist fantasy – *Billy Elliott* (2000), *Gosford Park* (2001), *Bend it Like Beckham* (2002) – and varieties of realism from brutal to lyrical – *Morvern Callar* and *Dirty Pretty Things* (2002), *Vera Drake* (2004), *This is England* and *Red Road* (2006), *Hunger* (2008). Danny Boyle is one of the decade's most versatile directors making an influential low-budget horror *28 Days Later* (2002) and the feel-good *Slumdog Millionaire* (2008) which wins eight Oscars, including Best Picture.

Art

The decade in British art is dominated by some very high-profile new gallery openings. In July, the Baltic Centre for Contemporary Art opens in Gateshead and welcomes 3 million visitors by the end of the decade. In 2003, Charles Saatchi opens a new gallery in County Hall on London's South Bank, before moving to premises on the King's Road in 2008 and then donating artworks from his collection worth £25 million to the nation. The White Cube Gallery in Hoxton moves to a new larger building in April 2000, and expands again in 2002 and 2006. The Whitechapel Gallery reopens in April 2009 after a major refurbishment which doubles its size. But perhaps the most dramatic gallery of the decade is Tate Modern, which opens in May 2000 to display more of the Tate's contemporary international collections and attracts almost 5 million visitors every year. A particular attraction is the massive Turbine Hall which houses large-scale installations by artists such as Louise Bourgeois (2000), Olafur Eliasson (2003) and Ai Weiwei (2010).

The Young British Artists (YBAs) continue to hold public attention. Damien Hirst's *For the Love of God* (2007), a platinum cast of a skull, studded with diamonds, is rumoured to have been sold for £50 million. In 2008 he holds an auction, *Beautiful Inside My Head Forever*, bypassing galleries altogether to sell directly to the public. The sale makes £111 million. Wild child Tracy Emin drifts into the establishment during the decade, becoming a Royal Academician in 2007 and voting Conservative in 2010.

New big names in the art world include the ceramicist Grayson Perry who wins the Turner Prize in 2003, Martin Creed who wins in 2001 for *Work No. 227: the lights going on and off* which indeed featured an empty room with the lights going on and off, and the anonymous graffiti artist Banksy, whose satirical stencil works intervene wittily in the urban landscape.

The low point for art in the decade comes in May 2004 with the fire that sweeps through the Momart warehouse in West London, destroying many (in)famous works by YBAs such as Emin, Hirst, Jake and Dinos Chapman, Gary Hume, Chris Ofili and Sarah Lucas.

4. Media

Television

Reality shows dominate the schedules and achieve massive audiences. *Big Brother* launches in 2000 and returns every year in the decade, with additional *Celebrity* editions from 2001. Talent-shows *Popstars* and *Pop Idol* (2001), *Popstars the Rivals* and *Fame Academy* (2002–3) are succeeded by *X Factor* (2004–) and *Britain's Got Talent* (2005–). *The Apprentice* (2005–) and a revamped *MasterChef* (2005–) focused on business and cookery respectively. *I'm a Celebrity . . . Get Me Out*

Of Here! (2002–), *Strictly Come Dancing* (2004–) and *Dancing on Ice* (2006–) involve celebrities completing tasks and being voted off the programme by the public.

High-definition cameras and broadcasting begin to change the feel of television through the decade with documentary series like *Planet Earth* (2006) and *Life* (2009) offering unprecedentedly sharp and detailed images of the natural world.

Critics and writers continue to lament the absence of the single drama but there are a few serious attempts to represent the nation to itself: *State of Play* (2003), *The Deal* (2003), *Party Animals* (2007), even the classic serial *The Way We Live Now* (2001), which finds in the 1875 Anthony Trollope novel a story for our times. *Spooks* (2002–11) captures the new world of secrecy, surveillance and terrorism. *Footballers' Wives* (2002–6) enjoyably skewers the celebrity WAG culture. The high-concept, time-travelling *Life on Mars* (2006) seems unsure whether the 1970s were a subject for mockery or nostalgia.

Celebrity

The determination of the media to end its stalking of celebrities after the death of Princess Diana in 1997 is short-lived and throughout the 2000s celebrities continue to be the staple topic for the tabloids. The vicissitudes of celebrity romances are followed as if they are a soap opera: the ups and downs of Ben Affleck and Jennifer Lopez (aka. 'Bennifer') are soon followed by Brad Pitt and Angelina Jolie (aka. 'Brangelina'); Tom Cruise and Katie Holmes compete for newspaper inches with Posh and Becks, Jay-Z and Beyoncé, Cheryl Cole and Ashley Cole, Jordan and Peter Andre, and Amy Winehouse and Pete Doherty. During Paul McCartney's messy divorce from Heather Mills, you could buy 'Team Macca' and 'Team Heather' t-shirts. More distressing stories are ghoulishly followed, including the emotional problems of Britney Spears and Lindsay Lohan, the scandals around Michael Barrymore and the trial in 2005 and accidental death in 2009 of Michael Jackson. Reality television generates people famous only for being famous, sometimes dismissed as *nonebrities*: the faces of Jade

20

Time-shifting

A phenomenon of the 2000s is a drift away from watching television live. One of the television highlights of the decade is the extraordinary high quality of American TV dramas like *The West Wing* (1999–2006), *The Sopranos* (1999–2007), *The Wire* (2002–2008) and *Mad Men* (2007–), but the scale of these series and their inconvenient scheduling mean that many prefer to watch them via DVD box sets. In September 2001, Sky+ is the first widely-available Personal Video Recorder, storing programmes not on a cassette but a hard disk. At the same time, as videos became obsolete, digital and internet technology make it possible to watch programmes afterwards on your computer. The BBC iPlayer, launched in late 2007, is instantly popular. In April 2010 alone, there are 123 million requests for TV and radio programmes.

Against this trend is the revival of 'appointment television' that demand to be seen live. In March 2005, writer-producer Russell T. Davies revives *Doctor Who*, which turns out to be one of the great successes of the decade. By catering simultaneously to adults and children, it is also credited with reviving Saturday night 'family' television. The rise of social media helps the revival of live television as viewers can connect via sites like Twitter to 'livetweet' about the shows.

Goody, Kim Kardashian and Paris Hilton are instantly recognizable, even if their precise talents are harder to place. When Jade Goody dies of cancer aged 27, her funeral is carried live on television.

Towards the end of the decade there is evidence that the pact between celebrities and the media is wearing thin. Two ferocious singles, Britney Spears' 'Piece of Me' (2008) and Lily Allen's 'The Fear' (2009), satirize and excoriate celebrity culture. Later, the phone-hacking scandal of 2011 will blow apart the myth that celebrity coverage was to the mutual benefit of celebrities and the media.

Comedy

It is a good decade for television comedy. The tone is set, at either extreme, by *The League of Gentlemen* (1999–2002) and *The Office* (2001–3); the former is brilliantly grotesque, cinematic, drawing on the tradition of the b-movie and Hammer Horror, at times genuinely chilling; the

21

latter is a mockumentary, with no laughter track, pared-down realistic performances, at times genuinely moving. Successors to *The League of Gentlemen* include *Little Britain* (2003–6), *The Mighty Boosh* (2004–7), *The Catherine Tate Show* (2004–9). In the spirit of *The Office* are *The Thick of It* (2005–), *Outnumbered* (2007–), Australia's *Summer Heights High* (2007) and the US's *Modern Family* (2009–). The US version of *The Office* (2005–), though broader and more traditional than its British counterpart, is a huge critical and audience success.

Stand-up comedy gets huge in the 2000s. Comedians like Michael McIntyre, Lee Evans and Peter Kay who, a generation before, might have played rooms above pubs, are now selling out sports arenas. Some complain that a harder edge is lost in the play for a broader public, but elsewhere one can still find comedians like Stewart Lee and Chris Morris, testing the boundaries of the form and the limits of what comedy can do. Several comedians attempt to shake off what they see as 'political correctness' and, with varying degrees of skill and intelligence, comedians like Jimmy Carr, Ricky Gervais and Frankie Boyle gain a reputation for outrageousness with jokes about women or the disabled.

Newspapers

Phone hacking: Timeline

Through the decade it becomes increasingly clear that some newspapers have used underhand or even illegal methods to get stories. These include intrusion and harassment in people's lives, hacking into people's phones, computers and bank accounts.

2003 Speaking to a parliamentary committee, Rebekah Brooks, editor of the *Sun*, lets slip that journalists paid police for information.

2006 Detectives investigating the reporting of private information relating to the Royal Family arrest the *News of the World*'s royal editor Clive Goodman and private investigator Glenn Mulcaire. Both are jailed in 2007 for phone-hacking. Andy Coulson, the paper's editor, resigns, but claims to have known nothing about their actions. The paper's publisher, News International, insist it was the work of one rogue reporter.

2007 Andy Coulson is appointed Conservative Party Director of Communications. James Murdoch – chief executive of News Corporation in Europe – pays £700,000 in an out-of-court settlement of a phone-hacking claim by Gordon Taylor of the Football Association, despite maintaining the Corporation's innocence.

2009 It is reported that up to 3,000 people may have had their phones hacked by journalists of the *News of the World*.

2010 A former reporter for *News of the World*, Sean Hoare, claims that phone-hacking was 'endemic'. Scotland Yard reopens its enquiry.

In 2011–12, the scandal grows enormously in scale. Andy Coulson is forced to resign from his Conservative Party job. He, Rebekah Brooks and many other journalists are arrested. Murdoch is forced to close the *News of the World* and withdraws his bid to acquire the television network. The Leveson Enquiry into press standards hears mounting evidence of corruption, collusion and law-breaking in the conduct of the press, and its links with politicians and police officers.

The press has a challenging decade. The decision of most national newspapers, early in the 2000s, to put most of their material free on their websites hits their sales. Tabloids see small dips in sales and most broadsheet newspapers see their circulations almost halve across the decade. In truth, the economics of the newspaper industry are changing, advertising accounting for more and more of a paper's revenue. Some newspapers are given away free, such as the *Metro* (1999–) and the *London Evening Standard* (from 2009), the increase in circulation allowing higher advertising rates. Newspapers like the *Daily Mail* focus considerable energies on their online content, calculating that high web traffic will pay off in advertising click-through rates. Rupert Murdoch takes the risk of placing online access to *The Times* behind a paywall; early figures are not encouraging, suggesting that the public has got used to getting news media content free and are disinclined to start paying for it again.

Murdoch has other problems through the decade, in particular the growing scandal of phone hacking (see box p. 22). Nonetheless the *Sun* remains the most popular daily newspaper of the decade, selling on average just over 3 million copies a day by the end of the decade, more than the *The Times*, *Financial Times*, *Telegraph*, *Guardian* and *Independent* combined.

Sport

British sport's three finest moments come in the 2003, 2005 and 2008. At the Rugby World Cup in 2003, England are world champions after a riveting final, ended with a last-minute drop-goal by Jonny Wilkinson. In 2005, the England cricket team win the Ashes for the first time since 1987, repeating the feat in 2009 and 2011. At the 2008 Beijing Olympics, Great Britain wins 47 medals, including 19 gold, its highest medal tally in 100 years. The news that Britain will host the 2012 Summer Olympics generates much public excitement and considerable building in the East End of London.

> 'They have a few drinks and probably the prawn sandwiches, and they don't realise what's going on out on the pitch. I don't think some of the people who come to Old Trafford can spell football, never mind understand it'.
>
> Manchester United captain Roy Keane complains about his team's middle-class fans (BBC Radio, November 2000)

Elsewhere, success is elusive. Britain's two great hopes in tennis, Tim Henman at the beginning of the decade and Andy Murray towards the end, find grand-slam success evading them. The perpetually troubled England football team fail to progress further than the quarter-finals at the World Cups in 2002 and 2006, do not qualify for the European Championships in 2008 and exit without much honour in the second round of the 2010 World Cup. Scotland qualify for no major international competitions in the decade and sink to an all-time low in the FIFA world rankings in 2004. Alex McLeish's brief stint as manager sees significant revival, including a convincing win against France and a steep rise in the world rankings.

The Premiership, however, continues to flourish, helped by the extraordinary injections of cash from television and from foreign businessmen like Roman Abramovich who takes over Chelsea FC in 2003, or Sheikh Mansour who buys Manchester City in 2008. Manchester United are, once again, the most successful club of the decade, topping the Premiership six times, winning the FA Cup in 2003 and the Champions League in 2008. Liverpool claim a famous victory in the Champions League in 2005, coming back from 3–0 down to win on penalties. Arsenal top the premiership in 2002 and 2004, on the latter occasion achieving the singular distinction of going the whole season without losing a game.

5. Science and technology

Science

The decade begins with the first draft of the Human Genome Project in June 2000, an ambitious project to map and identify the chemistry that defines every one of the c. 25,000 genes that make up a human being. The project is completed in 2003 and promises, in time, to find new ways to identify and treat diseases like cancer and Alzheimer's. Gene therapy and pharmacogenetics are key medical research areas of the decade. Neuroscience, meanwhile, grows in confidence – some say over-confidence – in its ability to account for every aspect of mental life by studying the activity of the brain.

Space exploration takes two new steps in January 2004 with the Hubble telescope's Ultra Deep Field images – which looked back through 12 billion years of space – and the landing of the Mars Rovers which will go on to show that water may once have flowed on the red planet. In 2006, the International Astronomical Union publish a definition of a 'planet' that sees our own solar system diminished, as Pluto is downgraded to a 'dwarf planet'.

At the other end of the physical scale, the Large Hadron Collider begins operation in 2008, seeking to empirically test the hypotheses of particle physics – in particular to find the 'Higgs boson', though the existence of that elusive particle has not been proved by the decade's end.

Technology

This is the decade of the internet. It stumbles at first with the bursting of the dot.com bubble. Many technology businesses in the early part of the decade find willing investors as the first wave of interest in the internet peaks. In 2000, 17 dot-com companies pay more than $2 million each for 30-second advert spots during the Super Bowl. Values spike on the NASDAQ index of leading technology shares in March that year and the only way is down. A sudden loss of confidence in this new technology sees share prices tumbling and wiping out a number of new companies including boo.com, startups.com and pets.com. Those businesses able to ride the storm – including eBay, Amazon and Google – emerge stronger than ever.

The World Wide Web is changing, meanwhile. 'Web 2.0' is a new phase in the evolution of the web, characterized by being much simpler to use, more intuitively designed, and a great deal more interactive. An icon of Web 2.0 is Wikipedia (2001–), a gigantic, user-edited, online encyclopedia the accuracy of which often rivals much more established print publications, though can be a target for mischief-making and vendettas. Second Life and MySpace are launched in 2002, YouTube in 2005 and in 2006 Facebook (initially restricted to schools and colleges) becomes available to anyone with an email address; by the end of the decade it is reported to have 360 million users worldwide. In March 2006, Jack Dorsey, founder of Twitter, sends the first ever 'tweet'; by February 2010, its users are sending 50 million tweets every day.

The culture of interactivity spreads to other media – television programmes encourage viewers to become citizen journalists by sending in their own photographs and images, newspapers urge readers to contribute to debates via comment boxes below the articles. The rise of immersive theatre events may be related to the impact of Web 2.0 on the public imagination. So decisive is this change that *TIME* magazine announced, in December 2006, that 'for seizing the reins of the global media, for founding and framing the new digital democracy, for working for nothing and beating the pros at their own game, TIME's Person of the Year for 2006 is you'.

The hardware for all this interactivity is the computer. In 2002 it was calculated that the one-billionth computer has been sold in the world. This figure is thought to have doubled by 2007. The decade also sees a multiplication of the devices on which the internet can be accessed. Smartphones, which can access the world wide web, handle email, offer games, as well as, occasionally, make phone calls, grow in popularity through the decade, spurred dramatically by the launch of Apple's iPhone in January 2007, which, with its touch screen and swipe-gesture operation (and, later, its proliferation of 'apps'), becomes one of the design icons of the decade. This was followed in 2010 by the iPad, which promises similarly to transform the tablet computing market. Apple announces that 42 million iPhones have been sold by the end of the decade, which, though huge, is still tiny when we consider that in mid-2010 there are thought to be 5 billion mobile phone connections worldwide.

Computer gaming

Games continue to grow in sophistication and popularity. *The Sims* launches in February 2000 and goes on to become the most successful PC game ever. *World of Warcraft* is the most successful of the new MMORPG genre (Massively Multiplayer Online Role-Playing Games). *Grand Theft Auto: San Andreas* runs into controversy in 2005 when hackers discover a minigame – the 'Hot Coffee' mod – intended to be inaccessible, in which the game's main character could end up invited back for sex by one of the in-game girlfriends. Games like *Silent Hill 2* (2001) and *Half-Life 2* (2004) show that computer games are not incompatible with emotional and intellectual complexity.

The ways in which games can be played transform with every new hardware release, including Microsoft's Xbox (2002) and Xbox 360 (2005), Sony's Playstation 2 (2000) and 3 (2005) and Nintendo's Wii (2006), which bring new levels of three-dimensional interactivity to the gaming experience. The advent of smartphones in the second half of the decade mean new mobile platforms for gaming 'apps'.

By the end of the decade, computers are continuing to get thinner and more portable; cloud-computing is the new thing, linking computers via wireless networks to data stored on the internet. The world wide web also emerges as a site of political struggle; the 2001 Patriot Act in the United States grants the government new powers to intercept e-mails and phone calls. In the same year, Wikileaks launches as a space to publish documents that governments and other organizations wish to keep secret and in 2010 is at the centre of intense controversy over its decision to leak sensitive diplomatic cables and documents about the War in Afghanistan.

6. Political events

The Labour Party remains in power for the whole of the decade. Indeed it is the first time Labour have won three full terms in office. Tony Blair comes to power in 1997 promising that 'we have been elected as New Labour and we will govern as New Labour'. What New Labour stood for is not always clear, but as the 2000s wear on it appears to involve a move to the centre of British politics, with a generally progressive attitude to personal morality, a mixture of neoliberalism for industry and higher public spending, and a decidedly traditional alignment in foreign affairs. Tony Blair's gifts as a communicator sustain the party through some of the decade, helped by the Conservative Party choosing a series of singularly inept leaders who, to put it mildly, fail to win a place in the public's heart.

Blair introduces several popular policies, including devolution in Scotland, Wales, Northern Ireland and London, and presides over an era of rising prosperity and low unemployment. He tentatively re-engages with Europe, introduces a minimum wage and oversees substantial investment in the NHS and school system. But his popularity never quite survives his decision to go to war in Iraq. In particular, the suggestion that we went to war on a false premise – to deprive Saddam Hussein of Weapons of Mass Destruction (WMDs) (which he turned out not to have) – damages his credibility. He is widely criticized for being too close to George W. Bush, an unpopular and divisive figure in the United Kingdom.

Blair's style of government is characterized by (a) 'sofa politics', a preference for discussion with close political friends rather than around the Cabinet table, (b) a 'presidential' style – he introduced monthly press conferences in June 2002, which appeared to bypass the House of Commons as the traditional place for major announcements and (c) a culture of 'spin'; New Labour is, for the most part, an enormously effective media operation, but the demands to keep 'on-message' are often criticized as over-simplifying politics and stifling debate.

> 'I ask you to accept one thing. Hand on heart, I did what I thought was right. I may have been wrong. That's your call . . . I have been very lucky and very blessed. This country is a blessed nation. The British are special, the world knows it, in our innermost thoughts we know it. This is the greatest nation on Earth. It has been an honour to serve it.'
>
> Tony Blair, announcing his resignation as Prime Minister, May 2007

A fourth feature of Blair's time in office is his increasingly strained relationship with his Chancellor, Gordon Brown. When the previous Labour leader, John Smith, died suddenly in May 1994, Blair and Brown agreed over a meal that Blair would stand for the leadership, but that at some future point would step down in favour of Brown. No formal agreement was made and it later becomes clear that the two men have different ideas about the timescales involved. Through much of the decade, Brown and Blair – and their respective supporters – are at loggerheads and the business of government is snarled up by their rivalry.

> **Cash for honours**
>
> The term refers to the suggestion in 2006–7 that life peerages have been offered to wealthy businesspeople in exchange for political donations. In 2005 a number of nominees for honours are rejected by the Appointments Commission amid rumours that several of them have made donations or loans to Labour. Lord Levy, the Party's chief fundraiser is arrested though later released without charge. Tony Blair is interviewed by the police three times as a witness rather than a suspect and while no prosecutions are ever brought, it tarnishes Blair's reputation. He is, after all, the man who once described himself as 'a pretty straight sort of guy'.

When Brown does eventually succeed Tony Blair, he brings a very different style to No. 10. His qualities as a Chancellor of the Exchequer – particularly his serious, dour demeanour – seem less attractive in a Prime Minister, especially compared to Blair's easy charm. He is much admired for his decisive handling of the Credit Crunch in 2008, but as the recession bites later that year, Brown seems ill-suited to keeping up the nation's spirits. It is, however, a sign of Blair and Brown's success as leaders that in the General Election of 2010, in the midst of a recession, with unemployment at a 15-year high, the Conservative opposition cannot muster a majority and is instead forced into awkward Coalition with the Liberal Democrats.

Timeline of events

2000: *Jan*, The third millennium begins with the opening of the Millennium Dome in Greenwich, the failure of the Y2K bug to wreak any of its predicted havoc; *May*, Ken Livingstone is the first elected Mayor of London, beating the official Labour candidate Frank Dobson; *Sep*, protests over the price of fuel see blockades of refineries and fuel distribution depots which leads, in turn, to some food shortages, school closures and rationing of NHS services; *Oct*, Scotland's charismatic First Minister Donald Dewar dies of a brain haemorrhage.

2001: *Jan*, Peter Mandelson, Secretary of State for Northern Ireland, resigns over allegations he had used his position to secure a UK passport for an Indian businessman Srichand Hinduka; *Feb*, outbreak of foot and mouth disease; *Jun*, General Election: Labour wins with a Commons majority of 167; *Sep*, 9/11, Tony Blair cancels planned speech to the TUC Conference; Iain Duncan Smith succeeds William Hague as Conservative leader; *Oct*, IRA begins decommissioning its weaponry.

2002: *Jan*, the Euro enters circulation but Britain stays out; *Jul*, Rowan Williams becomes the new Archbishop of Canterbury; *Dec*, Cherie Blair, wife of Tony Blair, forced to apologize after buying two flats with the assistance of a convicted fraudster.

The credit crunch

Through the 2000s, a number of mortgage lenders in the United States, encouraged by steadily rising house prices, issue a very large number of 'sub-prime' mortgages; that is, mortgages to people who may have problems making the repayments. The assumption is that even if they default, rising house prices will pay off the debt at a profit. When house prices begin to fall in 2007, these mortgages become significant liabilities. The problem is compounded by the complicated ways in which banks parcel up debts and sell them on. A group of mortgages might be bundled together, then parcelled up as asset-backed securities, with the promise that it will return its purchaser, at a future date, more than they paid for it; the purchasing bank might themselves rebundle and reparcel these and other debts and sell them on (in complex financial instruments with names like Collateralised Debt Obligations). When the crisis hits, the complexity of these assets means that the investment banks do not know who is holding these sub-prime mortgages, or, in the jargon, has 'exposure to toxic debt'. As a result, they stop lending to each other, for fear that, if you lend to a bank that then fails, you will not get your money back. In a market system, the value of any asset is determined by what someone is prepared to pay for it; since no one is prepared to buy or sell any financial assets, the banking system appears suddenly to have become completely worthless. The result is that governments in the United Kingdom, Europe and the United States are forced to pump huge amounts of money into the system, buying up bad debts, in an attempt to inject liquidity into the frozen system and restart the economy. While this avoids complete meltdown, the affair has two effects: first, the collapse of consumer and investor confidence leads to sharp declines in the market valuation of many industries, leading to job losses, falling output and substantial losses, which tips many countries into recession; second, the enormous sums required to prop up the banking system leave governments with substantial debts, which they will struggle to pay off.

2003: *Feb*, well over a million people take to the streets to protest against the coming invasion of Iraq; you now have to pay a Congestion Charge to drive in Central London; *Mar*, leader of the Commons Robin Cook resigns in protest at the Iraq War; 139 Labour MPs rebel in a vote on the war; Iraq War begins; *May*, Secretary of State for International Development Clare Short resigns over the Iraq War; *Jun*, a minor comedian gatecrashes Prince William's twenty-first birthday party dressed as Osama bin Laden; *Jul*, after a journalist claims that the dossier providing the rationale for the Iraq War was 'sexed up', the Ministry of Defence names weapons expert Dr David Kelly as the source. Kelly is found dead near his home in an apparent suicide; *Nov*, Michael Howard elected leader of the Conservative Party.

Banking crisis timeline

2007: *Jul*, Bear Sterns warns investors that they will get no money back because banks will not bail them out

Aug, BNP Paribas warns that liquidity has evaporated; banks are not lending to each other

Sep, Run on Northern Rock, the Government guarantees £56 billion of deposits

Oct, UBS announces $3.4 billion losses because of sub-prime investments; Merrill Lynch announces $7.9 billion exposure to bad debt

2008: *Jan*, House prices dropping, banks announcing losses, Bank of England offering clean money

Sep, In the United States, Fannie Mae and Freddie Mac are bailed out; Lehman Brothers file for bankruptcy; Merrill Lynch is taken over by Bank of America; Federal Reserve bails out AIG; Washington Mutual closed and sold; Bradford & Bingley nationalized

Oct, US House of Representatives passes a $700 billion bailout package; the UK Government introduces £50 billion bailout plus £200 billion short-term lending support; RBS, Lloyds TSB and HBOS nationalized at a cost of £37 billion

Nov, China announces $586 billion stimulus package; US Government saves Citigroup, at the cost of $20 billion; Federal Reserve injects another $800 billion into the economy

Dec, Recession announced in United States; $17.4 billion used to prop up Ford, Chrysler and General Motors

2009: *Jan*, United Kingdom enters recession

Feb, Barack Obama signs $787 billion bailout package

Mar, AIG announces that in the last quarter it lost $61.7 billion, the largest in US corporate history

---

2004: *Jan*, the Hutton Report sides with the government over the BBC in the David Kelly affair, to widespread public astonishment; *Jul*, Government passes legislation raising university tuition fees to £3,000; the Butler Report concludes that the case for war in Iraq was flawed; *Sep*, Scottish Parliament building opens at Holyrood; *Dec*, Home Secretary David Blunkett resigns over allegations he intervened to get a visa application approved for his ex-lover's nanny.

2005: *Feb*, Blair insists that he will stand for a third term; *May*, General Election, Labour wins a reduced majority of 66; *Jul*, London wins its bid to host the 2012 Summer Olympics; G8 Summit in Scotland; 7/7 London Bombings; IRA announces the end of its armed struggle; *Nov*, Labour defeated in Commons over Bill to increase maximum detention of terrorist suspects to 90 days; *Dec*, David Cameron elected leader of the Conservative Party.

2006: *Jan*, Charles Kennedy resigns as Liberal Democrat leader, admitting a drink problem; *Mar*, Labour wins vote in the Commons over school reform despite a backbench rebellion because of Conservative support; *Mar*, Scotland Yard launches investigation into 'Cash for Honours' allegations (see box p. 29); Government of Wales Act enhances the legislative powers of the Welsh Assembly

2007: *May*, Devolved government restored to Northern Ireland with the once-unthinkable leadership of DUP's Ian Paisley as First Minister and Sinn Féin's Martin McGuinness as his deputy; the Scottish National Party's Alex Salmond becomes First Minister of Scotland, leading a minority administration; *Jun*, Gordon Brown succeeds Tony Blair as Prime Minister; attempted terrorist attacks in London and Glasgow; heavy rains cause widespread flooding; *Jul*, Smoking is now banned in all indoor workplaces; *Sep*, a run on Northern Rock is the first major sign in the United Kingdom of the coming Credit Crunch (see box p. 31); *Oct*, when Gordon Brown decides not to call a snap general election, despite evidence that he would win, he is criticized for lack of decisiveness; *Dec*, Nick Clegg elected leader of the Liberal Democrats.

2008: *May*, Boris Johnson is elected Mayor of London.

2009: *Jan*, Britain is now in recession; *Apr*, Gordon Brown's special advisor is forced to resign over claims he plotted to smear Conservative politicians; *May*, the MPs' expenses scandal begins to unfold (see box below).

Expenses scandal

The convention is well established that MPs can charge office and some living costs to the state, but their expenses have always been kept secret. In May 2009, the *Daily Telegraph* gets a copy of MPs' expenses claims and begins publishing them, in advance of their official release later that year. The public are horrified by the dripfeed of extraordinary items that MPs are claiming for, which include swimming pools, furniture and, in the notorious case of Conservative MP Douglas Hogg, having his moat cleaned. It also becomes clear that MPs have frequently maximized their claims by repeatedly re-designating their 'second home', a practice known as 'flipping'. The scandal has several casualties, beginning with the Speaker of the House of Commons, Michael Martin, who is thought to have handled the scandal inadequately; more than 20 MPs resign from Government, or announce their decision not to stand at the next election. By the end of the affair, six MPs and peers have been convicted and imprisoned for making false claims. Perhaps the most serious casualty is the public's trust in its Members of Parliament. In response, the Government announces the formation of an Independent Parliamentary Standards Authority to examine MPs expenses and much tighter rules are drawn up governing what can be claimed.

World events

2000: *Jan*, the world celebrates the turn of the millennium; Vladimir Putin is elected president of Russia; *Feb*, Jörg Haider's far-right Freedom Party forms a Coalition government in Austria, to international consternation; *Apr*, In Zimbabwe, Mugabe pushes through a land reform bill, despite it being rejected by voters, and soon veterans of the war for independence are seizing white-owned farms; *Jul*, Concorde crashes in France, killing 113; *Aug*, the Russian submarine, K-141 Kursk, sinks in the Barents Sea, killing 118; *Sep*, Ariel Sharon's visit to the Temple Mount, an Islamic holy site, causes outrage, triggers the Second Intifada in which over 6,000 Israelis and Palestinians will be killed by the end of the decade; *Oct*, President of Serbia, Slobodan Milošević is overthrown and handed to UN in June 2001 (his trial for war crimes begins Feb 2002 and he dies in prison in March 2006 of a heart attack); *Nov*, US Presidential Election is indecisive, and recounts in Florida which seem likely to award the Presidency to Al Gore are eventually stopped by the Supreme Court, handing victory to George W. Bush.

'Let's roll'.

Todd Beamer, on United 93, rallying his fellow passengers to ground the plane, 11 September 2001

2001: *Jan*, George Bush is sworn in as the forty-third President of the United States; *Apr*, The world's first space tourist, Dennis Tito spends $20 million to spend 8 days on the International Space Station; *Sep*, 9/11 Attacks on the United States; *Oct*, Invasion of Afghanistan begins; *Dec*, Enron files for bankruptcy; a deepening economic crisis and rioting in Argentina forces the president Ferdinand de la Rúa to resign.

2002: *Jan*, George W. Bush's first State of the Union address denounces an 'Axis of Evil'; *Feb*, Hindu-Muslim violence in India, following a murderous attack on Hindu pilgrims in the Sabharmathi Express train; *Jun*, Israel begins constructing a wall along the West Bank, called a 'security fence' by Israel and an 'Apartheid wall' by the Palestinians; *Aug*, Iran's nuclear enrichment programme is revealed by a dissident.

'Every nation, in every region, now has a decision to make. Either you are with us, or you are with the terrorists'.

George W. Bush, speaking to Congress, 20 September 2011

2003: *Feb*, Space Shuttle Columbia explodes during re-entry, killing all seven crew members; Colin Powell presents WMD case to UN; a rebel uprising in Darfur, in the Sudan, marks the beginning of a six-year civil war and humanitarian crisis; *Mar*, Iraq War begins (see box p. 37); *Apr*, 'Road Map for Peace' developed for the Middle East but is not adopted; *Jul*, Valerie Plame is named in the press as a covert CIA operative in retaliation for her husband's criticisms of the War in Iraq. It transpires that her name was leaked by CIA and Bush Administration insiders. *Oct*, China launches its first space mission with astronauts aboard; Arnold Schwarzenegger elected governor of California; *Nov*, The Rose Revolution in Georgia overturns a rigged election; *Dec*, Saddam Hussein captured.

> 'There are known knowns; there are things we know that we know. There are known unknowns; that is to say there are things that we now know we don't know. But there are also unknown unknowns – there are things we do not know we don't know.'
>
> United States Secretary of Defence Donald Rumsfeld on the evidence for Iraq's WMD in February 2002

2004: *Feb*, a US-backed coup in Haiti removes President Aristide from office; *Apr*, Photographs are published revealing torture and prisoner abuse at Abu Ghraib prison, near Baghdad; *May*, ten new countries join the EU, seven of them from the former Communist Bloc; when rebel forces occupy Bukavu in the Democratic Republic of Congo, it triggers a new phase in the decade-long Congolese conflict that will kill over 4 million by the end of the decade; *Jun*, Shia insurgency in Yemen; *Nov*, George W. Bush is re-elected US President; the 'Orange Revolution' in the Ukraine overturns a rigged Presidential election; *Dec*, the Bolivarian Alliance is founded between various socialist and liberal democratic South American countries, intended as an alternative to the 'free trade agreement' model of international cooperation; an earthquake in the Indian Ocean earthquake causes a tsunami that leaves a quarter of a million dead.

2005: *Apr*, Benedict XVI succeeds John-Paul II as Pope; *Jun*, In referendums, French and Dutch voters reject the proposed Constitution for the EU; A religious and political hardliner, Mahmoud

Ahmadinejad, is elected president of Iran with 62 per cent of the vote; *Aug*, Hurricane Katrina floods New Orleans; Sep, after the Danish newspaper *Jyllands-Posten* publishes 12 cartoons depicting the Islamic prophet Muhammad, Muslims around the world protest, some attacking Danish and other Western embassies and burning flags; *Oct*, riots erupt in the suburbs of Paris in protest against the French police's treatment of French youths of African descent; *Nov*, Angela Merkel becomes the first female Chancellor of Germany; *Dec*, 11 million Iraqis vote in first democratic elections; *Dec*, the election of Evo Morales to the Bolivian presidency is the first of a new wave of socialist leaders elected in South America, including Ecuador's Rafael Correa in Oct 2006 and Paraguay's Fernando Lugo in April 2008.

2006: *Jan*, Hamas wins landslide in elections to the Palestinian Legislature; *Oct*, North Korea conducts its first nuclear test; *Nov*, Alexander Litvinenko died in London of radiation poisoning and it is widely alleged that Russian businessman Andrey Lugovoy is responsible; *Dec*, War in Somalia escalates rapidly; President Felipe Calderón of Mexico sends troops to deal with violence between drug cartels but draws the government into the Mexican Drug Wars; Saddam Hussein is executed in front of his jeering warders, some of them taking cameraphone pictures and videos.

The War in Iraq

After deposing the Taliban, why the United States's attention turns towards Iraq has been much debated. Some talk up a connection between Saddam Hussein and the 9/11 bombers, though no such connection exists. Others focus on the regime's human rights abuses. It is suggested that George W. Bush wants to complete the task of toppling Saddam Hussein that his father failed to achieve in 1991. Others see the US interest in Iraq to do with getting control of the region's oil supplies.

In the prelude to the invasion, attention focuses on Weapons of Mass Destruction. In 2002, UN Security Council resolution 1441 demands that Iraq comply with UN Weapons Inspectors. Iraq is reluctantly cooperative and on the eve of war, chief weapons inspector Hans Blix confirms that Iraq is complying with its commitments not to develop WMD. Nonetheless, the United States declares that the inspection process had failed and builds a 'coalition of the willing' which begins its invasion in March 2003.

In May 2003, President Bush stands on the deck of the USS Abraham Lincoln beneath a banner stating 'Mission Accomplished' to announce the end of major combat operations in Iraq. This is a touch premature. Over the next year the insurgency against the invasion (and sectarian attacks) intensifies and occupying forces and civilians become mired in an increasingly bloody civil war. In Fallujah, particularly, atrocities are carried out on both sides, the 'humanitarian' rhetoric of some of the war leaders undermined by photographs from Abu Ghraib prison detailing grotesque prisoner abuse. In July 2006, the UN calculates that 100 civilians are being killed every day. By the end of that year, the situation appears to have descended into chaos. At the beginning of 2007, Bush's new strategy, 'the surge', sees 20,000 additional US troops dispatched to Iraq. The initial response is a huge escalation in the insurgency, with almost 200 killed on a single day in April and almost 800 on 14 August 2007.

Meanwhile, a new democratic government in Iraq is elected in December 2005. In some areas, control is handed back to Iraqi authorities, and gradually, through 2007, the numbers of attacks and deaths decrease. British troops hand over control of Basra to Iraqi forces and in March 2009 Barack Obama, now President of the United States, announces that all US troops will have left the country by late 2011.

2007: *May*, Nicolas Sarkozy is elected President of France; *Dec*, The Treaty of Lisbon (a de facto constitution) is signed by all 27 members of the EU; Benazir Bhutto is assassinated in Pakistan.

2008: *May*, Dmitry Medvedev is elected president of Russia; Cyclone Nargis hits Burma killing over 150,000 people; *Jul*, Iran tests missiles that could reach Israel, sending oil prices to a record high of $147/ barrel; *Aug*, Russia and Georgia go to war for five days over South Ossetia; *Dec*, Bernie Madoff is arrested for conducting the largest Ponzi scheme in history, estimated at $65 billion; Operation Cast Lead: Israel invades the Gaza Strip, apparently to target those launching rocket attacks on its territory; up to 1,500 Palestinians are killed; the Zimbabwean inflation rate reaches 230,000,000 per cent.

2009: *Jan*, Barack Obama is sworn in as forty-fourth president of the United States; *May*, in Ireland, the Ryan Report into child-abuse in Catholic children's schools describes the problem as 'endemic'; *Jun*, after apparent irregularities in the Iranian Presidential election, the 'Green Movement' sees millions take to the streets to protest; *Oct*, At 830ms, the Burj Khalifa is now the tallest human-made structure in the world.

CHAPTER 1
THEATRE IN THE 2000s
Andrew Haydon

'What's so great about history? It's just one fucking thing after another.'

Contrary to this popular quotation, adapted to great comic effect in Alan Bennett's *The History Boys*[1] (2004), history is also quite a lot of things all happening at the same time in different places, with often difficult-to-measure impacts on other things.

In this chapter I intend to argue that British theatre enjoyed something of a qualified 'golden age' in the 2000s, both artistically and economically. While it could be claimed that by the end of the decade there had not been any single revolutionary moment – no *Look Back in Anger* or *Blasted* – a number of changes in the way that theatre was being watched, thought and talked about, were indicative of bigger underlying shifts, facilitating an ever-increasing plurality in the work available. Important elements among these changes include the interrogation and gradual problematization of a supposed antagonism between 'New Writing' and 'New Work' – the nominal division between newly written plays and almost any form of theatre that had been arrived at by another route – the embrace of 'alternative' or 'upstream'[2] elements and strategies by the 'mainstream', an increased internationalism in 'British' theatre and the emergence of entirely new channels for promotion and criticism on the internet.

To look at 'all the rest of British theatre in the 2000s' – apart from the work of the five authors covered in the subsequent chapters – is impossible. There is too much. So a certain amount of selectivity has been deployed here. Even with the dawn of live-streaming online, and the National Theatre's NT Live beaming productions to cinemas across the United Kingdom and beyond, the vast majority of theatre still relies on human bodies being in the same space at the same time. Evidence of productions relies on some of the bodies that shared that space with that performance creating some sort of documentation – be it written, photographic, recorded or filmed. One of the things this chapter reflects, therefore, is the subjective picture that I acquired living through the decade, working as a critic, living mostly in London, spending my Augusts in Edinburgh, and increasingly travelling to mainland Europe to see shows and attend festivals. It also reflects – and I hope reflects upon – concepts of 'importance' and 'success': shows that I saw or that I found 'important'; shows that I missed, that I subsequently felt I should have seen because of the importance attached to them by others.

I have tried to order this chapter in a number of ways, by picking at various 'types' of work, by looking at a number of key institutions and by examining the work of various individuals looking at verbatim theatre, work made using headphone, site-specific/sympathetic/ immersive work, the spaces in which work took place, a section on the Royal Court, the 'New Writing Industry' and funding, the concept of authorship, the National Theatre, criticism and then, to conclude, a selection of 'postcard' snapshots from autumn 2009. As a result, both chronology and thematic contiguity tend to hop back and forth. But if theatre, like a nation's press, is the sound of a culture talking to itself, then it makes sense that this conversation – like any conversation – will contain a few loops and double-backs. My hope is that from these skittering trajectories a broad overview of our theatre over the course of a decade emerges.

1. Verbatim

A good way to understand how theatre developed in the 2000s is to look at verbatim theatre. For Britain in the 2000s, this theatrical form had its most immediate precedent in the tribunal plays that were pioneered by the Tricycle Theatre under Nicholas Kent in the 1990s. Tribunal plays differ in kind from 'Verbatim Theatre proper' by virtue of their pre-existence as documents of events. They took the transcriptions of important political inquiries, edited them down to 'the good bits', gave them to actors and stood the whole thing up on stage in Kilburn. They were the essence of pre-In-Yer-Face 1990s political theatre: dour, grey and unimpeachably serious. They convinced through the sheer heaviness of their subject matter, and the fact that every word you were hearing had really been spoken by a real person in the real world. Audiences were not asked to perceive a metaphor, but to bear witness to a second-hand reality. Verbatim theatre moved beyond editing down transcripts of trials and inquiries that had already taken place and started conducting interviews and even inquiries of its own. Interestingly, this particular strand of the form's development took place at the heart of 'In-Yer-Face land', at Stephen Daldry's Royal Court.

The first example of the verbatim play in the 2000s is Robin Soans' *A State Affair* – interviews with residents of the Buttershaw Estate in Bradford where Andrea Dunbar had set her play *Rita, Sue and Bob Too* commissioned by Max Stafford-Clark as a companion piece for their revival of it in 2000.[3] The appeal of this new form was immediately obvious. A lot of 'political' playwrights already conducted interviews as part of their research; one of the best examples of whom was David Hare. A book of the interviews he conducted for his state-of-the-nation plays, *Racing Demon*, *Murmuring Judges* and the *Absence of War*, had already been published by Faber under the title *Asking Around*. The logical next step, rather than going to all the trouble of having to make up a vaguely fictional scenario populated with analogues of the people you have interviewed and the situations they had described, was to stage such interviews. It makes sense, then, that the next significant verbatim drama of the decade was created by Hare; again, like *A State Affair*, for Max Stafford-Clark.

The Permanent Way, a piece about the privatization of Britain's railways, opened in November 2003 in York and was shown at the National Theatre as part of its inaugural £10 Travelex Ticket Season. If *A State Affair* could be characterized as almost stupefyingly bleak, *The Permanent Way* had almost the precise opposite effect: 'I cannot remember when I last left a theatre feeling in such a state of pure fury. I intend a compliment. David Hare's dramatised documentary about the privatising of the railways is a theatrical red rag of an occasion,' wrote *Evening Standard* critic Nicholas de Jongh.[4]

42

Interviewed by Richard Boon at the NT on the subject of his adoption of the 'verbatim' documentary form, Hare is interesting in his response:

Boon You're a famously meticulous writer . . . How does that square with working with other people's words, when you have not interfered?

David Hare Well I have interfered . . . On some occasions, although not always, we had tape recorders . . . With certain characters, by changing everything I could make it into music which I think reflected what they wanted to say. But, when I did that, I always made sure they were entirely happy with it.[5]

In his next piece, Hare went further, mixing transcript with speculation for 2005's *Stuff Happens*, an epic-sized examination for the National Theatre of the players and reasons behind America and Britain's illegal invasion of Iraq in 2003. The title itself comes (verbatim, but decontextualized) from an offhand comment made by Donald Rumsfeld at a press conference regarding looting in Baghdad.[6] As well as mixing in speeches made at press conferences and on-the-record interviews, Hare also invented dialogue that he imagined being spoken in meetings behind closed doors. The result, while not quite Shakespearean in scope or theatricality, did at least present a timely, speculative account of one of the decade's defining stories.

Robin Soans also went on to create further verbatim theatre with *The Arab-Israeli Cookbook* for Erica Whyman's Gate Theatre (directed and co-gathered with British-Jewish director Tim Roseman and British-Lebanese director Rima Brihi). It was his follow-up to that piece which was to prove an early high-point of verbatim theatre in the 2000s. Out of Joint's *Talking to Terrorists* toured from late April 2005 before opening at the Royal Court on 30 June. My own review of the play for the website *CultureWars* was posted on 6 July.[7] On 8 July I was to discuss the piece in a panel event at the National Theatre,[8] with Aleks Sierz and the playwright Justin Butcher, who was doing good business with his own political farces *The Dubya Trilogy*. On the day, in between filing the review and taking part in the panel discussion, four

British-born Jihadist terrorists committed the worst bomb attacks on London since the blitz, and *Talking to Terrorists* suddenly became the most vital show in town.

Since 9/11 and George W Bush's 'War on Terror', discussion of terrorism had dominated a certain strata of discourse in 'political theatre'. This was why the piece had been made in the first place. The strength of *Talking to Terrorists*, especially in the context of the newly bombed London, was its admirably framed long-view. Not pandering to fears about The Threat of Islam™, *Terrorists* also interviewed (among others) the IRA member convicted for the Brighton Bombing of 1984, Conservative MP Norman Tebbit, who was injured in the attack, a member of the Kurdish PKK, a member of the National Resistance Army in Uganda and a psychologist who gives a fascinating, brief account of the intellectual structures behind terrorist organizations.

The invasion of Iraq, the war in Afghanistan, the detention without trial of terrorist suspects and 'unlawful combatants' in Guantanamo Bay and the siege of Fallujah all provided subjects for separate verbatim pieces in the 2000s. In 2007, the Tricycle Theatre made an intriguing addition to its own strand of tribunal plays, by essentially staging its own recording, and editing the results into the snappily-titled piece of verbatim, mock-tribunal theatre; *Called to Account: The Indictment of Anthony Charles Lynton Blair For the Crime of Aggression Against Iraq – A Hearing.*[9]

The most successful verbatim response to the Iraq war was not really 'verbatim theatre' at all, however. The newly formed National Theatre of Scotland's *Black Watch* was playwright Gregory Burke's follow-up to his acclaimed 2001 début *Gagarin Way*. The extent to which *Black Watch* was successful cannot easily be overstated. The reviews it garnered when it opened in Edinburgh 2007 speak for themselves:[10]

The foundation stone of Gregory Burke as a playwright is his grasp of different kinds of male relationship: camaraderie, community and rivalry are all present between his characters, but they are always talking the same language and wired for the same feelings. His new piece *Black Watch* fits this hypothesis perfectly.

(*Financial Times*)

The show gets away with its stylized, balletic-meets-bodyslamming battles (choreographed by Steven Hoggett of Frantic Assembly) because the acting is excellent and authentically mouthy. Director John Tiffany and designer Laura Hopkins also inject electrifyingly imaginative images.

(*Independent on Sunday*)

Even Quentin Letts in the *Daily Mail* could not disagree: 'For once, superlatives are no exaggeration. This is a stunning show. You emerge, after an hour and three quarters of this astonishing show, with your political dander twanging, your outrage tweaked.' While the piece also later gathered its dissenters,[11] it remains one of the undisputed stand-out milestones of theatre in the 2000s.

Also reflecting on life in the British Army, Sherman Cymru's *Deep Cut* interviewed a collection of those affected by the unexplained deaths of four young army recruits at the Deepcut barracks in Surrey. The play, which premièred at the Traverse Theatre, had arguably the greatest impact of any verbatim show of the decade. In a WhatsonStage interview with the author Philip Ralph, he noted, 'after its opening at the Edinburgh Fringe Festival in 2008, it reignited the campaign for a public inquiry into the deaths of four soldiers from gunshot wounds at Deepcut Barracks between 1995 and 2002.'[12]

By 2007, verbatim theatre was becoming *the* prevalent form for dealing with The Big Topics. Other significant additions to the genre included *Gladiator Games*, interviews surrounding the murder of a young Asian man in prison by the violent racist with whom he was made to share a cell; *The Trouble With Asian Men*,[13] Tamasha's examination of masculinity in Asian culture; *Stockwell*, a tribunal play looking at the inquiry into the shooting of innocent Brazilian Jean Charles de Menezes; and *My Name is Rachel Corrie*, an adaptation of the diaries of an American activist killed in Palestine. So pervasive was verbatim theatre that leading British playwright Dennis Kelly wrote a fascinating piece critiquing the form. *Taking Care of Baby* (Birmingham Rep and Hampstead Theatre, 2007) is a piece of verbatim theatre with a difference.[14] It opens with the words: 'The following has been taken word for word from interviews and correspondence. Nothing has been added and everything is in the subjects' own words, though some editing has taken place. Names have not been changed.' What this disclaimer does not tell the audience is that every word, every character and indeed the whole narrative, is made up. At no point is this crucial fact revealed. The story of *Taking Care of Baby* deals with the fictional 'Leeman Keatley Syndrome', which had significant similarities to the disputed cases of 'Münchausen's Syndrome by Proxy' – a theory put forward by Sir Roy Meadow as evidence that a number of mothers had been directly responsible for killing their children, which was discredited earlier in the 2000s. Kelly also makes a wider point about authorship. By having made up not only the 'testimonies' but also the 'facts', Kelly drew attention to the much-debated issue of how much editorializing went on in the creation of verbatim theatre, and also the wider way in which it could be seen to have provided a convenient way for dramatists to author their views on a particular subject under the guise of reportage.

*   *   *

Around the same time that the Tricycle's tribunal plays were emerging in Britain, in the United States, an actress called Anna Deavere Smith was creating one-woman-shows about the Crown Heights Riot (*Fires in the mirror* [1992]) and the Los Angeles Riots (*Twilight: Los Angeles*, 1992 [1994]) using a new technique for verbatim theatre. The basic approach was the same: identify a subject ripe for investigation; find people somehow connected to, involved in, affected by the subject; interview them. Where Deavere Smith's method differed was her use of the recorded material. Rather than transcribing the interviews and editing the words into a script which she or other actors could then perform, Deavere Smith edited the sound recordings themselves into the shape of the show, and then used these recordings as an integral part of her rehearsal process.

As well as making shows of her own using this method, Deavere Smith ran workshops on her technique in New York. One of these was attended by Mark Wing-Davey who is widely credited with bringing a new headphone back to Britain, where he ran workshops on it at The Actor's Centre starting in the late 1990s. One early result of these workshops was the little-known, little-documented Non-Fiction

Theatre company. The method came to prominence in 2003, when the young theatremaker Alecky Blythe's company Recorded Delivery opened a new verbatim piece featuring performers wearing headphones called *Come Out Eli* at the three-year-old Arcola theatre in Dalston, Hackney. The show explored the 15-day Graham Road siege in Hackney from Boxing Day 2002, during which 32-year-old Eli Hall had barricaded himself into his flat with a hostage and firearms. The show was seen by Patrick Marmion for *Time Out*, who declared it: 'the funniest, saddest, most ingenious show in London'[15] and transferred to the BAC in March 2004 for another run as part of the *Time Out* Critics' Choice strand.

Reviewing this transfer, Ian Shuttleworth in the *Financial Times* describes:

> The five performers wear Mini Disc players which carry the edit of the interviews, and rather than learning their lines they recite what comes over their earphones exactly as they hear it. It reproduces everyday speech patterns and intonations in a way no improvisation or devised work can ever quite do.
>
> It doesn't feel artificial, either. You spot things like the actors plugging into each other's machines for exchanges when dialogue needs to be closely synchronised, but it very quickly becomes just another condition of the production, no more obtrusive than the multiple role-playing (five players, more than 40 characters in 72 minutes: the play can only be as long as the maximum capacity of a MiniDisc [!]).[16]

And while Lyn Gardner, reviewing the original production in the *Guardian*, voiced concerns about the ethics of the approach,[17] *Come Out Eli* had put Recorded Delivery and Mark Wing-Davey's adaption of Deavere Smith's technique on the map. *The Girlfriend Experience* which opened at the Royal Court Theatre Upstairs in autumn 2008 before transferring to the main house of the Young Vic in 2009, moved the form forward. While Recorded Delivery's previous pieces had contained some fascinating, hilarious and candid interviews with its subjects – Blythe is clearly as talented an interviewer as she is a theatremaker – this was less a matter of interview, but of simple presence-in-the-room. *The Girlfriend Experience* opened a window on a group of sex-workers living and working in Bournemouth, talking not only to Blythe but nattering with each other. An early draft presented at the Royal Court's *Rough Cuts* season was almost Beckettian with its real-time waiting for the phone to ring, and bleak cycles of boredom and silence punctuated with paid-for sex. The final, more upbeat version had more laughs and set-pieces, but still presented a necessary, conflicted picture of sex-work in the twenty-first century.

It is after this chapter's remit closes, that the real apex of Alecky Blythe's career comes, with the 'verbatim musical' *London Road*, which premièred at the Cottesloe Theatre of the National in 2011 before transferring for a sell-out run at the NT's Olivier theatre in 2012.

*   *   *

Looking at one particular type of work being made in Britain in the 2000s, we see that vertabim theatre includes everything from small studios at the BAC or Arcola, and workshops at The Actors Centre, 'new writing theatres' like the Bush and the Hampstead, to the National Theatre's largest space on the South Bank and even the West End; everything from 'physical theatre companies' like Frantic Assembly to the ensemble of the National Theatre. It was performed in traditional and 'found' spaces. It covered topics from the urgent, pressing and national, to the minute, personal and unconsidered. The pieces were edited by a single hand or assembled collaboratively; minimally directed, or shaped into lavishly produced musical theatre. In short, verbatim theatre could be said to have touched on almost every possible way of working in modern British theatre.

2. Headphones

Developments in technology have a way of impacting on the sort of theatre it is possible to make – especially for young companies. Much of the form of Britain's radical theatre scene of the 1970s was attributable in part to the launch of *Time Out* and the Ford Transit Van,[18] as Chris

Megson suggests in his introduction to the 1970s edition of this series. In the 2000s it was the astonishing developments in digital technology that defined the decade. On the Edinburgh Fringe in 2000, for example, mobile phone ownership was not even the norm. By Edinburgh 2009 it was becoming unusual to find a mobile phone that did not include an MP3 player, a camera, a video camera and sound recorder *as standard*. And *everyone* had one. The iPod was ubiquitous and headphones were everywhere.

Alongside this boom in technology came a corresponding growth of work which made use of it. At the start of the decade 'multi-media' productions were still the oft ill-judged preserve of large, well-funded companies and buildings. By its end, you could hardly find a student production that did not incorporate video projections, live-feeds, homemade soundscapes and all manner of other technical wizardry. The fact that anyone with a laptop and some free, downloaded software could edit sound and video produced an unheralded revolution in theatre comparable to the early days of punk music. One striking new use this technology was put to was the creation of headphone-based theatre.

Theatre curator, maker and academic Andy Field suggests the artist Janet Cardiff's audio walks, which she started making in 1991, as the stepping off point for this new form,[19] citing her piece for Artangel *The Missing Voice (Case Study B)* (Whitechapel Gallery, 1999) as seminal for UK artists. In 2001 the company Blast Theory made *Can You See Me Now?*, a piece the company describes as 'a game' that made use of headphones and then fledgling GPS technology, premièring in Sheffield at the b.tv festival. This was followed by *Uncle Roy All Around You* in 2003 which developed the 'game' aspects of *Can You See Me Now?* It was 2007's *Rider Spoke*, playing at the Barbican as part of their BITE season that brought the company to wider attention. *Rider Spoke* is described as 'a work for cyclists combining theatre with game play and state of the art technology'. Field's review of the experience[20] is worth reading in full, but it concluded:

> There was a yearning here to create a beautiful journey through the city, a delicate network of small voices listening to each other.

49

To a degree the show achieves this. And yet, the time limitations and the sense of alienation from the technology, make you feel less like a player in a game and more like an audience member consuming a product, spending 60 minutes experiencing something that has the potential to be so much more.

At the same time that this strand of audience-of-one, site-specific or site-generic pieces were beginning to bloom, setting out in a different direction was Ant Hampton and Silvia Mercuriali's Rotozaza. In 1999 Rotozaza made a piece of performance called *BLOKE* – the first of the company's 'Theatre of Command and Response' (or TOCAR) pieces, spurred by a desire to see a non-actor friend perform on stage. The next TOCAR piece was a show for two similarly instructed performers called *RomCom* which premièred in 2003.[21] Thomas Frank's Notes on '*RomCom*' explain the piece:

> A male and a female actor meet for the first time on stage. They put on the headphones and act via prompts from a CD. A video projection is the only light source. Nothing is rehearsed.
>
> A man and a woman meet up, fall in love, get married, lose parents, get divorced and then can't stay alone . . . The enormous quality of the text by Glen Neath lies in its openness and fragmentary form . . . The tension of the show results from these two extremes: 'on the one hand, everything is pre-recorded on electronic media. A strict form where nothing can be changed. The stage situation on the other hand is completely opposite: nothing is secure, nothing to rely on.'[22]

A review in the *Glasgow Herald* suggested it 'resembles one of Godard's 1960's movies, full of jump-cut montages between close-ups of blank-eyed lovers and excursions into heavily captioned symbolism. As well as a comedy, it is a complex study of compatibility and communication.'

Tim Crouch arrived at his similar approach for performing *An Oak Tree* by an entirely separate route:

> I remember doing a short section of the *An Oak Tree* at a Paines Plough event at the Menier Chocolate Factory in early 2005 at an event curated by Mark Ravenhill, with Hannah Ringham as my second actor. In that, I had a tape cassette walkman with the main Father's speech on it (with spaces) and, at one point, I just asked her to put the headphones in, switch it on and deliver the speech. This was before I knew about the possible technology that would allow me to talk into the second actor's ears. . . .[23]

In 2007, Rotozaza unveiled their most groundbreaking work to date. The concept behind *Etiquette* is a simple extension of the TOCAR technique with one crucial difference – the two performers are also the only two audience members experiencing the show. The 'show' was two sets of headphones attached to the recorded script. Audience pairs would perform the piece to each other and that was (and still is – *Etiquette* is still touring, now in several languages) the whole of the show. The extent to which this redefined, or made explicit, the audience's responsibility for the creation of meaning within a piece of theatre underlined another of the major currents flowing through British theatre in the 2000s. Rotozaza christened this technique 'autoteatro'. Subsequent examples, *GuruGuru* and *Wondermart*, were unveiled by Rotozaza at Forest Fringe in 2009, and Ant Hampton and Tim Etchells' *The Quiet Volume* premièred outwith the scope of this chapter in the stunning, modernist library of the Humboldt Universität, Berlin in 2010.

Hundreds of examples of works using headphones began popping up. Unrelated to Rotozaza, in 2003 the artist Graeme Miller made *Linked*, a piece which was experienced by walking a three-mile route, along which 20 transmitters continually broadcast hidden voices, recorded testimonies and rekindled memories of those who once lived and worked where a motorway now runs.[24] In the later years of the decade the artist Duncan Speakman created, or maybe 'orchestrated', a series of pieces called Subtlemobs – in part a response to the vogue for 'flash-mobs' and 'silent discos'. The art group Platform made 'an interactive opera for one'[25] . . . *And While London Burns* (2006) imagining a walk round a post-environmental-apocalypse City – which again can still be downloaded.[26] Andy Field made *The Last Walk of Carlow Man* for a festival in Carlow, Ireland (2008); the brilliant performer, writer and sound designer Melanie Wilson made *Mari Me Archie*[27] (2009) as a companion piece to her show *Iris Brunette*, and David Leddy has made many such pieces, most notably within the 2000s *Susurrus* (2009).

While many of these pieces were designed to be experienced singly, and were often not limited to a specific time-frame and sometimes were not even anchored to a particular place, other headphone pieces still observed these once-vital rules of theatre. Shunt artist David Rosenberg's *Contains Violence* (2008), made for the Lyric Hammersmith, had its audiences stood outside on the theatre's first floor concrete terrace, watching a drama unfold in a disused office block opposite while listening to the soundtrack of what they were watching, live, through headphones. It was *Electric Hotel* (2010)[28] that made good on the promise of *Contains Violence* as critic Matt Trueman describes:

> *Electric Hotel* maintains all the mystery enforced by the glass partition by refusing us a closer inspection and keeping us at arms length, but its chief success is to make the barrier seem semi-permeable. This time Rosenberg, co-directing with choreographer Frauke Requardt, manages to draw us in. Or even: through. Simultaneously invested – even if still not quite empathetically – and utterly outside, our perspective multiplies: we're within and without, attached but adrift.

Similarly, the Leeds-based operation Slung Low made a number of staggering event-theatre pieces for which audiences definitely needed to be present at a specific time in a specific place to witness feats of visual bravura such as a body suddenly plummeting from the sky (*Mapping The City*, 2008) or huge explosions and hundreds of soldiers rushing across a quiet city square (*Beyond The Frontline*, 2009[29]), or chasing through underground car parks in Manchester or London pursued by vampires (*They Only Come At Night*, 2009). Of the latter, *Time Out* suggested: 'If the mark of great theatre is that it changes the way you look at the world, then Slung Low might just be the greatest theatre company around. . . .'[30] In the case of Slung Low, the audience received the majority of the sound for the pieces through noise-excluding headphones which were custom-made by the company, so they could be totally in charge of their audiences' aural experience.

As we see above, there is a lot of crossover between this headphone-based work and work made in/for found-spaces, with many headphone pieces granting audiences a certain amount of ambulatory freedom for their duration. Conversely, the first piece by young company non zero one (*Would Like To Meet*,[31] 2009) – who have subsequently made pieces for the Barbican, The Bush, and the National; making them perhaps the most 'theatre establishment' headphone-based company yet – required almost split-second timings for 'chance' encounters between their individual, aurally guided audience members to take place. As Field writes in a piece for *The Stage* on the subject:

> As headphones have become all-pervasive, we grow increasingly adept at utilising this technology – hearing voices or music whispered in our ears is becoming as familiar as settling into a theatre or cinema seat.
>
> Rather than the flourishing of a new genre, what I believe is happening is the ubiquity of this technology – meaning that it can emerge as a useful and imaginative solution to a diverse range of creative challenges. Not a single all-encompassing form, but an extension of a range of different ways of working.[32]

3. Sites

Another key trend in 2000s theatre was the burgeoning sector variously described as: 'site-specific', 'site-sympathetic', or 'immersive' theatre, with *Time Out*'s 2008 end-of-year round-up including the following entry: 'It's been a good year for . . . site-sympathetic theatre. Soon every theatre will be putting on performances in underground car parks and office spaces and using the main stages for storage.'[33] Plenty has already been written on the necessity of differentiating between these forms, much of it excoriating the lazy taxonomy which abounded in both journalism[34] and press-releases from companies themselves. My own rough guidelines, when writing about such work for publication, tended to be: site-specific theatre is theatre which has been, well, specifically made for a specific site (be it for reasons of the site's particular interest or resonances, its unique architecture or layout), site-sympathetic theatre is similar, except it could theoretically be moved to a different site without significant damage to its integrity. 'Immersive' differs slightly from the above two categories, since it describes the audience's relation to the piece, and is the most contested term, since the extent to which one has to be 'immersed' has been argued and counter-argued in numerous articles and blog-posts. This section looks mainly at the work of the two companies – Shunt and Punchdrunk – most famously identified with these various terms. Both the work and use of space by each company differs wildly, and neither company should be regarded as the first to have made a something akin to a promenade performance in a non-traditional theatre space.

*   *   *

The Shunt collective was formed in 1998 by Serena Bobowski, Gemma Brockis, Louise Mari, Lizzie Clachan, Hannah Ringham, Layla Rosa, David Rosenberg, Andrew Rutland, Mischa Twitchin and Heather Uprichard all of whom met on an MA course at the Central School of Speech and Drama. After graduating, they found a disused railway arch in Bethnal Green and began producing shows there.

The Ballad of Bobby François opened in late October 1999 to a tentatively enthusiastic review in *Time Out*[35] and Lyn Gardner for the *Guardian* declaring: 'This is fledgling work, but I reckon this company may eventually soar.'[36]

The piece went on to play at the Edinburgh Fringe in 2000,[37] where the company won a Total Theatre Award,[38] and then at The Drome as part of the London International Mime Festival 2001 where a young

Mark Espiner, then writing for *Time Out*, was smitten: '*The Ballad of Bobby Francois* is an astounding piece of theatre – an immersive experience . . . Shunt tip their hat at the De La Guarda style of theatre but provide a narrative to boot and carry it off with style. Radical, original, incredible. . . .'[39]

Thanks to all this exposure, the group's 2002 show, *Dance Bear Dance* – a terrifying, hallucinatory experience about global conspiracies based loosely on the Gunpower Plot of 1605 – was seen by Nicholas Hytner and Nick Starr, who were poised to take over as the artistic director and executive director of the National Theatre. In an interview with Andrew Eglinton for the *London Theatre Blog* some years later, Shunt member Mischa Twitchin recalls that Hytner and Starr

invited us to do something in one of the non-theatre spaces on the Southbank. We thought what could we possibly do there? But all credit to them, they acknowledged that, and when we found this space, Nick Starr hosted the negotiations with Railtrack in his office . . . They also supported us with a couple of fund-raising evenings . . . and, then, crucially the tickets for our first show here, *Tropicana*, were sold through their box office, so there could be credit card bookings in advance.[40]

In the same interview, Twitchin also described his company's ambivalence about the word 'theatre':

Like the company name, 'Shunt', the space doesn't say 'theatre'. It means the invitation to an audience can be part of the work, part of the dramaturgy, part of the scenography. The actual entrance to the space can be materially reinvented for any particular show. One of the things that the ten members of the Collective agree on artistically was that, even if any individual had an interest in working in theatres, there was a shared commitment to working in our own space. For the public – as distinct from the critics – the work needn't then be prejudged in terms of 'a night out at the theatre'.[41]

Within five years of forming, Shunt had moved from their modest space in Bethnal Green to the vast, strange network of man-made caves under London Bridge station – christened 'The Shunt Vaults', while tickets for their shows were being sold by the National Theatre.

*　*　*

The same year that Shunt moved to London Bridge, another young company was opening their version of *Macbeth* in an abandoned school in Kennington. Punchdrunk had existed as a company since 2000, but it was this show, *Sleep No More* (revived in New York in 2012), which was to prove their break-out hit.

Compared to Shunt, Punchdrunk's shows had much less of a common journey through them. Though the term 'installation' was bandied about in early Shunt reviews, there was still a sense of promenade theatre – of a cohesive, collective journey through the pieces. Punchdrunk were clear their objectives were different. The company declared themselves makers of 'immersive' theatre; audience members donned masks and were free to wander anywhere they pleased. Where Shunt used often dizzying sudden changes of perspective as part of their mise-en-scène, Punchdrunk relied upon an individual's curiosity and desire to unfold their own journey through a piece. Reviewing *Sleep No More* in 2003, Lyn Gardner observed:

> In the old school hall, the scene in which the ghost of Banquo appears at the Macbeths' dinner table is enacted with an idiosyncratic flourish. Another room offers you Birnam Wood, yet another the McDuffs' [*sic*] family home in the form of a doll's house . . . It is an evening that rewards the effort you put in. You could do it in an hour, but you could make a three-hour evening of it if you really wanted to see the full cycle. . . .[42]

Punchdrunk's next show, *The Firebird Ball*, found the company moving to Wapping, refining their techniques, and returning again to Shakespeare – this time *Romeo and Juliet* combined with Stravinsky's

Firebird Suite. Former BAC artistic director Tom Morris, in an interview with *WhatsOnStage.com*, described the piece thus:

> Nick Hytner and I went to see *The Firebird Ball.* I actually went twice. The first time I wandered around in this warehouse for two hours and I kept glimpsing extraordinary and mysterious things and had a wonderful time. I came out, met the director and realised I'd missed most of the show, so I went back and spent another two hours there and still didn't see everything that was going on. There's something very extraordinary not only about the quality of the work I'd seen but also about the fact it's the kind of work that you can really explore as a member of the audience. It is so rich that you can see a tiny bit of what's on offer and come away fascinated and excited.[43]

This interview forms the backbone of an article revealing that the National Theatre was to support Punchdrunk's next show, *Faust*.

As seen in the NT's alliance with Shunt previously, Nicholas Hytner was revealing himself not only to be a canny Artistic Director, but an astute operator in London's theatrical ecology. He knew the National Theatre had material resources it could offer to fledgling companies making their work off-site, and by doing so he allowed for a two-way flow of reflected glory: the NT got to look young and cool for promoting 'edgy', 'experimental' work, while the edgy experimental work-makers received access to a far wider audience and implied seal of theatrical approval 'from the grown-ups' (the word 'imprimatur' gets bandied about in several reviews). Shunt continued their alliance with the National Theatre beyond *Club Tropicana* to the present day. Tickets for Punchdrunk's next show were also sold through the National, but the show itself was installed in the BAC.

In any history of the 2000s in British theatre, Punchdrunk's *Masque of the Red Death* has to figure as a defining moment. David Jubb and David Micklem, the joint artistic directors of BAC, had just managed to wangle the use of the entire building, and they handed the whole thing over to Punchdrunk so the company could convert the entire rabbit warren-like maze of rooms in this nineteenth-century Town Hall into a kind of gothic nightmare for their loose adaptation of Edgar Allen Poe short stories. Writing a week after *Masque* had opened to the first-stringers of the national press, long-time supporter of the company Lyn Gardner wrote a blog for the *Guardian*. Writing largely as a corrective to Michael Billington's curiously needless qualifier that '[he] still [saw] this kind of magical mystery tour as an alternative to, rather than a substitute for, conventional drama', her re-review also hit on a far more crucial observation:

> What few of the reviews have mentioned is that this is a BAC co-production – and BAC has commissioned a number of artists including Kneehigh, Blind Summit, Julian Fox, Kazuko Hohki, [1927], and Hannah Ringham to create their own pieces as a response to Poe. These are hidden within the main show . . . Those with a detective's frame of mind can indulge in a treasure hunt created by Gideon Reeling and a mysterious BAC artist called Coney.[44]

If Punchdrunk's *Masque* contained this offer to a number of other artists embedded in its superstructure, then the roll-call of artists who appeared at the Shunt Lounge events almost demands a book in its own right. When the Shunt Collective were not producing their own shows in the Shunt Vault they curated The Shunt Lounge. At its worst, this resulted in the curious spectacle of some of Britain's most radical, visionary theatre-makers running one of the best late bars and clubs in London. But at its best, it provided brilliant spaces and technical resources for what felt like a near-endless roll-call of collaborators and young makers. To try to do justice to this apparently endless stream of invention is impossible. By the end of the decade, the popularity of Shunt and Punchdrunk had sparked a renewed fascination for theatremakers young and old for experimenting with the spaces in which they performed their work, but for experiments in one-to-one performances, and interactive theatre.

4. Ecosystems

As these new or rediscovered forms were emerging in this early part of the decade, just as significant was the changing landscape of spaces available to artists. Work flourished much more readily when people had somewhere they could put it on, and those spaces could even become an actor in the way the work was received, responded-to and understood. By 2000, it would also have been easy to argue the old fringe model – the network of rooms above, beside or below London pubs – was all but dead. Dead, or else – in the case of venues like the Bush or The Gate – elevated to 'Off-West-End' status by virtue of a solid critical profile and public funding.

The first new venue of the 2000s was the Arcola Theatre, founded by Turkish-born artistic director Mehmet Ergan and executive producer Leyla Nazli. In the 1990s, Ergan had set up the first incarnation of the Southwark Playhouse. In 2000 he opened the doors of a former shirt-factory on Arcola Street, Dalston, to a ticket-buying public. The venue rapidly became a huge success, due partly to canny programming (see *Come Out Eli*, above), but also thanks to the boost it was given early on by the simple fact that established theatre companies wanted to put their work on there. The Arcola had two main things going for it: first, it was firmly anchored at the heart of a diverse East London community, which meant companies like Out of Joint (*Macbeth*, 2004) and The Oxford Stage Company (*Cleansed*, 2005) now had ready-made access to a theatregoing demographic who might not have habitually trooped down to the West End for a show. Secondly, and more crucially, it had this fantastic warehouse-y space. It felt like a more exciting place to watch a play than the gilded proscenium arches or Cold War concrete bunkers on offer in central London. It had peeling paint, dusty floorboards and rusty girders. It had the romance of post-industrial dereliction that was to become another marker of so much theatre in the 2000s.

The original Underbelly venue in Edinburgh performed a similar function. Granted, it would be stretching the imagination to call the dank, only partly man-made network of caves and brickwork that used to be Edinburgh library's vaults 'post-industrial', but in its early days it shared the same kind of gloomy glamour. The work seen at the

59

Underbelly in the first few years was predominantly that of young, post-student companies specializing in what was then filed under 'devised' or 'physical' or 'visual' theatre: Warwick University's NSDF hit, the 'ballet about an autopsy'[45] *Witness Me*, graduate companies from Oxford University presenting bold versions of *Attempts On Her Life* and the Riot Group's recent Fringe hit *Wreck the Airline Barrier*, or the American dramatist Peter Morris' dark monologue inspired by the Columbine shootings, *Second Amendment Club*.

Another Edinburgh venue that made an indelible impression of British theatre's sense of the possible was Aurora Nova at St Stephen's. Despite only running from 2003–10, the venue – the main hall of a large, stone, deconsecrated kirk – booked some of the most important international work seen in Edinburgh in those years outside of the more forbidding (and certainly more expensive) International Festival. Fringe-goers were treated to a programme including work by the pioneering Russian 'science-theatre' of AKHE, the falsetto Berlin-cabaret of The Tiger Lillies, the mesmerizing dance-theatre of Do-Fabrik and innumerable other dance, visual, physical and clown-influenced performance companies, from mainland Europe and the United Kingdom.

Back in London, in 2002 the old Grace Theatre in Battersea, straight down the hill from the BAC, came under the management of Paul Higgins and was rebranded Theatre 503. Higgins' artistic directorship was remarkable. What he did, as soon as he got hold of the theatre, was to call up every theatre with a literary department and ask them about the best unsolicited scripts they had been sent but, for whatever reason, had not been able to stage themselves. The result was that during Higgins' four-year tenure Theatre 503 discovered some brilliant, important new writers such as Dennis Kelly and Phil Porter. Theatre 503 also became home to The Apathists, a group of six playwrights – Mike Bartlett, Nick Gill, Morgan Lloyd Malcolm, Duncan Macmillan, Simon Vinnicombe and Rachel Wagstaff – who had met on a variety of Young Writers' courses and wanted to commit to writing a new short piece for performance every month to be performed in front of a proper live audience. Although the group only ran for a year between March 2006 and March 2007, it produced a disproportionately fine body of work, and this freedom to experiment plainly impacted on the careers of those involved all of whom had become professionally produced playwrights by the end of the decade. Indeed, Mike Bartlett's play *Contractions*, later produced by the Royal Court and then on Radio 4, had its genesis as a piece for the Apathists. Another pub theatre that survived the death of the old fringe, and did so entirely without subsidy, was the Finborough. Nestled in the fork of an easily overlooked road near Earl's Court tube station, throughout the 2000s, under artistic director Neil McPherson, the theatre seemed to exist primarily as a kind of wet dream for Michael Billington, staging an astute mix of rarely-revived, lesser state-of-the-nation by well-known writers such as Priestley or Galsworthy, and straight-up personal but political new writing from up-and-coming playwrights like Jack Thorne, Sarah Grochala and James Graham.

The remit of the above two theatres could be seen to define one side of what almost became the defining theatrical schism of the decade – the split between 'New Writing' and 'New Work'. Representing 'New Work' – variously referred to as Visual Theatre, Devised Theatre and Physical Theatre were venues like the BAC and Camden People's Theatre (or CPT). Under its first artistic director of the decade, Tom Morris, the BAC pioneered an eccentric agenda running close to Morris' own idiosyncratic tastes offering a home for companies like the Cornish theatre group Kneehigh, the performance artists Kazuko Hohki and Frank Chickens and the heroically comic attempts to stage vast spectacles such as the *Dambusters, Ben Hur* or the *1966 World Cup Final* on stage. By the time Morris passed on the Artistic directorship to Davids Jubb and Micklem, artistic policy at the BAC had hardened into a 'no scripts' rule. Similarly, when Chris Goode was running the CPT he recalls his only instruction when he took over was to keep New Writing out of the venue. As Goode is also a writer, this illustrates the strange state of affairs that had arisen mid-decade.

Another home for this sort of work was the Lyric Theatre in Hammersmith. Writing on the occasion of Sean Holmes' ascension to its artistic directorship in 2009, Lyn Gardner observed:

Anyone at the Lyric Hammersmith on a Monday evening in March for the opening night of Gecko's *The Overcoat* would have

61

witnessed a curious sight. On one side of the foyer stood a large number of theatre-makers and producers, many of them involved in devised and visual theatre, who have been strongly associated with David Farr's outgoing regime. On the other side stood representatives of the UK's new writing scene, some of whom I suspect had not stepped inside the building for years. They were there because of the recent appointment of Sean Holmes as the Lyric's new artistic director. If you wanted a manifestation of the fissures that still run through UK theatre, then this seemed to be it.

I confess, reading this description of the Lyric, I was surprised since under David Farr, who had come straight from the RSC (and indeed opened his artistic directorship of the building with a transfer of his RSC production of *Julius Caesar*), and went on to produce work like an African-set version of Brecht's *Arturo Ui* which would not have felt out of place at the National. On the other hand, during the 2000s I also saw (among others): the Tiger Lillies/Improbable alt.theatre smash-hit musical *Shockheaded Peter*; the Frantic Assembly/Mark Ravenhill collaboration *pool (no water)*; a dance-theatre piece based on the Smiths' back catalogue called *Some Girls Are Bigger Than Others* by the briefly-popular mainland European company Anonymous Society. At the same time in the Lyric's studio, works by Spymonkey, Thirty Bird and Chris Goode's superlative *Longwave* contributed further towards making the Lyric an unconscious go-to destination for 'alternative' theatre in the 2000s. Similarly, The Drum Theatre in Plymouth also deserves credit as one of the major sponsors outside London of serious alternative theatre. So much so that its role as a commissioner and co-producer of work should be acknowledged far more widely than it has been hitherto.

* * *

Crucial to an understanding of the way work developed during this period is understanding the extent of the space and flexibility of programming at BAC and the Shunt Vaults, which meant many more artists could put their work in front of audiences, with the BAC popularizing the 'Scratch Night' where artists or performance groups could show embryonic forms of ideas to a largely sympathetic audience who would often be requested to fill in 'feedback forms' to let the artists know what they had liked, what they had not, and to give some ideas about how they would like the work to develop. This 'scratch culture' had its discontents. In an illuminating *Guardian* article from 2005 Richard Thomas – one of the team behind the massive hit *Jerry Springer: the Opera* – and Chris Goode offered *pro* and *con* positions. Goode (*con*) concluded:

> The defining cliché of Scratch culture is that, in it, artists are offered 'a safe space to fail'. But a safe space isn't the kind of 'risk-taking' environment that Scratch proponents espouse, of course: it's the reverse, a neutralised zone in which (necessarily) risk-averse organisations can release beta-versions of new products without exposing themselves commercially.
>
> The result is a generation of artists who talk endlessly about riskiness but can't say what's at stake; who are rendered functionally inert by a matrix of focus groups and safety nets; who conspire with venues and funders to evade the most pressing questions.
>
> All theatre should be like a good Scratch night. But Scratch culture won't get us there.[46]

Over the decade, writers also evolved a scratch culture of their own with the growth in popularity of the short play night. These self-explanatory events usually involved four or five young(-ish) or new(-ish) writers writing 20-minute playlets, sometimes in response to a theme – as with the theatre company Nabokov's *Present: Tense* events, or Theatre 503's *Rapid Response* nights. Alternatively, such evenings could act as a showcase for new talent, as in the case of DryWrite or the long-running Miniaturists events running for seven years now at the Arcola. They also sometimes worked as indicative statements of intent for more established companies like Paines Plough's *Later* and *Wild Lunch* series. By 2007 the influence of the short play night and scratch culture had reached as far up the food chain as the Royal Court and Hampstead Theatre with the former launching its own *Rough Cuts* seasons, which in the first couple of years included early versions of Laura Wade's *Posh* and Recorded Delivery's *The Girlfriend Experience*.

Another game-changing venue/organization/festival of the 2000s was Forest Fringe.

In 2006 the artist Deborah Pearson was asked by her friends at the Forest Café, a volunteer-run vegetarian café hidden away in the middle of Edinburgh, if she'd run a performance programme during the Fringe in the church hall above their café. Their only stipulation was that it couldn't be part of the official Fringe (a 'fringe of the fringe' as it would later be called by almost everyone apart from us) and that it would be free to everyone; there would be no charge for artists to 'hire' the space, it would be staffed by volunteers, and the shows themselves would be free for audiences. In 2008 Deborah was joined by Andy Field, who was involved in the first year of Forest Fringe as an artist. They got a tiny but important grant from BAC in London and used it to rent a flat that the invited artists could stay in. This festival was an unexpected and remarkable Edinburgh success, attracting hundreds of people to the old disused church hall and in the process winning a Herald Angel. So little was known about the venue that when the Herald newspaper decided to give it this award, the journalists were not actually sure whom it was they were supposed to tell.[47]

The reasons for Forest Fringe's success were manifold and simple. There was a hand-picked selection of companies and artists, like Bristol's Tinned Fingers, the Paper Cinema and Lucy Ellinson. Chris Goode did three afternoons of performance poetry including a complete reading of Alan Ginsburg's *Howl*, Kurt Schwitters' *Ursonate*, Cathy Berberian's *Stripsody* and his own *An Introduction To Speed Reading*. Chris Thorpe and Jon Spooner performed a double bill of solo pieces followed by a first work-in-progress of the new Unlimited show, *The Moon The Moon*; there was one of the first ever work-in-progress performances of Action Hero's *Watch Me Fall* (which Forest Fringe is, at the time of writing, taking as a finished piece to Dublin and Texas) and an event curated by the company Rabbit. A BAC One O'clock scratch programme included the very first experiment from American theatre company The TEAM for the project that became their popular 2011 show *Mission Drift*. And it was all effectively for free. It felt a world away from the plastic, corporate spaces of the 'Big Four' super venues (Pleasance, Gilded Balloon, Assembly Rooms, Underbelly).

Beyond these more obvious single venues, another crucial plank of Britain's theatre-going possibilities in the 2000s was provided by a number of festivals: the London International Festival of Theatre (LIFT), the Manchester International Festival, the London International Mime Festival (LIMF) and, added to these in 2007, the biennial SPILL festival, as well as the Barbican Centre's gradual expansion to a year-round rolling programme of its BITE festival. Alongside the Edinburgh International Festival and Edinburgh Fringe, these festivals gave vital exposure to international work that was otherwise still criminally under-represented in British theatres. Also worthy of mention is the National Student Drama Festival which continued to uncover some of the country's most exciting young theatrical talent before it had even left university, or even school/college, throughout the decade. Some of its most notable finds in the 2000s included the playwrights Lucy Prebble and Joel Horwood, the director Carrie Cracknell, the actors Ruth Wilson and Hattie Morahan.

Another important area is the growing influence that contemporary dance had on theatremakers in the 2000s. As we have already seen, the dance-theatre company Frantic Assembly played a crucial role developing the style of NTS' *Black Watch*. And in 2007 when Carrie Cracknell and Natalie Abrahami took over artistic directorship of the Gate Theatre they not only brought in choreographers to collaborate on their productions of classic and new European plays but also to generate new and exciting original pieces of their own, two of the most successful being Pierre Rigal's solo piece, *Press* (2008), and *I Am Falling* (also 2008) directed by Cracknell, choreographed by Anna Williams and written/dramaturged by Jenny Worton. Interestingly, both transferred to Sadler's Wells, a theatre dedicated to dance

65

performances, and consequently off the radars of most theatre critics, just as the Gate had hardly registered previously with the dance critics. But over the course of the decade the theatre, which also hosted pieces by influential choreographers like Pina Bausch, Alain Platel and Jérôme Bel, became an increasingly important destination for theatremakers. As Lyn Gardner observed: 'If a bomb had dropped on Sadler's Wells on the night of Bel's performance of *The Show Must Go On*, pretty well the entire, more radical wing of UK performance and theatre would have been wiped out at a stroke.'[48]

5. The Royal Court, the money and the new writing industry

If one took the propaganda for the 1990s as a theatrical decade seriously – the decade of 'The New Writing Explosion', of 'In-Yer-Face-Theatre', and so on – one might expect coming into the 2000s the new decade would be awash with violent, brash, young plays with the same feeling of vitality from the outset. In practice it felt slightly different. The buzz Stephen Daldry and Graham Whybrow had spun around the Court had been a hugely effective narrative, but it had run out of steam. It had been indicative rather than descriptive at the time; and now Daldry had moved on, anointing Ian Rickson to lead the Court back into the newly refurbished building. And Ian Rickson was a different man from Daldry. Depending on whom you ask, he was either a good, quiet man with a taste for small, quiet, introspective plays or just someone who had decided 'In-Yer-Face' was too much associated with Daldry's time at the Court, and wanted to make his stamp with smaller, more thoughtful, intimate plays. As such, the biggest buzz at the Royal Court in 2000 – the season that saw it return to Sloane Square – was the posthumous première of Sarah Kane's final play *4.48 Psychosis* and the Theatre Downstairs revival of her already seminal 1990s play *Blasted*. Looking back at the early years of the 2000s at the Court, we see there was a respectable enough trickle of new plays coming through, including David Eldridge's *Under The Blue Sky* (2000), Simon Stephens' *Herons* (2001) and Roy Williams' *Fallout* (2003), but the building was perceived to be in trouble. The online theatre magazine, *Encore*, painted a bleak, angry picture in 2003:

> Writers know that there is no vision at the heart of [the Royal Court]. Vision means a strong sense from the leadership of what type of writing they love and want to promote. Vision means a sense of the world, real and imagined, knowing what writing *does*, understanding its mysterious value. Vision can be artistic, it can be political; under previous reigns it has been both. But looking at the work over the last few years can you honestly say there is a sense of theatre in love with the work it produces? Look at the Court's recent programme: does anything connect those plays? Is there any kind of sensibility shaping that programme?[49]

Alongside this feeling of diffusion, another reason some of the Court's best work from this period has not shown up in surveys of the period is that some of the more inspired programming had not been written by British writers. Here we see how having nationality as a criteria in any survey of new work staged in a country over any given time period – or indeed applying the criteria of 'newness' when considering the theatre ecology as a whole over a period – proves crippling. During Rickson's tenure, alongside new work from British writers such as Lucy Prebble (*Sugar Syndrome*, 2003) and Laura Wade (*Breathing Corpses*, 2005) were the British premières of plays by Jon Fosse, Roland Schimmelpfennig and Lars Norén Downstairs and Vassily Sigarev and the Presnyakov Brothers in the Theatre Upstairs. Royal Court playwright Che Walker also suggests that under Rickson there was also a lot more racial equality seen in the playwrights coming up through the Court. Young black voices in particular were heard more clearly and more often. It is easy to forget that for all the underclass youth and violence in the plays of the alleged 'In-Yer-Face' movement, its prime movers were, for the most part, very white and middle-class, and had often studied theatre at university. Simon Stephens adds:

> Another thing about Ian Rickson's programming decisions is that they came out of his commitment, and this was a very

deliberate development from the Daldry era, to produce writers' second, third and fourth plays. He wanted not just to find first time writers, but to support whole careers. In this Richard Bean, Roy Williams, Marina Carr, myself and others really benefited. It wasn't 'radical' or 'sexy' but it did allow playwrights to develop and flourish over time.

There is also the question of production. Looking at Justin Mortimer's 2004 painting 'Three Royal Court Theatre Directors', alongside Stephen Daldry and Ian Rickson, seated and chummily clasping hands, it now seems surprising that the third director – pictured standing adrift from the two men, looking distressed with her hands clutched to her face; a kind of latter-day Cassandra – is the then Royal Court Associate Director Katie Mitchell. We might speculate that Mortimer's painting captures something of the frustration for a director like Mitchell in the European tradition at the writer-centred Court to the written playtext. Rickson and Whybrown also scrapped the old Young People's Theatre and refocused solely on writers, with this new scheme run by the energetic and determined Ola Animashawun. With hindsight, it could be argued that the single most far-reaching act Rickson performed during the whole of his artistic directorship was putting the charismatic playwright Simon Stephens in charge of the Royal Court Young Writers' Group. The names of the members of the groups Stephens taught tally more-or-less name for name with the list of some of the most successful young playwrights now working in Britain: Mike Bartlett, Lucy Prebble, Laura Wade, Jack Thorne and James Graham. Playwright Duncan Macmillan, another successful group member, suggests, 'there's a whole book waiting to be written about Simon's influence on a generation of young writers'. There is no doubt Simon was an inspiration: 'I think everyone was writing plays they wanted Simon to like.'[50]

Rickson's own productions included Beckett's *Krapp's Last Tape* featuring Harold Pinter in the title role and a 'celebrity-cast' production of Chekhov's *The Seagull*, although it was cynically suggested this last served more as a calling card for his re-entry into the world of freelance directing. The production subsequently transferred to Broadway. More strange, though, was the spectacle of the Royal Court celebrating its 50-year anniversary at the home of the English Stage Company (or at least, the fiftieth anniversary of *Look Back in Anger*) with the première *Rock 'n' Roll*, a new play ostensibly about Pink Floyd and the failure of communism, by Britain's most famous Tory-voting playwright Tom Stoppard – a playwright with no prior association with the theatre. In protest, Caryl Churchill withdrew her permission for the Court to also stage a revival of her 1979 play *Cloud Nine*,[51] although she maintained her links with the theatre, and her new play *Drunk Enough To Say I Love You?* premièred later that year. Reviewing the play I suggested we should

> view *Drunk Enough To Say I Love You?* as a satire on *Rock 'n' Roll*'s romantic-comedy exaltation of the overthrow of the Eastern Bloc and the triumph of capitalism, expressing disgust at the crimes and tactics of the winning side . . . Taken in isolation, *Drunk Enough* . . . seems perversely one-sided; viewed as a companion piece to *Rock 'n' Roll*, it begins to sound a lot more like the other side of longer debate.[52]

This anniversary year sums up the patchwork contradictions of Rickson's time at the Court. In April, Simon Stephens' *Motortown* opened, directed by Ramin Gray with movement by the leading Israeli choreographer Hofesh Shechter and an electric performance from regular Court actor Danny Mayes; and in November there was Churchill's furious anti-American, anti-Western, anti-war play. In between, there was a West-End-transferring money-spinner by a Tory playwright.

* * *

Beyond the walls of the Royal Court there were changes taking place around the very concept of new writing. In 1997 Britain elected its first Labour government in 18 years. At the end of 1998 Secretary of State for the Department of Culture Media and Sport Chris Smith announced a massive increase in funding for the arts.[53] The fact the new government even wanted to give this impression of increased public spending on the arts contributed to a new atmosphere of confidence.

More importantly, in 2000 the government also commissioned and received the Boyden Report into regional producing theatres. The study was long, thorough and drew a number of conclusions, which could best be summarized as: investment in theatres will result in more, better theatre in the regions. To its eternal credit, the government listened to the recommendations of the report, and more money was made available to the Arts Council for regional theatres. As Michael Billington notes: 'The result was an exponential leap in funding over the next three years: increases of 91 per cent for Sheffield theatres, 112 per cent for Newcastle's Live Theatre, 72 per cent for the Bolton Octagon. Admittedly, this was putting back money lost over the previous decade and increases also bottomed out in ensuing years. But theatres large and small benefited hugely from the post-Boyden boom.'[54]

If the government and the Arts Council had then left that money to percolate, perceptions of England's funding body may have remained rosy for the rest of the decade. However, alongside the extra money and the good intentions, there was also a perception of micro-management incompatible with the business of making theatre. The end of Mike Bradwell's theatrical memoir *The Reluctant Escapologist* turns into a lengthy attack on Arts Council England: 'Since the departure of Sue Timothy, I felt there was no one at the Arts Council who understood what the Bush was for, or valued our contribution to the theatrical wealth of the nation. What they did want from us, however, was a Cultural Diversity Action Plan.'[55] Even more pragmatic voices conceded ACE had done a poor PR job implementing their enthusiasms regarding outreach and diversity. Both were laudable aims: to oppose greater access to the arts for the poor, the elderly, the disabled, ethnic minorities – everyone beyond a narrow band of the affluent, white middle-class – is bigotry, pure and simple, but criticisms from theatre-makers focused on way in which the Arts Council attempted to achieve these objectives, while the right-wing press, opposed to the very principle of all but the smallest public subsidy, seized on this discontent with glee. The era of 'box-ticking' was born.

70

When in 2007, the Arts Council announced a series of retrenchments of funding, notably the proposed cutting of funding to the Bush Theatre by 40 per cent and by 100 per cent to the National Student Drama Festival, there was a widespread outcry. Equity called an emergency meeting at the Young Vic, and in early January 2008 a vote of no confidence in the Arts Council had been delivered. Subsequently, appeals were heard, many of the cuts rescinded, and the worst catastrophes were averted. It was clear something very fundamental needed to change at the Arts Council. To the eternal credit of Barbara Matthews, who took up the new post as Head of Theatre just before the funding storm of 2007/08 broke – and as such had nothing to do with those decisions – the situation was turned around, and rapidly. Matthews' most simple observation was the Arts Council had somehow found itself positioned as 'the enemy' in the mind of theatre-makers, which was both counter-productive and unnecessary. The Arts Council was, after all, *their* funding body and an advocacy organization representing the interests of artists and theatres to Government. Peer-review panels were reintroduced (across the arts) and 'relationship managers' established. From my own inside perspective (both sitting on a pilot theatre peer-review panel and talking to both Arts Council employees and theatre staff), it was remarkable how quickly the change of culture took hold following the resignation of Peter Hewitt and his replacement Alan Davey's insistence on transparency and consultation.

Flashing forward to 1 April 2011, the Arts Council that dealt with the first set of cuts to arts spending by the new Conservative and Liberal Democrat coalition government is unrecognizable from the organization that had so disastrously delivered the 2008 spending review. Commentators and artists alike agree that, with a few painful exceptions, the revivified Arts Council had made an incredibly good job of an almost impossible task. That the Conservative/Lib-Dem coalition then set about further cutting and dismantling ACE lies outwith the scope of this chapter, but one need only look at back to the landscape described by the Boyden Report with which the 2000s began to understand where this cutting will lead.

* * *

Going back to the arrival of the new money, which was combined with a change in the rubric on *how* lottery money (distributed separately through Grants For The Arts) could be spent on 'non-core' activities, we see it coincided with the buzz of excitement around New Writing. As a result, much of the new money available to theatres was channelled into the creation or expansion of literary departments. It is worth wondering, if Labour had won the General Election in 1992 instead, how Britain's theatre scene would have looked today. However, the creation of 'The New Writing Industry', as it came to be known, played a key role in the way Britain's theatre ecology developed in the 2000s.[56]

Aleks Sierz's survey of New Writing 'Pure' during this decade, *Rewriting the Nation*, offers the conclusion: 'If you can blame playwrights for failing to write [different kinds of] plays, you also have to hold theatres to account for neither commissioning them, nor taking steps to widen their rather narrow repertoire of plays.' (p. 237) Reviewing *Rewriting the Nation*, I suggested, 'this might be a fair assessment to make at the end of a book which had actually considered the total output of any given theatre, including the foreign plays, the revivals, the new writing which isn't "New Writing", the devised work and everything else. But this isn't that book'.[57] Sierz had already dismissed all plays with a historical setting thus: 'History plays can also act, in the words of director Ramin Grey, "as a corrective to our own myopic and self-regarding times". True, but more often they are costume dramas with little relevance to today,' and describes one of the decade's most popular new plays *The History Boys* as 'simply not contemporary'. While partial, Sierz's definition is sadly not just a work of imagination. Through the decade, it often seemed that the guidelines for what constituted 'New Writing' became more and more narrow by the month. Part of the problem was this definition of – capital N, capital W – New Writing, essentially constituted a genre all of its own. In doing so, it marginalized other new plays, not to mention new work, which did not conform to its specifications. Typically, the New Writing play would be naturalistic, contemporary and set in a very specific (usually underprivileged and urban) social milieu. It would generally have a small cast, a perfunctory storyline and forgettable characters. Its point was to offer some kind of an insight into the living conditions and social issues within a particular disadvantaged community. The problems of this sort of social drama are captured in Dan Rebellato's review of Michael Billington's book *State of the Nation*: 'The austerity of Billington's insistence on content – because that's what's really at stake here – is at the cost of many things which have often been considered key to the theatre. Form, theatricality, poetry, metaphor, all of these things are either ignored or dispensed with summarily.'[58]

A number of 'New Writing theatres', including the Royal Court and the Soho, ran writers' groups targeted at members of particular social groups or ethnic minorities with awkward titles like 'Unheard Voices'[59] or 'Giving Voice'.[60] While such schemes had the necessary effect of diversifying the overall pool of writing talent in British theatre, there was a concern that the writers they recruited could be trapped by the narrow confines of what they were asked to write about, and all too often fed little more than an appetite for 'the new', only to be discarded before a second commission. Similarly, while the Royal Court's international programme was admirable in its reach, it did also suffer from two different cultural imperialisms; on one hand, sometimes timidly importing only those plays from other countries that already most resembled British New Writing plays and at the same time exporting the *social issue* New Play model abroad, with workshops encouraging foreign playwrights to write plays offering snapshots of life in their country – again often by shining a light on a particular social problem – which could be easily digested by a British audience. That Britain had other models of playwriting and making theatre, or that other countries had different traditions of writing, let alone of staging work by their writers, sometimes did not figure enough in its thinking.[61] This model of commissioning work did uncover writers who outstripped the deadening model through which they had entered the profession. It also resulted in a lot of first commissions and no follow-ups. The most notable catastrophe for this model of community-engagement New Writing was Gurpreet Kaur Bhatti's *Behzti*, a new play commissioned by Birmingham Rep, hoping to engage with its local Sikh community. The play, which depicted sexual abuse being conducted in a Gurdwara, resulted in the local Sikh community rioting the play off-stage, breaking the windows of the theatre, and sending death-threats to the playwright.

* * *

Dominic Cooke's press conference announcing his first season at the Royal Court in February 2007 resulted in a surprising number of headlines: 'Courting controversy'[62] 'Royal Court discovers the middle-class hero'[63] 'New director to satirise audience'[64] 'Les miserables at the Royal Court throw out kitchen sink drama'[65] – proving the most unexpected, confrontational thing anyone could have imagined the Royal Court doing was putting on a bunch of plays about middle-class liberals. On one level, Cooke's off-the-cuff soundbite was just a neatly provocative umbrella under which he could discuss the flagship shows of his opening season: Mike Bartlett's *My Child*, Polly Stenham's *That Face* and American Bruce Norris' *The Pain and The Itch*. But the thinking behind it ran deeper. Ramin Gray recalls:

> This is how [Cooke] sold it to us. He said: 'I've been down at the RSC and I've done these Shakespeare plays' – and I really buy his argument – 'when you do a Shakespeare play you're dealing with the king, or you're dealing with people with power. Modern plays tend to be about people at the bottom of the heap. Why don't we flip that around and look at the people who have power? Let's interrogate that.' And it came out as: 'I want to do middle-class plays about middle-class people', but in conversation with him that was a much more interesting way of putting it.[66]

More exciting than the surprise change of milieu was the sudden blast of fresh air that blew through the programming. All the writers in that first season were making their British professional débuts. And, as the plays started opening, it was discovered they were also remarkably good, with a real range and difference of textures in the writing. What was noticeable in first play of the season – former Apathist Mike Bartlett's professional début, *My Child*[67] – was that, having spent seven years since university writing plays, staging them and knocking up new ideas at a remarkable rate for the Apathists, Bartlett's coming-of-age play could not have been leaner. The Theatre Downstairs had been converted into a kind of oversized London Underground tube carriage by Miriam Buether. Numerous scenes cross-cut under a remorseless lighting state. Watching the première, it felt like the Court had caught up on about ten years worth of writing experiments in a single hour. And, while Polly Stenham's *That Face*[68] lacked quite the same finesse in terms of technique, the combination of its writer's extreme youth, the play's emotional punch and an excellent cast (including Matt Smith and Lindsey Duncan), along with its upper-middle-class setting, made it wildly popular – so much so that it transferred to the West End the following year. The season was rounded-off with the unprecedented, at least in recent times, scratch events: the Royal Court Rough Cuts season. And as the autumn season was announced – new productions of seminal European classics *Rhinoceros* and *The Fire Raisers* downstairs and a whole pile of new international plays upstairs – there was a buzz and a warm glow around the Court that had been missing for a very long time. Ramin Gray again:

> When Dominic came in he did basically what Graham had been saying for years and years, which was 'programme the thing actively, bring in some exciting voices from outside to goad on English writers, and put on a blast of English writers who no one had ever heard of'. I mean, there was a lot of stuff that had built up on the Young Writers' Programme and Dominic brilliantly . . . I mean, it was all there in the larder, Dominic just unleashed it.

2008 kicked off to a lacklustre start, with a low-rent UK première of David Hare's *The Vertical Hour*, which had already opened in New York the previous year with a movie-star cast. There was also a remount of Fiona Evans' age-gap, pupil-teacher, dirty-weekend Edinburgh hit, *Scarborough*, which had been doubled in length by copying and pasting the whole script and reversing the genders in the second half. Caryl Churchill's translation of Olivier Choinière's *Bliss* (originally: *Félicité*) directed by Joe Hill-Gibbins was a more intriguing, provocative proposition – a story told by multiple voices in which Céline Dion becomes an abused child, becomes a boneless Wal-Mart worker who vomits herself inside out and becomes Celine Dion again. An 'Upstairs Downstairs' season saw Marius von Mayenburg's *The Ugly One*, Anupama Chandrasekhar's *Free Outgoing* and Bola Agbaje's *Gone Too Far*, transfer to the larger Downstairs theatre through the summer.

If 2008 suffered by comparison to 2007 then the last year of this book's scope at the Royal Court sees the theatre going out on a high. The first show of the new year was *Shades*, a promising début from Alia Bano in the form of a sassy, perky, feelgood rom-com set in London's Muslim community, while Downstairs a week or so later the British première of Marius von Mayenberg's *The Stone* opened, launching a season of German plays set within a single white cube set. However, it was the next play to open on this set that really caught fire. Caryl Churchill's seven-page play *Seven Jewish Children* must hold some sort of record for the number of column inches generated per page of playtext as the charge that the play was anti-Semitic was vigorously debated back and forth across countless newspapers and websites. Coinciding with a similar row about Islamophobia in Richard Bean's *England People Very Nice* at the NT, London's subsidized theatre never seemed to be out of the news. The vigorously divided views on the follow-up to *The Stone*, Mark Ravenhill's *Over There* – boasting luminous performances by the twins Luke and Harry Treadaway – felt almost lacklustre by comparison. The German season was quickly followed by an even more ambitious undertaking, a season of plays by the excellent, difficult, avant-garde American playwright Wallace Shawn, including the UK première of his latest piece, *Grasses of a Thousand Colours*, a three and a quarter hour near-monologue in which Shawn himself, taking the role of narrator, relates a tale in which he seems to end up having sex with and beheading a talking cat. The piece, and indeed the season, received a lukewarm critical reception at best.

Then something amazing happened to the Royal Court. There was no particular reason to suspect that Jez Butterworth's little-awaited follow-up to his recent Royal Court plays, the underwhelming *The Night Heron* (2002) or *The Winterling* (2006), would be any different, but *Jerusalem*, directed by the returning Ian Rickson, proved to be a late contender for play of the decade. The main reason was a towering central performance from the former actor-manager of the Globe Theatre, Mark Rylance. Indeed, were there more space, Rylance's career across the decade – from a near-definitive, but overlooked Hamlet in 2000 through to his barnstorming creation of Johnny Byron – would make for another interesting way of tracking the tastes and perceptions of the British theatregoing public. That *Jerusalem* went on to conquer the West End and then Broadway, and ensured that demand for Butterworth's 2012 follow-up *The River* was such that the Court completely rethought its approach to ticketing, speaks for itself. More satisfying for this narrative is the final triumph for Ian Rickson's time at the Royal Court, the justification of his continued faith in Butterworth as a playwright and the unique partnership in the way that the play eventually evolved between them and with their remarkable leading man.

6. Authors

As a result of the increased interest in the New Writing Industry, allied with Britain's long-standing cultural tendency to 'serve the text', plus the apparent distaste of British mainstream critics (and indeed some British playwrights) for 'director's theatre', the rise of the New Writing Industry also gave the impression of flourishing at the expense of the art of directing. In the following section, I examine some of the assumptions this division between 'writer' and 'director' throws up, and how it obscures the question of 'authorship'.

Two of the most important directors working in Britain in the 2000s were Katie Mitchell and Rupert Goold. In fact, as we have already seen, Mitchell – almost a decade older than Goold – was already a well-established director by 2000, directing *The Oresteia* at the National Theatre and Martin Crimp's *The Country* at the Royal Court where she was an associate. But, although only a few years into his career, Goold was also already a jobbing director with credits at the Salisbury Playhouse, the Gate and the Hampstead Theatre under his belt. What is most interesting about a comparison between these two directors is both the difference of their approaches and the divergent trajectories and markers of success that their careers follow. In his speech at the opening of the 2011 Stückemarkt at Berlin's Theatertreffen Simon Stephens explained Ramin Gray's oft-made point about the unspoken 'endgame of theatrical cultures'.[69] 'In the German speaking world to have a production invited to Theatertreffen as a representation of one of the ten highest manifestations of excellence is a goal to which many aspire. In Britain it's different. In Britain the endgame is the possibility of a commercial transfer.' By the end of the 2000s, Goold had seen several of his productions transfer to the West End, and a couple even to Broadway and towards Hollywood. Meanwhile, Katie Mitchell had become the only British director to win a place at Theatertreffen with her first piece for Schauspielhaus Köln, her 2009 production of Franz Xaver Kroetz's *Wunschkonzert*.

* * *

In 2002 Goold was appointed as the artistic director of the Royal and Derngate Theatres in Northampton. The list of shows which he staged there – *Arcadia*, *Betrayal*, *Waiting for Godot*/*The Weir*, *Othello*, *Insignificance*, *Summer Lightning*, *Hamlet* – is an ordinary enough list of plays, but it was the increasing verve and playfulness Goold brought to bear on these texts which marked him out. In 2003 the *Daily Telegraph*'s Dominic Cavendish noted:

> The Northampton Theatres' young, dashing artistic director's revival of *Othello* has so much to commend it, it's hard to know where to begin. Why not, then, at the sensational start, when Iago and Roderigo are revealed framed within a car interior, one in military uniform, the other in dapper 1940s civilian dress? Behind them, dots of light flicker then fade into the distance, delightfully pastiching cinema techniques of the time. At a stroke, the production signals that we're in for some extremely eye-catching visuals, and that it has a firm, if arch, sense of period. . . .[70]

When Goold made his Shakespearean début for the RSC[71] a few years later with a production of *The Tempest* starring Patrick Stewart, he rethought Prospero's isle as a frozen Arctic tundra. And it is this sort of original thinking, combined with his acute grasp of text, that could be said to define Goold's style. While often painted as an 'auteur'[72] (not a complimentary term in mainstream British critics' books), in fact Goold's productions are not driven by a 'concept' as they might be in the work of his mainland European counterparts – rather than directing his productions as attacks 'against' the texts of the plays, he instead finds new ways through which the texts can be rediscovered by audiences.

Around the same point as his RSC Shakespeare début, Goold also finished at Northampton to take over from Dominic Dromgoole as the artistic director of the Oxford Stage Company (Dromgoole was going to The Globe on the south bank). He renamed the company Headlong, and set about transforming it from an easily overlooked producer of mostly lacklustre, dispensable versions of the classics into one of Britain's most vital companies, producing work seen nationally and internationally, commissioning and importing some brilliant new plays, and making radical reinterpretations of classic texts. The first Headlong production I saw was the Headlong transfer from Northampton to the Hampstead theatre of *Faustus*[73] in 2006. Goold, along with his regular collaborator and dramaturg Ben Power, had radically rewritten Christopher Marlowe's sixteenth-century text, eviscerating the original and adding a whole new second storyline about the infamous Young British Artists The Chapman Brothers and an imaginary vision of them creating their *Insult to Injury* pictures, in which they painted over original Goya etchings. It was stylish, iconoclastic and said more about what our souls could be, and how we might sell them, than any straightforward 'proper' production of the Marlowe is now likely to.

Following his production of *Rough Crossings* (Lyric Hammersmith and tour, 2007) adapted by novelist Caryl Phillips from the book by Simon Schama, it was Goold's next show that temporarily established him as a critical darling. Opening in Chichester, transferring to the West End and then Broadway, Goold's *Macbeth*,[74] was set in a vision of Stalinist Scotland/Russia, and starred Patrick Stewart as Macbeth. It was a combination of playfulness, intelligence and sheer clarity that made this *Macbeth* so exciting, though. Set in a grimy, white tiled basement designed by Anthony Ward, it owed more to modern horror films than to Jacobethan England and managed to make this most familiar of plays feel newly written, even though, unlike *Faustus*, barely a single line had been rewritten. More left-field was Headlong's production of *The Last Days of Judas Iscariot* (Almeida Theatre, 2008), a new American play by Stephen Adly Guirgis, which imagined a trial in the afterlife of the titular betrayer of Christ, played out in downtown New York. Beneath this immaculately realized production was a highly original new play.

Six Characters in Search of an Author (Headlong/Chichester/ West End, 2008) found Goold and Power back on the same extreme-intervention form they had displayed with *Faustus*. The production took Pirandello's 1921 piece of pioneering meta-theatre and setting it in the makeshift studios of some documentary film-makers. Rather than feeling like redundant contemporaneity for no other reason than a fear that audiences can only identify with people dressed like them, it created a new set of resonances and meanings to the questions posed by Pirandello's original.[75] By contrast, Goold's production of Harold Pinter's *No Man's Land* (Gate Theatre, Dublin/West End, 2008) did not change a thing, yet, according to the *Guardian*, 'ushers us into the strange, spectral world that characterised his productions of Shakespeare and Pirandello'.[76]

Later in 2008, however, Goold fell foul of the critics. He had been commissioned by the Everyman Theatre to direct a new production of *King Lear*[77] as their contribution to Liverpool's European City of Culture status, starring one of the theatre's most famous actors, Pete Postlethwaite. Goold's response to the commission, and to the play, was to set his *Lear* in a rolling history of the city of Liverpool, beginning in the 1970s, with Lear as a brown-suited trade-unionist, dividing his kingdom by means of a massive train set. The critics set upon it with venom. Billington decried 'a production full of short-term effects rather than long-range vision . . . elevation of bright ideas above coherence. . . .' and 'the show's constant surrender to momentary effects and facile theatricality'.[78] And yet, on coming to London, the piece opened to a six-star review in *Time Out* and sell-out audiences. The point was that as well as delivering a watchable, moving *King Lear*,

Goold and his team had also authored a new, visual dimension which lent the play an additional set of resonances.

* * *

If the trajectory of Mitchell's career over the decade sounds less dramatic – with fewer takeovers, coups and less entrepreneurial swashbuckling than Goold's – then the sheer fineness, precision, experiment and surety of the work produced more than makes up for it. Put simply, Mitchell is Britain's finest director of European classics, a revelatory director of new plays (she is responsible for most British premières of new plays written by Martin Crimp and increasingly Simon Stephens), an excellent director of opera and, working in collaboration – often with Leo Warner and Gareth Fry – she is also one of Britain's (and Europe's) foremost experimenters with the latest video and sound technology.

In his study of Mitchell's career in *Contemporary European Theatre Directors*, Dan Rebellato relates:

> By the turn of the century, Mitchell . . . managed to secure a fellowship to go back to Europe and renew her studies of theatre processes and training . . . Through the early 2000s, Mitchell looked again at Stanislavski, but widened her attention to take in, amongst other things, the latest discoveries in neuroscience, the history of painting, contemporary dance theatre, the ideas of the Dogme 95 movement in cinema and the performance experiments of John Cage.[79]

Looking at the spread and diversity of Mitchell's work over the decade, it is possible to trace a number of developments within it. In 2002, for example, her production of Jon Fosse's *Nightsongs* at the Royal Court – playing in a double bill with Martin Crimp's *Face To The Wall* (later a part of *Fewer Emergencies*) – elicited an interestingly conflicted review from Ian Shuttleworth, who describes the Dogme influence: 'lighting and sound [are] mixed live on the night, no props unless absolutely essential, rehearsals continuing right through the run so that every performance will be a little further on from the last. It's an exciting approach . . . The interest is all in the process that keeps these deadening events alive as theatre'.[80] While at the National Theatre later that year, Lyn Gardner, describing her more Stanislavskian *Ivanov* praised, 'Mitchell's wonderful and wonderfully acted production . . . Paule Constable's spine-tingling lighting is all lengthening, hardening shadows that make people look like ghosts.'

Throughout the decade it could be argued there was an increasing divide between Mitchell's reputation for hardcore naturalism (in her productions of *The Seagull* and *Women of Troy*, Mitchell had rooms built off-stage where her actors would continue to be 'in character' even while not visible to the audience) and her increasing flair for 'experiment'. In the former category, productions of *Three Sisters* (2003), *Iphigenia at Aulis* (2004), *The Seagull* (2006), *Women of Troy* (2007) and *The Pains of Youth* (2009) – all at the National Theatre – in fact questioned the boundaries of uninterrogated, mainstream, naturalistic theatre, deploying actual room-volume-speaking in large theatres, moments of almost dance-theatre for minutely detailed scene changes and even, in *Women of Troy*, a moment where lighting and sound effects combined to create the impression of a vast 'fourth wall' opening before the characters could directly address the audience. Conversely, in the category of more 'experimental' work – *A Dream Play* (2005), *Waves* (2006), *Attempts on Her Life* (2007), . . . *some trace of her* (2008) and *After Dido* (2009) – there remains a rigorous adherence to Stanislavskian principles of naturalistic acting, and the presence of live Foley, video cameras, microphones and the live creation of special effects were to enhance and highlight this realism. In this latter category of work we see the extent to which Mitchell also authors the work she directs, and see that while it is usual to write about Mitchell's work as the product of a single directorial vision we should also understand her work as the product of a collaboration with not only the writer, but with her team of set, costume, sound, light and video designers. Like Goold, despite her greater acclaim in Europe, Mitchell remains a very 'British' director, still rarely – at least during the 2000s – 'attacking' a text she directs, but instead sympathetically opening it up to best emphasize those parts of it she finds most interesting.

While it may seem counter-intuitive to spend so long discussing the work of two directors in a series nominally focussed on 'Modern British *Playwrights*', within the mainstream Goold and Mitchell offer two of the clearest examples of how directors also 'author' a piece of theatre. Even aside from the obvious moments where they collaborate on creating their own *written* texts, there is a process of *wright*ing a play embedded in the heart of their directing processes.

* * *

Looking at these two careers in isolation, we notice something else about the way the theatre ecology functioned in Britain in the 2000s. Not only writers but also directors moved between buildings. Audiences could follow the work of their favourite writers and directors from venue to venue as easily as they could build affinities with specific buildings. And yet, while the Young Vic offered an imaginative programme that boosted London's stock of exciting director-led work (early highlights including Michael's Boyd's *Henry VI*s and *Richard III* as part of the RSC's first history plays cycle in 2001 and David Lan's revival of *A Raisin in the Sun*), the boutique houses of Michael Attenborough's Almeida – which until 2002 had been a powerhouse of invention under Jonathan Kent and Ian McDiarmid – and the Donmar Warehouse under Michael Grandage (also from 2002) produced mostly staid, unimaginative revivals and very flat new plays. Similarly, while the Bush followed a very particular path, first under Mike Bradwell until 2007, and then under Josie Rourke (until 2012), it did manage to keeping on discovering and providing a home for some of Britain's best playwrights (discoveries during this decade include Jack Thorne, Nick Payne and Adam Brace, while plays by Simon Stephens, Dennis Kelly and Richard Bean proved it remained a go-to destination for more established writers). Conversely, the Soho Theatre under Lisa Goldman (2006–10) gave the impression of a beleaguered receiving house, often forced to take whatever happened to be around in order to pay the rent. Ironically, this perception of the respective merits of their artistic policies actually made little difference to the hit and miss nature of the work seen – Suspect Culture and Graeae's touring production of Dan Rebellato's *Static*, which I saw at the Soho (for the FT),[81] remains one of the most moving plays I saw in the 2000s.

* * *

A further difficulty that attempting to discuss 'directors in the 2000s' throws up is the extent to which a reliance on pigeon-holing can warp our perceptions of a decade's theatre. Another of the most important and influential directors working in Britain in this decade was the plawright, poet, theorist, deviser, teacher and blogger Chris Goode.

The production which brought Goode to public attention was a revelatory version of *The Tempest* from the Edinburgh Fringe in 2000. The production gained immediate attention for the simple fact it was performed in the audience's own Edinburgh accommodation, but this was more than a simple gimmick. Lyn Gardner's review captures the magic of the piece:

> As far as Goode is concerned, people's homes are simply the best place to perform a play that is all about changing perceptions, altered states and geographical confusions, allowing him and the cast to take the audience on a journey in which the familiar becomes disconcertingly unfamiliar. . . .
>
> There is something infinitely touching about watching Miranda and Prospero's murmured conversation from just a foot away, and hearing Shakespeare being spoken not declaimed. And that is why this *Tempest* works. It is transparently honest and shiningly sincere. You long for the lovers to be happy, ache for Ariel to be free and when Prospero promises to give up his magic your heart gives a wistful lurch. I have never seen a Tempest that has been quite such fun or moved me quite so much. At the end we sit in pitch black for a few seconds, slightly stunned.

Averaging about five productions a year every year of the 2000s Goode's subsequent output cannot be easily summarized. The following year in Edinburgh saw the première of his first collaboration with Unlimited

Theatre, *Neutrino*, and a production of *Twelfth Night* at CPT. Work in 2002 included the first outing of his long-running one-man show *Kiss of Life*, a 'devised piece' for the Traverse in Edinburgh called *Napoleon in Exile*, and *The Big Room* for CPT. 2003 saw credits as director for Julia Barclay's *My First Autograce Homeography 1973–74*, as co-devisor with Unlimited for the follow-up to *Neutrino, Could It Be Magic?* and co-devisor/writer of *his horses* with Exit Strategy at CPT. Subsequent pieces over the decade could be divided up under similar labels, separating the 'devised pieces' (*Escapology*, 2004, *Longwave*, 2007, *Hey Mathew*, 2008) from the 'plays' (*Weepie*, 2004, *Speed Death of Radiant Child*, 2007, *King Pelican*, 2009); the one-man-shows (*Nine Days Crazy*, 2005, *Hippo World Guest Book*, 2007, *Infinite Lives*, 2008, *The Adventures of Wound Man and Shirley*, 2009) from the occasional radical production of an extant play (. . . *Sisters*, after Chekhov's *Three Sisters*, 2008) or the direction of another performer's work (Harold Finley, *Rhymes, Reasons and Bomb-Ass Beats*, 2006). As a sub-category, we might also divide again pieces made for performances in their audience's homes, such as the 'devised' *Homemade* (2005) or the 'solo-show' *We Must Perform a Quirkafleeg!* (2006).

A selective list of titles gives no real impression of the work, only of the sheer amount of it. And, there is little generalizing that can be done. *The Adventures of Wound Man and Shirley* was a one-man-show which toured extensively from 2009. It featured Goode standing in a giant-sized set of a young boy's bedroom and telling a deceptively sweet tale about a young boy called Shirley who meets a living, walking illustration from a renaissance medical text book depicting all manner of battle wounds. That the piece might have gently explored transgressive homosexual inter-generational desire, while also presenting an incredibly touching coming-of-age narrative, and all the while feeling its way round the edges of liveness in performance, perhaps begins to capture the difficulty of describing Goode's work. By contrast, *Longwave* featured two bearded performers (Tom Lyall and Jamie Wood) in a more-or-less silent devised show in which two scientists in a shed in remote Arctic conditions, perform a series of inscrutable experiments on what look like plasticine haggises at the same time demonstrating a tragic inability to communicate with each other which concluded with a Captain Oates-like departure and an incredible sense of loss and wonderment on the part of the audience. And this in turn was different to *The Speed Death of Radiant Child* at The Drum Theatre in Plymouth. About the only critic who saw the piece was Lyn Gardner:

> Even though this is played out on a conventional set in a traditional theatre building, that is about the only thing that is orthodox about it. [The piece] works its way through a body of evidence that not only links the characters . . . but also connects the Windscale nuclear disaster of 1957, the death of actor River Phoenix outside Hollywood's Viper Club, artist Keith Haring's iconic image of the Radiant Child and Caravaggio's great homoerotic picture of Doubting Thomas putting his finger inside Christ's open wound. The piece is emotionally raw and suffused with an almost religious intensity. Watching it is like feeling the protective layers of skin being peeled from your body to reveal the bloody wounds beneath. . . . this is a play that burns the retina with the glare of its huge ambition.[82]

From this small sample giving impressions of only three pieces, we can at least discern the enormous range and scope of Goode's project in the 2000s. Impossible to pin down as simply a writer, or a director, or a performer, Goode deserves significantly fuller critical study than he has thus far received.

7. National Theatre

'What director of the National Theatre wouldn't merit a place on a "most influential people in theatre" list, for heaven's sake? (Answers on a postcard marked "Trevor Nunn Competition" to the usual address, please.)'[83]

History has not been kind to Trevor Nunn's time as artistic director of the National Theatre. Taking over from Richard Eyre in 1997, and succeeded by Nicholas Hytner in 2003, he is now remembered chiefly for putting on a lot of musicals. In the last three-and-a-bit years of his tenure, the part with which this chapter is concerned, he did at the very least hold the reins while some good and/or interesting work passed through the building. David Edgar's *Albert Speer*, Joe Penhall's *Blue/Orange* and Mark Ravenhill's *Mother Clap's Molly House* all premièred. Visionary Canadian director Robert LePage's *The Far Side of the Moon* visited, and the runaway success that was Gregory Burke's first play *Gagarin Way* also transferred from the Traverse Theatre. And there were solid, popular revivals of Gorky's *Summerfolk* and, well, some musicals.

Encore Theatre Magazine took a less charitable view:

> plays like *Mutabilitie*, or *Battle Royal*, or *Remember This*, or *The Villain's Opera* look like the work of a theatre has lost any sense of what it wants to do. They were ill-matched to their theatres, underdeveloped, did not appear to have emerged from any sharpening dialogue with the theatre . . . At Sir Trevor's National Theatre there seemed to be no real policy for new writing. Jack Bradley is a good man but he has evidently struggled with an artistic directorship with no instinctive sympathy for the new play.[84]

More important, and certainly more indicative of the shape of things to come was the Transformation season. In 2002 Nunn hit on the bright idea of constructing two new, slightly different 'Loft'-style spaces ingeniously imposed upon the Lyttleton. Ticket prices were brought down and the programming was explicitly aimed at grabbing the attention of a younger audience. Former artistic director of the Gate Mick Gordon was put in charge as artistic director of these two new spaces. In retrospect Gordon's programming looks inspired. A great mixture of urgent, sinuous, topical new writing from great emerging playwrights (Roy Williams, Richard Bean, Moira Buffini) alongside an astute mixture of physical, visual and dance theatre (Kathryn Hunter, DV8, Matthew Bourne), and some slightly less successful good-ideas-on-paper (Jeanette Winterson and Deborah Warner's *Power Book* and any play by Tanika Gupta).

Looking back over the season at the time Michael Billington grudgingly accounts it only a partial success:

> Judging by the National's own statistics, it would seem to have had some success. The 13 shows have played to about 70% capacity. (Intriguingly, one of the most popular was the critically assailed version of *The Birds*.) More importantly, just over half the total audience has been under 35.
>
> But has the season, under Mick Gordon's direction, been an artistic success? Here the results have been more mixed . . . my impression has been of a dominance of style over content. I remember images from the shows I saw rather than emotions or ideas; my eyes were consistently dazzled, but I left spiritually untransformed.[85]

In this article, as much as in the programming on which it comments, we see seeds of a conflict that was to flare up around the NT again during Nicholas Hytner's time as artistic director.

*   *   *

Writing in the *Guardian* in early July 2002, Tom Morris, responding to the question 'is this an exciting time for British theatre?', replied:

> In a way, the most exciting time for theatre is when there is the least going on. Radical invention requires a clean slate . . . So the more tired, conservative and celebrity-driven you think theatre has become, the better the opportunity to make it buzz. The extraordinary thing is that for the first time in 25 years, there is new Arts Council money available to do it with. If I were Nick Hytner taking over the National . . . I would be leaping with excitement at the opportunities to create something new: not something poised, snappy and chic – as some seem to think the best new theatre is – but something dirty, passionate and wild. If you see Improbable Theatre, Richard Thomas, Frantic Assembly, Complicité and Tom Waits being commissioned to

make new work in these spaces, you'll know they're on the right track.

Less than a year after the article was printed, Nicholas Hytner had made Tom Morris an associate director at the National Theatre, and Richard Thomas and Stewart Lee's *Jerry Springer: The Opera* – originally seen as a scratch at Morris' BAC – had transferred to the Lyttleton; to a riotous chorus of approval:

> There could be no clearer sign that the National Theatre is under new management than the arrival of *Jerry Springer – the Opera*. It's filthy, it's funny, it's brilliantly original and, taken all in all, about as much fun as you are likely to have with your clothes on.[86]

Within a couple of years, Improbable and Complicité had also produced shows there. Hytner's own first production at the National as artistic director was also a calculated bit of iconoclasm; dressed in modern British army fatigues, opening only weeks after the United States/ United Kingdom invasion of Iraq, the brilliant black actor Adrian Lester played Henry V to yet more acclaim. Even if the production itself was a little ordinary it was an important statement of intent; here was an NT regime with its sights clearly trained on the twenty-first century. It is likely, looking back over these first six years of Nick Hytner's time as Artistic Director of the National Theatre, everyone will choose different highlights, but part of the brilliance of Hytner's regime was its fleet ability to cover all the things people thought a national theatre should be covering, and at the same time introduce new things no one had realized were essential until they arrived, all combined with a commitment to artistic excellence and experimentation.

As well as work by companies and directors already discussed, there was also excellent work from Marianne Elliot, who won a Best Director Evening Standard Award for her production of Ibsen's *Pillars of the Community* (2005) and who, with her production of *St Joan* in the Olivier (2007), went on to spearhead the National's move to reclaim the works of George Bernard Shaw for the twenty-first century; proving plays which had long been regarded as fusty and too wordy could not only be brought back to life, but could prove fascinating mirrors of our own times. Similarly, Nicholas Hytner's revivals of classic plays, most notably in *The Man of Mode* (2006), demonstrated for a play to reflect modern society it need not have been newly written. Indeed, Hytner had a particular flair for reflecting contemporary mores in old texts seen again in his productions of *The Alchemist* (2006) and *Major Barbara* (2008). Beyond this, alongside Katie Mitchell's Chekhovs, the National also looked to Russia with Howard Davies' fine revivals of Gorky's *Philistines*[87] (2007), Peter Flannery's adaptation of the Russian film set in the era of Stalin's purges, *Burnt By The Sun* (2009) and Bulgakov's *The White Guard* (2010), and Africa for Rufus Norris' imaginative production of Wole Soyinka's *Death and the King's Horsemen* (2009).

Although curiously overlooked as a new writing building, the National did in fact stage numerous new plays throughout the decade, as well as works previously discussed elsewhere in the chapter, it had enormous artistic and/or critical successes with Kwame Kwei-Armah's *Elmina's Kitchen* (2003), Simon Stephens' *Harper Regan* (2008) and Martin McDonagh's *The Pillowman* (2003).

And then there was Alan Bennett's *The History Boys* (2004), which was a phenomenon all of its own. Nominally about a group of boys studying for their Oxbridge exams in Sheffield in the 1980s, it was plainly set in a romanticized vision of Bennett's own youth, with the updated setting thrown in so Bennett could make amusing mischief at the expense of contrarian television historians. Hardly even a play, so much as a set of extended, and gently funny sketches, some songs, and a slight plot playing a younger, more cynical teacher off against an older, more idealistic one, something about its diffident comedy captured the country's imagination and it sold out the National, then the West End, and then national tours, before becoming a film.

In 2005, a short way into Hytner's time at the NT, a group of writers calling themselves The Monsterists, including David Eldridge, Rebecca Lenkiewicz, Richard Bean and Moira Buffini, formed an artistic pressure group for theatres to start letting living writers write 'big plays'. They demanded: 'The elevation of new theatre writing from the ghetto of the studio "black box" to the main stage; Equal access to financial resources for plays being produced by a living writer (ie equal with dead writers); Use of the very best directors for new plays; Use of the very best actors for new plays.'[88] Plainly Hytner was listening carefully, as over the next five years, all opening on the National Theatre largest stage, with excellent casts, directors and resources behind them, came the remarkably varied fruits of the Monsterists: David Eldridge's *Market Boy* (2006), Rebecca Lenkiewicz *Her Naked Skin* (2008), Richard Bean's *England People Very Nice* (2009) and Moira Buffini's *Welcome to Thebes* (2010) – a play about Romford market in the 1980s, a play about the suffragette movement, a history of multicultural Britain focusing on London's East End and a mash-up of Greek classical tragedies re-imagined in contemporary Africa.

Alongside these diverse and quirky new commissions, the NT also did sterling work with adaptations of children's books as Christmas Shows. No consideration of the decade's theatre would be complete without noting the sheer verve of commissioning a (two-part) adaptation of Philip Pullman's *His Dark Materials* trilogy, replete with giant puppet armoured polar bears and daemons, or the immensely popular follow-up adaptation of Jamila Gavin's *Coram Boy* (2005). But it was in 2007 that this strand of commissioning went global. Adapted by Nick Stafford, directed by Tom Morris, Marianne Elliot and in collaboration with the Handspring Puppet Theatre Company the National Theatre's version of Michael Morpurgo's *War Horse* is the most widely seen, and surely one of the best-loved, theatre shows of the decade. Telling the story of a young boy and his quest to find his horse after it is pressed into military service in World War One, the real triumph of *War Horse* was its revelatory use of puppetry to depict the horses. Review after review rhapsodized about the skill of the – visible throughout – puppeteers, and how you somehow forgot they were even there. This marriage of what had been, only a few years earlier, deemed 'alternative theatre' techniques with mass audience appeal was Tom Morris' finest hour at the National, confirming his desire for 'the opportunity to create something new: not something poised, snappy and chic' had been entirely correct.

* * *

91

A similar trajectory to Morris' can be traced for the small Cornish theatre company Kneehigh across the decade. I first saw the company in 2000 doing their rough theatre, almost adult-panto-like version of *The Red Shoes* in 2000. The last time I saw Kneehigh during the period in question was eight years later in the West End with a version of the classic British film *Brief Encounter* (2008). Orchestrated by a lusciously be-wigged, cross-dressed narrator who prodded a cast of men with grimy vests and underpants and the heroine around a rough wooden stage, *The Red Shoes* had all the hallmarks of a particular brand of 'alternative' theatre at the beginning of the decade. There was the almost mandatory clownish debt to L'Ecole Jacques Lecoq, accordion-playing, and almost certainly some battered leather suitcases being flung around – refugees from whatever Eastern European show had first inspired their ubiquity. Eight years on, the company's trademark clowning and healthy disrespect for their source material had not dimmed and *Brief Encounter* subsequently transferred to New York where it was described by New York Times theatre critic Ben Brantley as: 'surely the most enchanting work of stagecraft ever inspired by a movie'.[89] *The Red Shoes* was followed by a touring version of *The Wooden Frock* (2003) and then a production of *The Bacchae* (2004). This latter was already supported by the National Theatre, although for its London dates it played at the Lyric, Hammersmith.

The Lyric, Hammersmith, was also the London home and co-commissioner for Kneehigh's Angela Carter adaptation *Nights at the Circus* (2005) their version of Shakespeare's *Cymbeline* (2006), co-produced with the RSC as part of its Complete Works season. Their second show for 2006, *Rapunzel*, retrod the same ground as *The Red Shoes*, and much that followed. Lyn Gardner noted: 'despite the silly songs, the cross-dressing, the wild boar poo, a pair of comic-book villains who turn out to have hearts of gold, and a rabbit of monstrous size, it is not *just* a merry romp . . .'[90] [my italics]. And so, all had been mostly well for Kneehigh. They had a loyal, established audience, they had regular touring partnerships, typically taking in the West Yorkshire Playhouse, Bristol Old Vic and Lyric Hammersmith, and as such they tended to be reviewed by second-string critics (such as Lyn Gardner) who were broadly in tune with their aesthetic. Until,

92

that is, *A Matter of Life and Death* opened at the National Theatre in 2007.

Kneehigh were another Tom Morris import to the NT. They enjoyed house-room during his tenure at the BAC, and given their growing profile it made sense to bring them in-house to the Olivier to give them a chance to show what they could do on a stage with a greater magnitude. *A Matter of Life and Death* was adapted from Powell and Pressburger's 1946 film by Kneehigh artistic director Emma Rice and Tom Morris. It also featured a performance from noted Icelandic aerialist Gísli Örn Garðarsson, who was part of the company Vesturport, who also enjoyed previous success at the Lyric Hammersmith with their version of *Metamorphosis* and at the Barbican with a circus-inflected version of Büchner's *Woyzeck*. *A Matter of Life and Death* opened to a muted-at-best response from the first-string critics. This, following on from the downright hostile response from some quarters to Katie Mitchell's *Attempts on Her Life*, led to one of the most infamous off-stage theatrical scandals of the decade.

8. Criticism

National Theatre artistic director Nicholas Hytner's mischievous accusation that Britain's theatre critics were 'Dead White Males'[91] did not appear in a vacuum. Granted, his subsequent clarification[92] made some fair and reasonable counter-points to his original claim that they had a problem with female directors, but the phrase itself would not have gained the enormous and immediate traction it did[93] without some ghostly feeling Hytner had merely said out loud something rather a lot of people had been thinking for rather a long time.[94]

By 2007 British theatre criticism had reached a crisis point. The first-string critics for all the major broadsheets, were white, middle-class, mostly Oxbridge-educated men with conservative tastes in theatre. The personal tastes of a single critic are an occupational hazard of having theatre reviewed professionally. The problem by 2007 – perhaps something that had been a problem for considerably longer – was that the combined personal tastes of *all* the first stringers no longer represented a significant proportion of the theatre-going public.

Writing and researching this chapter, for example – particularly in the case of performances I did not see myself – often felt like a case of having to negotiate with some very unreliable narrators. I heard from friends and colleagues about how good such-and-such a specific show was, and how it must be included in any consideration of theatre seen in Britain in the decade, and then I try to find a review which reflects this, only to discover one did not exist.

Thanks to the old-fashioned, hierarchical way British theatre criticism was ordered, the chief critic of a newspaper would mostly see those shows that were most economically important. That is to say: West End shows, openings at the National Theatre and the RSC, other large theatres in London, and leading regional theatres; while a paper's 'second string critic' would travel more to the regions, would see more work in smaller theatres and on the fringe.

This meant – as we have seen in the cases of Kneehigh, or Shunt, or Punchdrunk, or the NT Transformation Season – when a first-string critic was confronted with work which had moved out of venues more usually covered by the second-string critics, he – and it was *always* a 'he' – was suddenly face-to-face with already enormously popular companies whose progress he had not witnessed, and whose work was frequently not to his taste. There was a tendency for this work either to be attacked – witness Michael Billington's two-page attack on Shunt in *State of the Nation*[95] – patronized – as with *A Matter of Life or Death*[96] – or, most annoyingly, for it to be praised condescendingly, as with Punchdrunk's *Masque of the Red Death*.

The crucial difference from earlier spats between critics and a theatre or company was that in 2007 there was now an alternative. For a while, since approximately 2000, there had been a gradual growth in online theatre reviews. British Theatre Guide and CultureWars being two of the earliest sites, along with the early move online of *What's On Stage* magazine and best, in terms of quality, if not quantity, the excellent *Encore Theatre* magazine, since the advent of 'Web 2.0' – the point where it became incredibly easy for anyone with a computer and an internet connection to publish their own reviews on a blog, and to publicize their writing using new social media sites like Facebook and Twitter – there had been an explosion of theatre blogs. Early adopters included theatre makers like Chris Goode,[97] David Eldridge[98] and Andy Field[99] whose blogs all quickly became required reading for anyone with the slightest interest in theatre. Popular blogs from America and Australia like George Hunka's *Superfluities*[100] and Alison Croggon's *Theatre Notes*[101] turned the 'blogosphere' into an international conversation. And there were the West End Whingers – the camp, comic, anonymous theatre-reviewing double-act who briefly had commercial producers running scared with their acerbic skewerings and refusal to abide by the press night embargo on reviews for the simple reason they were buying their own tickets and could therefore do what they liked. In October 2007 the *Guardian*, which by this point had already been running its own 'theatre blog' for about a year, instituted a weekly column called *Noises Off*, which offered a 'best of the blogs' overview[102] In 2010 the Whingers made *The Times*' 'Luvvie List' of the 50 most influential people in theatre.[103]

Being a self-confessed farce-fancier, Billington must have relished the way that every time he reviewed a show by an avant garde company – say, Punchdrunk,[104] or Katie Mitchell's *Waves*,[105] etc. – his opposite number at the *Guardian*, Lyn Gardner, would write a blog contradicting it and essentially re-reviewing the piece. Similarly, when the national critics panned Mitchell's production of *Attempts on Her Life*, the National Theatre's press department led their press quotes with excerpts from the intelligent, appreciative online reviews. The game had suddenly changed.

Articles imagining 'bloggers versus critics' became de rigueur,[106] and would bemoan the challenge to 'the professionals' posed by 'amateurs', but judged by content, the best of the theatre blogs were rapidly outstripping the professionals by virtue of having the time and space to do more than immediately reel off a 300-word response with a star-rating.

Even now, it still feels as if the dust has yet to fully settle. In 2007 somewhere between the 'Dead White Males' furore in May and Michael Billington's piece 'Who Needs Reviews?'[107] in September, denying 'blogs' could or would replace 'critics', the landscape of theatre criticism in Britain had changed irrevocably.

9. Autumn 2009: Postcards from the end of the decade

At the Royal Court, transferring from Chichester, Rupert Goold directs Lucy Prebble's second play *ENRON*. The all-singing, all-dancing, extravaganza depicts the intricacies of the corruption and collapse of the American energy company with an assured theatricality. The tagline reads: 'There was a warning: its name was ENRON'.

Over at the Lyric Hammersmith, Sean Holmes' tenure as artistic director kicks off in style with Simon Stephens' new play *Punk Rock*, a two-hour slow, tense, build into a sudden frenzy of deafening violence. It feels like a raw, exciting statement of intent. At the time, no one could have guessed that three years later it would explode quite so spectacularly with the phenomenon that was *Three Kingdoms*.

The National Theatre present a sensitive, stripped-down British première of Tadeusz Słobodzianek's *Our Class*, presenting a British audience with a rare look back down the corridor of European history to a point in Poland's national story with which Poland herself was only just beginning to come to terms. A story told, crucially, not for a British audience, or mediated through British eyes, but written by a Pole for Polish audiences.

At the BAC Andy Field presents a scratch performance of *the other night i dreamt the world had fallen over* as part of their David Lynch season. A piece mostly consisting of a series of instructions to its audience playing on a giant video screen on the stage where the performers might usually be expected to stand. The piece talks about a riot or a revolution taking place in the streets outside the theatre.

Shunt open their new show, *Money*, in a new space in which they had constructed a giant, three storey, custom-made set. Led around it, the audience watch a surreal adaptation of Zola's *L'Argent* in which the set, the sudden way that the audience's perspective was violently altered, where a swimming pool disappeared to reveal a family living room three floors below, becomes as important as the words being spoken by the performers.

At the Royal Court Upstairs, performer Tim Crouch's *The Author* opens, seating two banks of audience members opposite one another, with four performers sat among them asking 'Is this all right? Can I go on?' while ripping to shreds the violence and abuse and *research* of the in-yer-face movement.

At the National Theatre, David Hare's *The Power of Yes* looks again at the financial crisis. It has the subtitle 'A dramatist seeks to understand the financial crisis' and began with the words: 'This isn't a play', which are spoken by Anthony Calf, who played 'David Hare'. While the dramatic properties of the text are not well-served in Angus Jackson's men-in-grey-suits production, Hare proves he still has a keen eye for the story of the moment.

Chris Goode revives *Hippo World Guest Book* at the CPT, charting the life of the website from its utopian beginnings, through a period where dissenting voices abuse hippos, other guest book users and each other, until a point where the site is been abandoned entirely by humans, the only postings by spambots advertising online gambling sites, and blank, anonymous posts. The piece suggests a process of inevitable collapse and entropy; beyond this, something more remote and intangibly sad.

Katie Mitchell opens two productions within a month of each other at the National Theatre, first a dark, painstakingly naturalistic version of Ferdinand Bruckner's 1923 play *Pains of Youth*, with scene changes apparently inspired by Pina Bausch, and then a brilliant, unexpected, playful, sublime staging of the Dr Seuss children's book *The Cat in the Hat*, signalling the growing interest in better theatre for young people.

At the Barbican, London audiences are treated to Toneelgroep Amsterdam's *The Roman Tragedies*, Ivo van Hove's revelatory back-to-back stagings of Shakespeare's *Coriolanus, Julius Caesar* and *Antony and Cleopatra*, in a production that invites audience members onto the stage to sit amid the plays as they are performed, becoming at once living scenery and up-close observers.

Back at the Royal Court, Mike Bartlett's play, *Cock*, finds the Theatre Upstairs audiences sat gathered close up to the action in a small wooden amphitheatre as the performers in James Macdonald's production turn in perfect, realistic performances, while resolutely not undressing where the script said they were undressed, and totally removing any pretence at naturalism.

* * *

That autumn, the aspects of the past ten years discussed in this chapter had finally begun to weave together to create new possibilities for the next decade of theatre in Britain. A future where old divisions between 'New Work' and 'New Writing' had turned into fertile breeding grounds for collaboration. Where narrow 'Britain's Best' nationalism had learned to embrace and to love internationalism. Where even the most rigid theatre spaces had begun to question their relationship with their audiences. And where a progressive spirit of inquiry and confident uncertainty had begun to replace condescension and refusal.

CHAPTER 2
PLAYWRIGHTS AND PLAYS

1. Introducing the playwrights

The five key playwrights featured in this book came to public attention between the mid-1990s and the mid-2000s. Playwrights continue to develop and change throughout their writing lives and where they begin has often very little to do with where they end up. This has two impacts on the way we might understand these particular writers. First, we can offer only snapshots of how their work looks to us now. T. S. Eliot remarked that with every new work of literature, the canon of existing literature moves around to accommodate it. This is even more the case with writers' own works. A new play can force our attention to neglected features of earlier works, as in the way that Simon Stephens' move towards formal experiment might encourage us to pick up the signs of structural playfulness in the early plays. In the case of startlingly original writers like Harold Pinter or Sarah Kane, the work, as it unfolds, teaches audiences and critics how to watch it, and it is only after seeing later work that the earlier writing can be properly understood. In some cases, conversely, a promising early start can seem less impressive if that promise fails to be fulfilled later on. All artistic judgements are, in some sense, provisional – there will never be a final answer to how good a play is – but in the case of these writers, in some cases, barely a decade into their writing careers, our judgements must be doubly so. Their next plays could transform our understanding and appreciation of their work.

The second impact of their contemporaneity is that they need much less introduction. While a reader in the 2010s might need some context to get a grip on what John Osborne was trying to do when writing *Look Back in Anger*, they will likely share in some of the cultural assumptions and reference points of these writers. When, in

Punk Rock (2009), Chadwick Meade enters in a new coat and Bennett greets him with the words 'Holy fucking Moly on a horse, it's Kanye West!',[1] the writer Simon Stephens can be reasonably confident that an audience will know enough about Kanye West's occasionally outlandish fashion sense to get the joke. Author and audience, in large part, share a cultural context, and, in that respect, introductions are unnecessary. Each of the five playwrights that follow are briefly introduced in the course of the essays.

SIMON STEPHENS*
Jacqueline Bolton

1. Introduction

Richard Do you believe in the intransience of love?

Jimmy You what?

Richard What about the communicability of the human spirit?

Jimmy Those are very odd questions.

Richard They're about the most important questions in the whole fucking world, Jimmy. Give me an answer.[1]

In returning repeatedly to these, the most important questions in the whole fucking world, Simon Stephens's search for answers has generated some of the most significant drama of the early twenty-first century. An increasingly insistent presence not only on main stages across the United Kingdom but also in repertoires across Europe, Stephens's fascination with the potential and the struggle of individuals to negotiate transience, to locate and communicate a self, to understand and to be understood, animates a now extensive oeuvre, the sometimes brutal gesture of which is matched always by a generous compassion for its subject(s). While rooted in the recognizable realm of the everyday, these plays nevertheless spar with this quotidian reality, deflecting commonplaces and challenging reflex judgements. Stephens writes, moreover, with an acute sensitivity to the potential and the struggle of communication inherent in the act of theatre-making itself. The 'communicability of the human spirit' – a concept bruised and fractured within contemporary studies of the postdramatic – is a potential cleaved to by these plays, but the substance, the merit and the resilience of this spirit within the spaces carved out for it by contemporary society remains an ongoing enquiry.

Too open, too exposed, too vulnerable, perhaps, to be described as 'chronicles' of their age, Stephens's plays invite empathetic engagement with the despairs, doubts, betrayals – and *hopes* – of a society often fearful to acknowledge these 'everyday' presences.

With a precision satisfying for this volume, Stephens pinpoints his playwriting career as beginning in earnest on 1 January 2000. After several years of writing 'a series of terrible plays', it was Stephens's ninth, *Bluebird*, which secured him his first professional production as part of the 1998 Royal Court's Young Writers' Festival, 'Choice'.[2] Stephens was working as a secondary school teacher at Eastbrook School, Dagenham,[3] when the Royal Court's then Artistic Director, Ian Rickson, invited Stephens to become Playwright in Residence at the Royal Court for 2000/2001. Since committing full-time to writing Stephens has averaged a play a year, winning the Pearson Award in 2002 for *Port* and the Olivier Award in 2005 for *On the Shore of the Wide World*. He has been Playwright in Residence at the Royal Exchange, Manchester (2001) and the National Theatre, London (2005) and between 2001 and 2005 he was Writers' Tutor for the Royal Court's Young Writers' Programme. In only ten years of writing professionally for the stage, Stephens's plays have been translated into over a dozen languages: Catalan, Croatian, Danish, Dutch, Finnish, Flemish, French, German, Japanese, Korean, Polish, Russian, Spanish and Portuguese to date. An ongoing collaboration with German director Sebastian Nübling is currently establishing Stephens as a major contemporary dramatist within German-language theatre; in 2007, the popular theatre journal *Theater Heute* voted Stephens Best Foreign Playwright.

It is, perhaps, worth pausing over Stephens's popularity among audiences and critics in Germany, as the naturalist, or realist, traditions within which his plays have been received in the United Kingdom are traditions that German theatre cultures, over the course of the twentieth century, have critiqued and often rejected. I introduce this idea not in order to speculate upon the many and varied reasons for Stephens's success within German-language theatre – Stephens himself attributes it to having 'a great German agent'[4] – but to suggest that Stephens's plays evince a sensibility which tests and perhaps revises

102

established ideas of naturalism even as they subscribe to a naturalistic rationality.

> I'm drawn to naturalism because I want to make sense of the world. I have a deep interest in humanity. I have faith in the power of story and I think a simple story told with honesty and with rigour is the essence of theatre.[5]

Naturalism and realism are notoriously diffuse terms, their distinction made hazier by the common substitution of one phrase for the other. It is perhaps more accurate to identify naturalism as one particular strand of realism, but common to both terms is what Stephens here identifies as an interest in humanity and a faith in dramatic narrative: if naturalism attempts to reveal how heredity and environment govern individual lives, realism seeks to depict histories and social worlds as 'realistically' as possible. From the violence against nature enacted by the damaged teenagers of *Herons* (2001) through to the peripatetic wanderings of a wife and mother estranged from her family in *Harper Regan* (2009), the ways in which individual identities are shaped by history and geography constitute a red thread running throughout Stephens's oeuvre. Place is often depicted in these plays as a kind of extension of the self, a proposition treated, however, with some caution: the sense of identity, purpose and belonging imparted by 'home' can at the same time delimit and deny opportunities for change, growth and renewal. In their depiction of lower- and lower-middle-classes in urban settings, their reliance upon colloquial, demotic speech and their siting of action in a recognizable 'here and now', Stephens's plays also sit comfortably with established traditions of social realism.

Stephens came to prominence at the Royal Court only a few years after the generation of playwrights branded 'in-yer-face' transformed the critical and commercial expectations of British 'New Writing'. His plays share a similar intellectual milieu to that of his immediate predecessors, succinctly summarized by Paul in *Motortown*: 'God. Law. Money. The left. The right. The Church. All of them lie in tatters. Wouldn't you be frightened?' (p. 171).[6] Characters in Stephens's plays do not pronounce upon or argue the relative validity of a coherent political stance, but rather demonstrate an ongoing improvization of moral, societal and familial values, an improvization engendered by the twentieth century's erosion of such ideological certainties as organized religion, elected government and the nuclear family. In addition to shared thematic concerns, much of the bad language, brutal imagery and 'gritty realism' contained within Stephens's plays might also qualify for inclusion under the in-yer-face banner, from the underlying threat of disaffection and violence in *Christmas* (written 1999, produced 2003), *Port* and *Country Music* (2004), to the depiction of a teenage boy anally raped with a bottle in *Herons*. There are, however, important distinctions to be drawn between Stephens's plays and many of the headline plays of the mid-1990s, distinctions related precisely to the spectator-performance relationship identified with in-yer-face theatre in the book of the same name by Aleks Sierz.

Sierz locates the specifically 'experiential' nature of an in-yer-face sensibility as inhering in 'any drama that takes the audience by the scruff of the neck and shakes it until it gets the message'.[7] Drama is quite literally 'in-yer-face' when, as a member of an audience, you feel 'your personal space has been invaded', when the performance before you 'threatens to violate [a] sense of safety'.[8] In Sierz's account, the activity of experience is contrasted against the passivity of speculation: 'unlike the type of theatre that allows us to sit back and contemplate what we see in detachment, the best in-yer-face theatre takes us on an emotional journey, getting under our skin'.[9] An in-yer-face 'journey' may be readily described as one of provocation and confrontation, discomfort and outrage, a sustained strategy of 'shock tactics' deployed in order to 'more aggressively aim at making audiences feel and respond'.[10] Sierz also attributes to the best of these writers a 'transformation of the language of theatre', the introduction of a new dramatic vocabulary which 'threw off the dead hand of literature and created a distinctively theatrical language'.[11] The corporeality of the metaphors employed by Sierz – 'scruff of the neck', 'personal space', 'under our skin', even 'dead hand of literature' – echo and reflect the centrality of the body and, specifically, its violation within much 'in-yer-face' drama. While the analyses of society, ethics and sexuality advanced by these plays may profoundly differ, their depiction of transgressive actions – the dismemberment and dumping of Ezra's body in Jez Butterworth's *Mojo* (1995); the sexual violence inflicted upon/desired by Gary in Mark Ravenhill's *Shopping and Fucking* (1996); the systematic mutilation of Carl in Sarah Kane's *Cleansed* (1998), to give just three examples – seem designed to deliver, in Ken Urban's striking phrase, 'a kick in the arse, a jab in the eyeball and a punch in the gut'.[12] Sierz's analysis of in-yer-face theatre identifies a dramatic writing which perceives and deliberately exploits the live dynamic of performance – the bodily co-presence of actors and spectators – in order to engender a profound discomfiture which might shock audiences out of a deadening complacency. It is significant that agency in the performance-spectator relationship as construed by Sierz's account lies unequivocally with the former at the expense of the latter: the performance 'shocks' while spectators 'are shocked'. The theatrical language Stephens has developed over the past decade similarly exploits the performance-spectator relationship, but his dramatic vocabulary neither divorces the experiential from the speculative – the 'active, involved' body from the 'passive, detached' gaze – nor predicates its formal strategies upon an assumed, or implied, apathy or ignorance in its audiences.

In contrast to a dramaturgy of coercion, invasion and violation, Stephens's construction of character and narrative invites audiences into a process of observation, selection and comparison in order to interpret a story from the individuals, events, dialogue and images presented to them. The invitation to engage empathetically with the drama does not straightforwardly flatter or indulge the audience; depending upon the play, or even on a certain moment within a play, this 'invitation' might better be read as a provocation, an entreaty, or a dare to the audience to recognize themselves and/or their loved ones. Departing from the attempt to maintain an appearance of seamless surface reality, Stephens's brand of naturalism exposes its artifice through an acute acknowledgement of the audience's role in creating the dramatic fiction. His ongoing revision of naturalistic models seems to refute any notion of an objective, uniform transmission of meaning or affect *from* the stage *to* the audience, acknowledging instead the theatre event itself as a third term in the process of meaning-making. The play-texts of *One Minute* (2003), *Motortown* (2006) and *Pornography* (2008) 'give it up for performance' – in both senses of relinquishment and celebration – subtly inscribing the moment of performance within the text itself.[13]

2. *One Minute*

Commissioned and directed by Gordon Anderson for Actors Touring Company, *One Minute* was first produced at the Crucible Theatre, Sheffield, in June 2003 and transferred to the Bush Theatre, London, in February 2004.[14] Anderson's commission set Stephens the challenge of writing 'a play that didn't necessarily work along the normal structures of narrative logic, so that scenes contrasted and juxtaposed with one another in a way that was organized but not necessarily defined by narrative cogency'.[15] The resulting play-text takes the genre of detective fiction and turns it inside out, jettisoning the plot-driven 'hero's journey' of a Raymond Chandler and relocating the act of 'deciphering' from within the play's fiction to the dynamic between performance and audience.

Touched by the abduction and murder of schoolgirl Milly Dowler in March 2002, *One Minute* is in part the story of a police search for a missing child.[16] Set in London, the play depicts DI Gary Burroughs and his assistant DC Robert Evans investigating the disappearance of Daisy Schults, daughter of Dr Anne Schults. Beginning in January, the play spans a 11-month period: in April the search is scaled back, in August a body is found and in November Gary, Robert and Anne visit London Zoo together to say their goodbyes. Orbiting and, at times, colliding with the police investigation are Catherine Denham and Marie Louise Burdett. Marie Louise contacts the police claiming to have seen Daisy two days after she disappeared; this sighting, it transpires, is Marie Louise's invention. In a manner befitting the play's 'sense of the city, its randomness [and] its parallel worlds',[17] despite Catherine's friendship with Gary – he is a frequent visitor to the bar where she works – she never finds out that he is investigating the Schults case; nor does Gary ever learn that Catherine flat-shares with Marie Louise. A meditation upon loss, grief and consolation, the doubled absence at the heart of *One Minute* – a missing girl whose image is never seen – is complemented by a dramaturgy which withholds the depiction of key narrative events, shifting these potentially climatic scenes to the periphery of the play in performance. Stephens:

> I remember seeing a friend of my wife's mother whose daughter died in adulthood. I remember seeing her shortly after her daughter died and it was like she had, literally, had a hole cut out of her stomach. It was like I could fucking see right through her [. . .] I wanted to construct the play as a police investigation but I wanted to somehow take the 'whole' out of the heart of it [. . .] What I decided to do was to imagine the middle of that story taken away, and just show the edges of it. So that all the scenes take place around the edges of the grief [. . .] I had this sense that if I did that, the form would dramatize the grief.[18]

A conventional conflict-driven narrative might be expected to dramatize the pursuit of a suspect, the identification of a body, the interrogation scene; it might be expected to examine the strained relationship between Anne and her husband, or the fantasist aspects of Marie Louise's character. Instead, Stephens allows an 'emotional space and light into the structure of the text',[19] by positioning these significant incidents and relationships 'around the edges' of the drama, in the gaps *between* scenes. By avoiding explicit depiction, the pain, emptiness and confusion which suffuse the story of *One Minute* appear not so much as fixed, quantifiable, known emotions as dynamic, amorphous, unutterable experiences. The underlying sense of helplessness, or impotence, which differently inhabits each character in *One Minute* finds its counterpart in a recurring sense that we, the audience, have arrived on the scene 'too late': scenes begin with half-finished conversations, or shortly after some sort of confrontation has occurred: when Gary tells Anne that her daughter's body has been found, we enter the scene only *after* Anne 'has stopped crying' (p. 56). A sense of 'the vast unresolvedness of things'[20] similarly infuses scenes which evade conclusion by ending abruptly, by ending on a question or by simply trailing off into silence: 'All right. This is what happened to me today:' (p. 22); 'Tonight, Gary. You coming or what?' (p. 28); 'I understand, you know? People get. . .' (p. 39). It is typical of the play's openendedness that even as Anne ends her communication with Gary and Robert, the police investigation is ongoing.

A mixed critical reception greeted *One Minute*'s experiment with 'narrative cogency'. While welcomed and praised by critics such as Jeremy Kingston, Ian Shuttleworth and Benedict Nightingale, the play was also decried by Fiona Mountford, for example, as 'frustratingly elliptical'.[21] Patrick Marmion declared that Stephens's 'short, oblique scenes' were 'no substitute for direct conflict and robust characterization',[22] and Charles Spencer pronounced that Stephens 'seems wilfully to have thrown away potentially powerful dramatic material'.[23] Spencer accused Stephens of failing to 'do justice to the visceral terror of his theme' and, on the strength of his aversion to the play, went so far as to speculate upon the playwright's personal life: 'I may be wrong about this, but I have a strong hunch that Stephens has no children of his own, for I cannot believe that any loving parent could write with such arty attenuation on so harrowing a subject'.[24] Spencer here equates what he identifies as Stephens's waste of 'powerful' material with a failure to stage the 'visceral terror of his theme', and attributes both flaws to an apparent lack of understanding, experience and empathy on behalf of the playwright.[25]

The remarks of these critics provide an interesting meta-commentary on positivistic habits of playwriting and spectating, raising questions as to how writers 'credibly' represent the experience of extreme emotion as well as how audiences experience the representation of extreme emotion as 'credible'. It might be that Stephens's alleged waste of material is better described as a refusal to exploit for the sake of dramatic expediency the 'harrowing anxiety' which attends real-life abductions.[26] In this sense, *One Minute* works antithetically to what might be termed the 'consumer aesthetics' of an in-yer-face gesture which delivers, via the 'visceral' spectacle of grief, pain or fear, an immediate 'hit' of morbid pleasure, thrilling terror or prurient fascination. Rather than 'calcify' these emotions in a particular representation, the mimetic realism of *One Minute*'s individual scenes works in concert with an overarching dramaturgy which 'allow[s] these feelings to situate themselves *beyond* the world depicted by the play'.[27] *One Minute* asks of its audiences an active engagement which goes beyond a fixed empirics of dramatic representation, and towards a liberated dynamic in which the play's 'absences and misconnections *are* the meaning, which we inhabit in our own ways as the characters do in theirs'.[28]

Unlike Stephens' previous plays, the writing process for *One Minute* was informed by a series of workshops, spread across eight months during 2001–2, using actors drawn from the Actors Centre, London. Devising a variety of acting and writing exercises, director and playwright worked with these actors to imagine situations, settings, characters and objectives, on the back of which Stephens later produced the first draft of *One Minute*. One exercise devised by Anderson directed the actors to specific locations in London and asked them to keep a 'sensory diary of the walk'. Anderson:

The idea for the sensory diaries came from my experience of a sudden bereavement in my family. During that time I travelled around London trying to maintain my day-to-day, and I was struck by how difficult articulating grief actually is. London just looked different to what it had the year before, to the point where I wondered if it was just a place constructed in our minds by all our different experiences. So the London I saw was actually physically different to the London the person walking next to me saw [. . .] with their new love, or their new job, or whatever was occupying their thoughts at that moment. I knew that constructing a play about the 'events' of this bereavement would say nothing about the experience; that's why, within the workshops, I was looking for ways of expression that would unlock the articulation [. . .] I wanted to explore this thing where you hear something terrible, or you hear something amazing in life, and you have to just sort of trudge through London with it fresh in your mind. So I said 'what I want you to do is to imagine you're this character and imagine you have this news on your journey home. And I want you describe London without talking about what the news is'.[29]

These sensory diaries directly inspired the inclusion of five monologues dispersed throughout *One Minute*, short direct-address speeches in which each character describes a journey home. As with the play's opening scene, where Marie-Louise mistakes Catherine for a shop assistant, some of these monologues were generated directly from the workshops; both Anderson and Stephens attest that the gorgeous details of 'flashing lights on trainers' and 'only diabetic toffee' were directly provided by the actor improvising Marie Louise:[30]

> **Marie Louise** So I'm coming home and I'm walking down the side of the theatre where, where, where *Les Miserables* is playing [. . .]
>
> Just near there I see a younger boy holding hands with his mother. He's got this soft blond hair and he's very excited. Stamping his feet up and down like a robot or something. And there are these lights on his trainers which I think, I just think is fantastic. [. . .]
>
> I get onto Oxford Street, heading up to Oxford Circus and before I get there I, this is a bit naughty, I decide that I'm going to go into Thornton's [sic], there. I really want to buy some toffee. I just have this this this this urge. So I've decided, really decided, that I'm going to have this toffee. But in the shop, I get there and in the shop they only have diabetic toffee. That's all they have. In the whole shop! [. . .]
>
> I go into Top Shop. I don't buy anything. [. . .] (pp. 22–3)

The impact of journeys and journeying upon the individual is a recurrent theme across Stephens's oeuvre. As Sarah Frankcom, co-Artistic Director of the Royal Exchange, Manchester, observes, Stephens's plays are often examinations of 'what you can learn from journey[ing], what people experience from changing their circumstances [. . .] how journeys can be your undoing or how they can be your salvation'.[31] The journeys in question may be literally geographical, but they might also be figuratively emotional, sexual, intellectual or criminal; the apparently innocuous question 'What's the furthest you've ever been to?' can hold many connotations.[32] The concept of 'journey' implies also its opposite. It is typical of Stephens's greater interest in 'fallout' than 'event' that the dramatic focus of his 2006 'anti-anti-war play', *Motortown*, is not the British Army tour of Basra recently completed by its protagonist, Danny, but the shattering impossibility of this character's 'return' to civilian life.

3. *Motortown*

[Playwriting] is *not* a linguistic profession, it's a behaviourial profession. My subject isn't what people *say* to each other; it's what people *do* to each other that interests me.[33]

In the introduction to his second volume of work, Stephens describes the five plays collected there as profoundly informed by 'two ruptures'.[34] The first of these ruptures occurred on 11 September 2001, when members of the militant Islamic group al-Qaeda hijacked four American passenger planes, crashing two into the Twin Towers of the World Trade Centre, New York. The United States, supported by the United Kingdom, responded by declaring a 'War on Terror', an offensive which included the invasion of Afghanistan.[35] The second rupture occurred on 7 July 2005, when four British-born Muslim men detonated four bombs across the London Transport Network. The stated motivation for the bombings was the United Kingdom's ongoing involvement in the Iraq war, also known as the Second Gulf War.[36] Having spent six months planning the play, the week in which Stephens wrote *Motortown* was the week of the London bombings – a week that also saw London stage the Live 8 Concert and win the bid for the 2012 Olympics.[37] This extraordinary week for the capital would provide the pretext for Stephens's next play, *Pornography*. While notably different in form and affect, both *Motortown* and *Pornography* may be read as uncompromising critiques of a culture in which devastating acts of violence are understood as the symptoms, not causes, of a society in political, cultural, ecological and moral chaos.

In stark contrast to *One Minute*, *Motortown*'s eight tightly-contained episodes ricochet from one pivotal event to another. When the play begins, Danny has bought himself out of the army and is staying with Lee, his autistic brother, in Dagenham. Any hope Danny has for a

111

fresh start with his ex-girlfriend, Marley, is instantly dispelled by Lee's opening line: 'She doesn't want to see you. She told me to tell you' (p. 143). Danny visits Marley anyway, who tells him she wants nothing to do with him. Danny buys a replica gun, goes to London to get it converted, and pays Marley another visit.

Danny I've got something for you. I went out, into town, up London, this afternoon and got a present for you. I've not decided whether you're gonna get it yet. (p. 177)

Danny does not shoot Marley. He abducts the black teenage girlfriend of the man who converted his P99. He takes her to Foulness Island, where he tortures and shoots her. On his way back to Dagenham he stops off for a drink at a hotel bar in Southend, where he is propositioned by a married couple of swingers. The play ends with Danny back at Lee's flat; Lee knows what Danny did, and it is almost certain that he will turn in Danny to the police.

In many ways, the tensions and contradictions that reverberate throughout *Motortown*'s taut narrative – Stephens is adamant it is 'a love story' – crystallize the profound moral complexity that continues to surround the United Kingdom's involvement in the Iraq war.[38] In contrast to the editorial line widely adopted by the British media during the 2000s, *Motortown* refrains from condemning the war, displaying instead a distinctly ambivalent attitude towards the arguments constructed by anti-war rhetoric; attitudes sharply satirized in Stephens's portrayal of the smugly liberal swingers, Helen and Justin (pp. 189–202). Stephens:

There was something about the anti-war movement that [. . .] unnerved me. It was a movement that seemed to be based on a separation of the war from the international context that surrounded it. It managed, at times, to argue its way into defending the sovereignty of a mass murderer. I was not an unapologetic advocate of the war in any way and was sensitive to many arguments made against it. But it struck me as childlike not to see the war as symptomatic rather than causal. It wasn't that the war was a monstrosity born out of a salvageable world. The world felt malign to me. The war seemed symptomatic of that.[39]

Some commentators have long argued that the First and Second Gulf Wars were wars over access to, and control over, oil reserves located in the Middle East. The contradiction Stephens explores in *Motortown* confronts the unpalatable but unavoidable fact that a fundamental condition of sustaining the economic framework of Western capitalist democracy is secure access to this oil. If oil is a global resource, then war is a global responsibility. As *Motortown*'s director, Ramin Gray, argues:

All these people [on the 'Million' march against Iraq, 16 February 2003] walking down the road holding their lattes and wearing their t-shirts and saying 'no war, no war'. Don't they realise that their lattes and all the wealth they have comes from the oil that is being pumped out of the Middle East? Don't they see the irony of that position?[40]

Despite the play's attack on the woollier aspects of a knee-jerk liberalism, critics almost unanimously read *Motortown* as a standard critique of the dehumanizing effects of war. Stephens, however, is clear that he 'wanted to write a play which inculpated more than it absolved [its audiences]'.[41] Any criticism espoused by the play is directed less towards the army than the culture of which it is an extension:

I think it is easy to imagine the military as being hermetically sealed and separate from our culture, to view military atrocities as being something that are not our fault [. . .] but it is a myth. If those boys are violent, chaotic or morally insecure, it's because they are a product of a violent, chaotic and morally insecure culture. It's inaccurate to dismiss them as being part of something else.[42]

To attribute Danny's motivation for abducting and killing a teenage girl to a process of brutalization within the army is, for Stephens, to conveniently overlook the pervasiveness of violence and chaos within our own society. 'I don't blame the war', Danny tells us in the play's

113

closing moments. 'The war was alright. I miss it. It's just you come back to this' (p. 209).

The stage directions for *Motortown* state 'the play should be performed as far as possible without décor' (p. 142), and Ramin Gray indeed directed the play's premiere at the Royal Court on a spare stage that exposed the Theatre Downstairs' imposing back brick wall. Starkly lit by an overhead bank of bright white lights, a square of white tape on a grey dance floor demarcated 'onstage' and 'offstage'. Actors remained visible throughout the play; when not engaged in a scene they sat around the edges of the square, watching the play unfold. The set consisted of a dozen plastic chairs, arranged by the actors to suggest different locations. The rearrangement of chairs itself became a pronounced feature of the production, with Gray engaging the skills of choreographer Hofesh Schechter: 'What I wanted between each of the scenes was a spritzer that would wipe the audience's aesthetic palate. We used the image of a man plunging his head into a bucket of water, and between each scene he comes back up [gulping for air]. That's the choreography'.[43]

We might describe Gray's *Motortown* as setting a psychological realism typically allied to 'illusionist theatre' against a staging which consciously utilized 'anti-illusionistic' techniques of a Brechtian epic theatre. Dan Rebellato, however, has recently interrogated this concept of 'illusion' in ways more productive for an analysis of the representational strategies put into play by Gray's production. Rebellato contends that it is a mistake to refer to representational theatre as illusionistic, pointing out that 'in illusions we have *mistaken beliefs* about what we are seeing. No sane person watching a play believes that what is being represented before them is actually happening. We know we are watching people representing something else; we are aware of this, never forget it and rarely get confused'.[44] In place of illusion, Rebellato suggests that the relationship between stage and fiction instead works in terms of metaphor: 'in metaphor, we are invited to see (or think about) one thing in terms of another thing [. . .] when we see a piece of theatre we are invited to think of the fictional world through this particular representation'.[45] When, for example, the audience is invited to see (or think about) the fictional locations of *Motortown*, an explicit 'non-identity' of stage and fiction is in process: we see four

114

chairs placed in a particular arrangement and actively engage in 'seeing' Lee's flat, Paul's high-rise apartment or the Northview bar. The relation between the chairs and location they represent is not mimetic but metaphorical; there is a vast aesthetic distance between the material reality of these chairs and the fictional reality they gesture towards.[46]

Extending this logic, we can say that actors serve as 'metaphors' for characters: the actor Daniel Mays, for example, is a *metaphor* for the character of Danny. In productions such as Gray's *Motortown*, however, in which actors were cast closely to character type, this relationship between actor and character might be better described as *metonymic*. The aesthetic distance between the 'thing we see' (signifier, actor) and the 'thing we are invited to think about' (signified, character) is very slight; the former successfully substitutes for the latter, and vice versa. Stephens himself attests that he is 'fascinated' by 'the directness between an actor and performance and the character'.[47] An early draft of *Motortown* contains a stage direction (omitted from later drafts) suggesting that the characters' names should be those of the actors; indeed, Stephens wrote the part of Danny specifically for Daniel Mays.[48] In performance, the striking *non-identity* between stage and fiction in terms of design threw into sharp relief a posited *identity* between character and actor, a dynamic which concentrated and consolidated the psychological realism of the actors' performances. The implied proximity of 'actor' to 'character' sustained in performance was particularly exploited in *Motortown*'s graphic depiction of torture, as the production arguably conspired to make the race and gender of the actors playing Danny and Jade profoundly and inescapably 'present'. As the audience watched a white male threaten a black female, stage reality seemed fleetingly to *vie* with dramatic fiction: watching 'Danny' abuse 'Jade' uncomfortably approximated to watching 'a Daniel Mays' abuse 'an Ony Uhiara'. The text itself slyly references this terrifying entanglement of actuality and imagination:

Danny Now here's a question for you. Is this really petrol or is it water?

He opens the canister. Holds it open, under her nose, for her to sniff.

What do you think? Jade? What do you think? Answer me.

115

Jade I don't know.

Danny No, I know. But have a guess. What do you reckon?

Jade I think it's petrol.

Danny Do yer?

Jade It smells like petrol.

Danny Are you sure that's not just your imagination?

Jade No. I don't know.

Danny Your imagination plays terrible fucking tricks on you in situations like this. (p. 187)

What's *really* inside the canister is, of course, water – Health and Safety would see to that – but as the performance of *Motortown* pressurized perceptual distinctions between actor and character, actuality and fantasy, such distinctions became strangely, productively, difficult to sustain.[49] For a critical few moments, disbelief was not so much suspended as *tested*: when Danny taunted Jade about her imagination playing tricks on her, he may as well have been taunting the audience. As reviewer Matt Wolf noted:

Gray blurred the boundaries between art and life to such a disturbing extent that audiences at the end had to pause a moment before applauding. On opening night the leading man, Daniel Mays, even spun himself quickly around before taking his bow, as if that action might in an instant shed the scar tissue in which so scary a play is steeped.[50]

That which Gray's production alluded to, the character of Paul baldly states: 'You see, when you can't tell the difference any more between what is real and what is a fantasy. That's frightening, I think' (p. 169). Danny's actions in *Motortown* might, in fact, be attributed less to a notional 'brutalization' in warfare than to a desperate horror at 'the discrepancy between the certainty of the insurgents against whom he had been fighting, and the valueless sprawl of the country he came

116

home to'.[51] Unable to recognize the country he fought for, Danny fatally misrecognizes the lines between military activity and civilian life.

4. *Pornography*

> For me, character is so important. We understand ideas through the behaviour and actions of individuals. I hope people can recognise themselves in the characters they're watching. Even in a play like *Motortown* where you see a lot of violence, I think there's hope in it, and it's a hope created by self-recognition [. . .] That continued attempt of people to form relationships with characters and with each other in this context is very hopeful. Although we do live in pornographic times, people still see the potential to need intimacy and seek it out.[52]

The need to 'seek out intimacy' provides a thoughtful definition of the collective gesture of *One Minute*, *Motortown* and *Pornography*. Intimacy, of course, takes many forms and inspires many relationships: sexual, cerebral, physical, emotional. These intimacies may be described as reciprocal states between lovers, friends and/or family: private realms inhabited by individuals who know and are known by one another. Commitment to psychological realism in creating and writing character, however, can invite another manifestation of intimacy that, in theory, may be forged in a public space, between complete strangers, one or more of whom are, bizarrely, fictional: the sense of intimacy engendered by an instance of 'self-recognition' in the theatre. The 'hope' created by self-recognition is, perhaps, a hope sprung from the idea that enabling such recognition to take place is a fleeting moment of sincere communication and understanding between individuals. The 'communicability of the human spirit' mooted by Richard in *Bluebird* is a potential to be fulfilled in performance, as we recognize aspects of ourselves, or of our loved ones, in the actions or words of a fictional character. This moment is not always a pleasurable experience; self-recognition may well make for uncomfortable viewing as we are surprised, dismayed or perhaps shamed by the actions or behaviours

117

with which we find ourselves identifying. Recognition is, moreover, rarely, if ever, total: the ability to disassociate as well as associate with images and ideas is a vital condition of life as well as art. Nevertheless, the empathy required for a sense of intimacy to manifest itself in the theatre is, arguably, a *humanizing* energy: to recognize one's 'self' in an 'other', is to encounter, joyfully or reluctantly, an unexpected commonality.

Pornography suggests itself as a play inspired by a sense of 'living in pornographic times'. The play-text takes the form of four monologues, two duologues and one list offering short descriptions of the 52 people killed in the 2005 London bombings. Each scene presents 'a story of transgression'.[53] A woman leaks a confidential report to her company's nearest competitor; a schoolboy attacks a teacher; a brother and sister enter into an incestuous relationship; a British-born Muslim walks onto the London Underground with a bomb in his rucksack; a male university professor attempts sexual relations with a female former student; an elderly woman knocks on the door of a stranger; and, in a wryly self-referential twist, information about the victims of the London bombings is lifted from a BBC website and used as material for a play.[54] The seven discrete scenes of *Pornography* refract the events of 7 July 2005 through characters and stories which work individually and together to explore what Stephens has described as his 'inability to share people's incredulity' that the 'boys who bombed London were British by birth':

> Rather, it seemed logical to me. Their actions seemed to be absolutely a product of the same Britain I'd grown up in. They were born and raised in a Britain built by one prime minister who denied altogether the existence of society and another who made a passionate plea for understanding to be valued less than unthinking condemnation of others. I wanted to write a play that put a terrorist action on equal footing with many of the other flaws and ruptures I saw around me.[55]

Pornography depicts a culture in which understanding and intimacy are lacking, refused, misread or (deemed to be) perverted. In its observation and dissection of the small, seemingly-insignificant iniquities of everyday life, the play dramatizes the devaluation and insidious erosion of qualities such as tolerance, trust, generosity, kindness and empathy. Values and lexicons forged in the crucible of consumer capitalism infiltrate private as well as public spheres, co-opting everyday relations into miniature narratives of transaction and exploitation. Business interests intervene between husband and wife: 'The Triford report is nearly finished [. . .] We actually did have to sign a contract that forbade us to speak even to our spouses about what was going on. It's a legally binding contract' (p. 218). Television formulas hold images of the weeping bereaved 'in our gaze for a good twenty seconds before the cut' (p. 232). Marketing spiel substitutes for individual judgment: '[Lenny's] got one of those three-wheeled pushchairs. It has fabulous suspension. It makes it ideal for city street life' (p. 216). Live 8 and the Olympics manufacture compassion and solidarity, promoting international harmony while a nation fractures from within. Characters are isolated within their family, exploited for personal gain, alienated from their own bodies. They observe, rather than inhabit, their actions, words, instincts and emotions.[56] They repeatedly fail to recognize if someone is laughing or crying.[57] *Pornography* presents these characters as individuals 'scorched by a need and an *inability* to connect' (my italics).[58]

This is the culture of dislocation and disaffection, Stephens seems to suggest, from which transgressive actions ensue. In this reading, *Pornography*'s title refers less to sexually explicit material per se than to the underlying *suppression of empathy* which enables its consumption: it is the inability, or refusal, to imagine what it is like to be 'the other' which enables individuals to commit acts of sexual, physical, emotional or economic violence. As Sean Holmes, director of the UK premiere of *Pornography*, proposes:

> To consume pornography, you have to deny the humanity of the person that you're looking at on the screen or in the picture. You don't think about that person, what they had for breakfast or the fact they may have kids, you're just looking at them as a thing to give you pleasure. I think the same thing applies if you're

119

trying to kill a load of people on a tube: you just can't ask those questions – the questions that the *play* asks.[59]

The transgressive actions of the characters in *Pornography* invite the unimaginable to interrupt and disrupt the imaginable. As (destructive) gestures of defiance against the routinized, standardized, commodified experiences of the everyday, these transgressions suggest both a dangerous estrangement from lived reality and a passionate desire to transform it. In situating suicidal mass murder on the extreme end of a spectrum which encompasses sexual harassment and assault, *Pornography*'s critique is directed less at the individual than at the iniquities and inequalities which breed hatred, bitterness and fear within an increasingly atomized society. By refusing to condemn its characters, *Pornography* stages its own defiant gesture against pornographic times, 'forcing us to feel and understand the complexities of each character – even if they're a suicide bomber who we would rather not know about'.[60] *Pornography*'s intimate portraits of character and situation present a difficult, complex but, ultimately, familiar world. We might argue that 'empathy' in *Pornography* moves beyond mere formal device to achieve a thematic resonance in performance, interrupting and disrupting the 'unthinking condemnation' – marginalization, ostracization – of the play's transgressors. The empathetic impulse forms fleeting relationships between character and spectator, transient associations in which difference can perhaps be evaluated alongside unexpected, unlooked for, perhaps unwanted, commonality.

The decision to focus on character in this brief account of *Pornography* may seem puzzling, given that on the page there are, in fact, no named characters. The stage directions which precede the text inform us that: 'this play can be played by any number of actors' and that 'it can be performed in any order' (p. 214). In these respects, *Pornography* would appear to be the most formally experimental of the three plays discussed here. Commissioned by the Deutsches Schauspielhaus, Hamburg, and written specifically for Sebastian Nübling to direct, Stephens's play-text interestingly crystallizes some of the contrasting approaches to playwriting and theatre-making between English and German-language theatre cultures.[61] In Germany and, indeed, in many countries across mainland Europe, a play-text is often regarded as a point of departure rather than a destination to reach. In line with a director's vision for a production, an existing play-text may be rewritten, edited, spliced, fused and/or collided with other texts; a play-text is regarded as less a *blueprint* than a *stimulus* for performance. Knowing that 'writing for Sebastian would likely involve him intervening in the text', Stephens decided:

. . . to create a text that allowed intervention rather than discouraged it, to produce a text that he could really take apart and interrogate and reinvent. And cut! Which is something that seems completely counterintuitive for any English playwright who operates in a theatre culture where the play is everything.[62]

Indeed, the open structure of *Pornography*, its refusal to delineate characters and its deliberate appeal to directorial intervention were choices which in 2006, according to Stephens, 'seemed to bewilder many readers in England'.[63]

I couldn't believe how difficult it was to get that play placed in an English theatre [. . .] I remember talking to Nick Hytner about that play and he said to me 'I couldn't really read that. There are no character names or stage directions – it's not really a play is it?' Sebastian Born at the National said exactly the same thing. He couldn't read it.[64]

Without character names to nominally 'define' its speakers, *Pornography*'s mixture of narrated and enacted action may initially appear confusing on the page, yet this blending of modes is not so radically different from what Stephens achieved with *One Minute*; indeed, the degree to which 'form dramatizes content' in both *One Minute* and *Pornography* is striking. 'Bewildered and frustrated by people's reluctance to produce [*Pornography*]', Stephens drafted another version of the script in an attempt to 'seduce some English theatres into producing it'.[65] Significantly, none of the text itself was altered: Stephens simply inserted character names before the dialogue and spliced the episodes to form a new sequence of scenes which formed a chronologically linear narrative.[66] He retained the list of people killed in the London bombings and new stage directions suggested that this section could 'be performed by all eight actors, or displayed as text or played over a soundtrack. It could be performed using all three methods simultaneously'.[67] When Sean Holmes came to direct *Pornography* in 2008, this was the script that was taken into rehearsals. After encountering some difficulties with the revised version, however, director and actors decided to create their own adaptation, a decision that Holmes affirms ran counter to his usual practice as a director: 'that was new for me, this thing of inventing, having to invent [a structure] – I'd never normally be so presumptuous to think that my structure could be better than the writer's'.[68]

Interestingly, while Nübling's German-language production edited and rewrote some scenes – the sexual relationship between brother and sister, for example, became a story of incest between two brothers – the play's formal structure remained intact. The set for *Pornographie*, designed by Nübling's long-term collaborator Muriel Gerstner, comprised of half a dozen school tables and chairs set before an enormous, half-finished, metal mosaic depicting Brueghel's painting of the Tower of Babel – a biblical image powerfully symbolic of cultural division, miscommunication and confusion. When not directly involved in the action onstage, actors attempted to complete this mosaic. Tiles, scattered like debris about the stage, were slotted into wooden frames which, at particular points during the action, were hoisted onto incomplete areas of the image by two or three actors working together. It was, according to Stephens, 'the best design I'd ever had. It had a visceral theatricality to it, as well having an intellectual presence. The necessity and impossibility of completing the mosaic seemed, to me, to be thematically relevant'.[69]

Since *Pornography*, Nübling has staged Stephens's adaptation of Alfred Jarry's *Ubu Roi* (2010, Theater Essen, co-production with Toneelgroep Amsterdam) and his 2009 play *Punk Rock* (2010, Junges Theater Basel). In September 2011, Nübling premiered Stephens's epic, trilingual *Three Kingdoms* in a three-way co-production between Teater No99 (Tallin, Estonia), the München Kammerspiele (Munich,

122

Germany) and the Lyric Hammersmith (London, England). In the view of Ramin Gray:

> Simon's [collaboration with Nübling is] a two-way street, because Simon's really responded to what he's experienced over there [. . .] What's happening between Nübling and Stephens is really important and, I'd say, unique or unheard of so far. A relationship between an auteur European director and a British playwright? That's probably worth a chapter in itself.[70]

Stephens' career as a playwright is indeed distinguished by a willingness and enthusiasm to work collaboratively, whether writing for directorial intervention with *Pornography*, inviting a choreographer into rehearsals for *Motortown* or improvising with actors for *One Minute*. In 2005, Stephens embarked upon what would become a five-year process of collaboration with playwrights David Eldridge and Robert Holman, resulting in the jointly-authored play *A Thousand Stars Explode in the Sky*, produced at the Lyric Hammersmith in 2010. Stephens suggests that you can 'sniff the influence of [that] collaboration' in the plays he has written since 2005, citing these writers' 'boldness of theatricality' and 'linguistic openness' as key inspirations for his work: 'I don't think I would have written Seth Regan's final monologue in *Harper Regan*, for example, if I hadn't worked on *Thousand Stars*'.[71]

Stephens's interest in collaboration stems from a refreshing mix of pragmatism and idealism. On the one hand, playwriting is a craft and the playwright an artisan: 'you have to take responsibility for yourself, as a writer. If you think you're going to sustain a writing career by only writing from within, from extracting plays from your soul, then you're not going to get very far [. . .] collaboration stokes the fire'.[72] On the other hand, there is perhaps something about the nature of collaborative processes which resonates with recurring concerns in Stephens's writing. To work collaboratively is, after all, to affirm the importance and significance of trust, of respect and of generosity; communication and understanding are integral to the process, as is a collective spirit of curiosity and enquiry. To work creatively in the theatre, whether as a playwright, director, actor, designer, musician or, indeed, as an audience member, is to embrace and engage with these intangible energies, in order to collectively explore their potential. The last word rests with Stephens:

> Theatre is an innately optimistic profession. It's a profession born out of optimism. For you to write for theatre is very different from writing poetry or writing novels because it's built on the optimistic possibility that when you give your play to a director not only will they not fuck it up but they'll make it better. And when they give it to actors not only will they not forget your lines but they'll make your lines sing. And then when you put that in front of an audience not only will they not close off to it but they might open up and let it in. And that's a fucking optimistic process. And it's built on faith. On the faith that people can be better together than they can be apart. I don't think there's anything ironic about that optimism.[73]

TIM CROUCH
Dan Rebellato

'The word is the ultimate conceptual art form.'[1]

1. Introduction

On either side of the stage stand two actors. One of the actors, dressed in a glittery waistcoat, is playing a hypnotist who is, in turn, playing a mother in distress; the other, despite not having seen the script before, is playing a grieving father, their lines being fed to them by the first actor. The scene is the climactic moment of Tim Crouch's *An Oak Tree*: the father has come to the place in the road where their daughter was killed in an accident and has become convinced that his daughter has been transformed into one of the oak trees standing by the road. His wife pleads with him to see sense: 'it's a tree, Andy, it's just a fucking tree,' she says. 'Our girl is dead, love. She's dead'.[2] Between them stands the contested tree, though what we actually see is a piano stool, one of the few items of stage furniture that have had to stand for everything in the world of the play. As the debate unfolds between the two parents, the audience is asked to see the piano stool as a tree and then that imagined tree as the couple's dead daughter. It is an intensely moving scene about terrible loss, survival, longing and despair, but it is also a scene that interrogates and affirms the transformative mechanics of theatricality, and it is the audience's effortful act of imagination that fills the theatre with profound feeling. The scene is typical of the work of Tim Crouch, one of the most daring, playful and challenging theatremakers to emerge in the 2000s.

Tim Crouch is a playwright and performer all of whose work asks searching questions about theatre, plays and performance and the kinds of relationships we all have with the world and with each other. His

125

plays and his own performances in them have a tight unity and some of the most interesting puzzles they generate and the questions they ask emerge from his own theatrical presence. Although he has worked as a theatremaker and performer since the 1980s, he emerged as a writer only in 2003; by the end of the decade, he had produced nine plays, five of those for children. The four plays for adult audiences are *My Arm* (2003), *An Oak Tree* (2005), *ENGLAND* (2007), and *The Author* (2009). He appeared in all of the plays and toured with them internationally, receiving sometimes acclaim, sometimes furious denunciation. *The Author* received wildly opposed reviews, frequent audience walk-outs, heckling and angry letters to its author.[3] By contrast, no less a figure than Caryl Churchill chose *An Oak Tree* as her play of the decade, writing: 'It's a play about theatre, a magic trick, a laugh and a vivid experience of grief, and it spoils you for a while for other plays'.[4]

Tim Crouch's plays in performance are absurdly funny, fiercely intelligent and terribly moving adventures in theatrical storytelling and, while one can see overlapping concerns between his work and that of other writers and theatremakers, he remains a unique figure. A number of different early experiences contributed to his writing his first full-length play. His parents are teachers and Crouch has credited their influence on his determination to write for young audiences, his appetite for education, discussion and workshops as he develops his work, but also, as an actor, 'how to control a space and how to control a group of people'.[5] His interest in storytelling was extended by a period of work as the official storyteller for the Woodcraft Folk in the late 1990s. He brings to theatre a long interest in the visual arts and debates around conceptual art and theatre and his plays emerge as much from conceptual questions as more personal impulses.[6]

His turn to playwriting was stimulated by his growing dissatisfaction with the position of the actor in British theatre. Crouch studied Drama at Bristol University before forming a theatre company, Public Parts, a collective, socialist, devising company which toured successfully for some years before he decided to refine his performing skills and enrolled on a postgraduate acting course at Central School of Speech and Drama. There he worked with David Bridel, an actor, teacher and director, who instilled in Crouch the notion of the 'authorial actor': someone who does not merely execute someone else's creative ideas but is a co-creator who shares responsibility for the whole performance.[7] But for the next few years, working as a professional actor, he found the structures of conventional theatremaking blocked the ability of the actor to take this kind of responsibility. While working on a National Theatre education tour of Churchill's *Light Shining in Buckinghamshire* in 1997, the rehearsal process involved the actors being asked to break their roles down into psychological objectives and units of intention, in the Stanislavskian manner. They 'actioned' all their lines and 'hot-seated' their characters.[8] But all of these exercises served to restrict the actors' responsibility to nothing more than their own characters; on tour, the play's politics resonated strongly with the then-General Election campaign, but in post-show discussions the actors found themselves ill-equipped to discuss the political ideas behind the show.[9] The modes of theatrical production disempowered and disenfranchised the actors by systematically excluding them from creative responsibility for the whole production.[10] Although Tim Crouch is the focus of this chapter, that, too, is to distort his way of working. 'I'm not a solo artist,' he has insisted[11] and indeed his work is developed with some key collaborators, crucially a smith[12] and Karl James, who direct, advise and develop the work.

All of these different experiences – the early political work, the storytelling, the interest in conceptual art and his dissatisfaction with the power structures around conventional acting – converged in Crouch's first play. 'I had a story,' he has said, 'I needed to tell it and all the ideas I'd been worrying about for the last 20 years fell into that story'.[13]

2. *My Arm*

The play emerged from a workshop at the National Theatre Studio that explored making objects act. 'We performed scenes using fire extinguishers, coffee cups, chairs, whatever was lying around. The objects were manipulated by actors who were instructed not to get emotionally involved with either their object or the scenario in which their object was engaged,' Crouch explained.[14] The first outcome of these experiments was his play for young people, *Shopping for Shoes* (2003),[15] which concerns two teenagers, Shaun and Siobhan. Shaun is obsessed with designer trainers but Siobhan is more interested in politics. When they go bowling, Siobhan throws away his 'Nike Air Jordans Mark One', but Shaun discovers he does not mind because he has fallen in love with her. The witty theatrical device of the play is that all of the characters in the play are represented only by their shoes. The paradoxical journey of the play is that we are continually asked to imagine characters based on their shoes, yet the argument as the show develops is not to judge people by their shoes. At the end of the play, the two protagonists discard their shoes, leaving them visually unrepresented on stage. It is a performance, then, about imagination as a free space beyond materialism.

These theatrical ideas are explored even more intensively in *My Arm*. The story is fairly simple: one day, a boy decides to put his arm above his head and thereafter never takes it down. Despite the efforts of family and friends, he keeps his arm in the air, even as his muscles begin to waste. He is an object of fascination for the art world, images of him forming the basis of paintings and installations, and eventually he becomes a kind of art work himself. However, his atrophying arm causes complications and heart disease, and barely 40 years old, he dies. The story is absurdist in its central conceit, yet the writing insists on its realism, keeping the practicalities of this bizarre feat always in the foreground. *My Arm* is a one-man show: Tim Crouch addresses the audience directly and describes the events of the play in the first person. The convention is of the autobiographical performance and indeed, at the Edinburgh Festival where it premiered, there were two press releases: one was 'about a play by Tim Crouch' and the other was 'about a man who has lived with one arm above his head coming to Edinburgh to tell his story'.[16] The mode of the performance, together with Tim Crouch's then-relatively anonymous persona, encouraged the assumption that this was his own story.

However, at no point in the performance does Tim Crouch raise his arm above his head. This immediately causes some dissonance between what is being offered to the eye and to the ear. As the show develops it is clear that the boy never took his arm down and so this autobiographical performance is both non-autobiographical and also is not respecting the basic conventions of impersonation. As the show develops, the dissonances intensify: at one point Crouch, discussing the medical complications, tells us: 'I conceded to having this finger removed' showing us his non-amputated finger apparently as evidence (p. 39). Later he describes an operation he undergoes following a failed suicide attempt: 'you can see the scar,' he says, lifting up his shirt to reveal his unscarred back (p. 42). Recalling another moment, he explains that his hair 'was shorter than it is now' (p. 43), though Crouch's head is completely shaved.

In addition, at the beginning of the performance, he asks the audience to provide his props: they are reassured that the objects will be in plain sight at all times and 'treated with care and respect'. These objects – keys, cameras, wallets – are kept in a tray on stage and at various points Crouch introduces them to illustrate the story and to stand in for other characters and objects from the story; when two adults, enraged by his caprice, attack the boy, they are represented through the objects. The fact that we know that they have come from the audience ensures their arbitrariness: if Crouch had come in with a random collection of his own objects, it would have been possible to think that fleeting affinities between the objects and the things they stand for might be intentional.[17] But here, though we are directed to look at the objects – Crouch even has a video camera set up so that we can see them 'properly' – the whole of the stage picture resists being understood in terms of its visual resemblance to the fictional world. The only thing on stage that is vaguely representational is an Action Man doll that stands in for the boy on occasion and does, indeed, have its arm in the air,[18] and part of the work of the audience is to combine the image of the doll with Crouch's own body, arm resolutely unaloft.

Crouch's performance style is an important contribution to the play of signification at work in the show. He is a skilled performer who deliberately – and skilfully – strips his performances of anything that would separate him from the audience. He does not do a warm-up; he does not get into character; the play has never been rehearsed as such. He presents the lines of dialogue vividly but without very strong characterization, emotional colour or physical embodiment. The vocal style is even, assertoric, clear. His performance is, as Stephen Bottoms describes it, a 'relatively neutral canvas' on which the audience can paint.[19] The effects of this are multiple. First, it challenges the hierarchical separation between actor and audience. Crouch has described 'placing the audience in a dark space [. . .] getting them to sit still and quiet while we subject them to indulgent and impersonated fantasies' as 'an abuse of power'.[20] By refusing to assert his authority over the performance 'it becomes a community of ownership rather than "the actor and the company own this, and you own that"'.[21] Second, it offers a space for the ideas of the play to be experienced more freely, not tied down to visual particulars. Third, as he discovered when working in the National Theatre workshop on objects, when a chair 'played' a character in a scene, rather than lowering the emotional temperature, as one might expect, 'this detachment often had the effect of heightening the emotional charge of the scene'.[22] Fourth, by removing the duty of the stage to *resemble* the fictional world, it allows us to experience the stage images for their own sake; that is, it permits us to experience the performance in aesthetic terms and not only in terms of meaning and representation.

This can sound as though *My Arm* is a rather abstract exercise, but these unusual theatrical devices deepen and enrich the story being told. Indeed, all of these transformations in the relationship between stage and auditorium are echoed thematically in the play. The blankness of the mode of theatrical production corresponds to the blankness of the boy's existential act. His decision to raise his arm above his head is notably empty of significance. He makes no direct attempt to explain why he makes this strange decision. He recalls child psychiatrists trying 'to work out what the big idea was' (p. 34), but insists to his friend Anthony, 'in fact, it wasn't any idea at all' (p. 33). This boy's blank decision becomes a *tabula rasa* on which parents and friends, artists and psychiatrists write. As such it becomes replete with multiple, rival meanings. In the play's vision of a culture, furiously determined to explain, to pin down and normalize any action, there is something disruptive and transgressive about a meaningless act.

But more, *My Arm* present selfhood as a kind of fatal side-effect of culture. To the boy with his arm in the air, rather than the act issuing from a sense of self, the act seems to *produce* a selfhood that he had previously lacked: 'I realized for the first time where I ended and the rest of the world began – I felt sharp, delineated' (p. 32). But where this begins as a joyful discovery ('I was the boy with the arm' (p. 31)), he is soon a victim of his public identity and, eventually, expelled from it, when an art dealer pays $250,000 for exclusive rights to his image as he lives and possession of the famous arm after he dies (p. 46). The cultural obsession with understanding the boy with the arm literally assists in the death and dissection of the boy with the arm.

This complicates the relationship between the theatrical language and the story. Crouch's rejection of the Stanislavskian tradition of acting (which proceeds from the inside out, creating action out of a vividly and internally realized sense of character) connects with the way the boy's action produces a vivid internal sense of self, rather than the other way round. This action, which takes place 'without his conscious understanding',[23] also has resonances with Crouch's deliberate effacement of apparent intentionality, his embrace of arbitrariness, which places part of the performance outside his conscious control. As such, Crouch's blankness stands in, effectively, for the boy's blankness, each giving the other significance, though of an indeterminate kind.

Similarly, just as the adults in the play manufacture meanings in their desire to understand the boy and his raised arm, the audience fills in the gaps in performance with their own associations, experiences and ideas. But this is not a wholly comfortable association, given the brutality of the adult world's attempts at 'understanding'. This becomes particularly acute in the play's presentation of the art world. We are, at moments, given reasons to think that some of the conceptual art made with the boy's image is pretentiously fraudulent, particularly those created by his friend Simon; the latter's slogan 'Art is anything you can get away with' is written up and displayed prominently through the second half of the show. This cannot help but make us wonder if the performance itself is a kind of practical joke. Yet, the very indeterminacy that this generates in the audience, offering and withdrawing its own responses, continually reassessing the value and significance of its own spectatorship, is absolutely characteristic of conceptual art practices.

Crouch likes to refer to Marcel Duchamp, perhaps the original conceptual artist, who declared that 'painting should not be exclusively retinal or visual; it should have to do with the grey matter, with our urge for understanding'.[24] In other words, art must not solely appeal to the eye but to the mind as well. *My Arm* intensifies the drama of the mind and the eye, requiring an active audience engaging in complex acts of selection and transformation of what they see to populate a complex and imaginative picture of the fictional world.

A word of caution though. It may seem as if Crouch and his collaborators have imported a series of conceptual art techniques from outside the theatre; but it is worth remarking that these apparently experimental and eccentric techniques are what theatre uses all the time. In a play, we are continually invited to look at one person as if they are someone else, to see a stage cloth as a battlefield, or a stage wall as a horizon. There is no particular reason to assume that the relationship between the stage and the fictional world should be one of resemblance; in fact, most stage sets do not significantly resemble the worlds they represent. But even when they do, there is no more reason to think that the theatre is at its purest when it resembles the world than there is to think that language is at its purest when it is onomatopoeic. All theatre involves a kind of imaginative transformation of the visual material before us into something else.[25] It is for this reason perhaps that Crouch and his collaborators sometimes playfully refer to their work as 'pure theatre', 'more theatre' or 'very theatre'.[26]

3. *An Oak Tree*

Crouch wrote the first draft of *My Arm* very quickly, in 'response to the loss of my faith in acting and in me as an actor',[27] a spirit of melancholy that permeates the text. He sent it to Caryl Churchill and Mark Ravenhill who both encouraged him to put the play on; Ravenhill went further and recommended its publication to Faber & Faber, before it had been produced. In the text, simply to force himself to make another piece of work, Crouch added the note that his next project would be *An Oak Tree, 1973.*

The title is taken from a piece by Michael Craig-Martin, which Crouch has described as 'the most important theatre text I know'.[28] It is a surprising description because the piece is not obviously a theatre text at all. It is an art work comprising two elements: one is what appears to be a glass of water on a shelf; the other is a printed text that appears to be a series of questions posed to the artist, and his answers. In the course of these replies, he explains that in this art work he has, without altering its appearance, changed a glass of water into an oak tree. In response to further questions, he insists that he does not mean the glass of water has become a symbol of an oak tree; it is actually an oak tree. Nor has he merely called the glass of water an oak tree; he has changed it: 'It is not a glass of water any more. I have changed its actual substance [. . .] The actual oak tree is physically present but in the form of the glass of water'.[29] *An Oak Tree, 1973* is a landmark work of conceptual art and its mischievous profundity lies in its questioning of the limits of artistic intentionality, the connection of words to things, the importance of the visual as a guide to the essence of experience. And these are, after all, key questions for theatre, which regularly deals in transformation, pretence, words and images.

Tim Crouch's *An Oak Tree* transforms Craig-Martin's questions into a complex exploration of loss and the ethical significance of the imagination. As with *My Arm*, the story is straightforward (and odd): a stage hypnotist, distracted while driving, kills a teenage girl walking to a piano lesson and listening to music on her headphones. Some months later, her father attends the hypnotist's act. The hypnotist brings him onstage, defensive and angry. But the father just wants to tell him that Claire is okay. He knows that she has been transformed into an oak tree by the side of the road where she died. Transformation is at the heart of the play in a number of ways. It is there in the father's belief in his daughter's apotheosis but also, more tackily, in the acts of imaginative transformation that form the core of the hypnotist's act. It is there in the way the performance transforms the mundane stage furniture – little more than a stack of black plastic chairs, a speaker on a stand, and a piano stool – into a range of characters, locations and scenes, functionality transformed into intensity.

The most striking way in which we glimpse this transformation is in the second member of the cast. *An Oak Tree* is a two-person performance, but the second actor has never seen the script before and is different at every performance. The actor meets Crouch an hour before to test levels on the microphone and get a feel for the performance, still without seeing a script. Through the show, Crouch guides the second performer on what to do, either by handing them a clipboard with a section of dialogue on, prompting them through an earpiece, or simply instructing them out loud in what they say. Near the beginning of the show, adopting the role of the hypnotist, Crouch, his syntax stumbling a little, tells his imagined audience, 'Firstly, I will never lie to you. You will see no false nothing false tonight. Nothing phoney. No plants, no actors. The people you will see on stage tonight, ladies and gentlemen, apart from me, will be genuine volunteers' (p. 63). And the hypnotist's promise is kept throughout: Crouch introduces the volunteer second actor and explains their situation. The means by which the theatrical convention works are never hidden from us, so there can be no falsehood or phoney pretence. We are entirely 'in' on the rules of the performance.

There is something superficially Brechtian about Crouch's staging conventions. Brecht felt that laying bare the artifice of theatre encouraged audiences to judge more critically the actions of the characters and indeed the decisions of the creative team in putting the narrative together. By rejecting impersonation and the total immersion in character, Brecht hoped to prevent an audience from getting drawn uncritically into the reality of the fictional world. Crouch has spoken similarly about performance style, rejecting bravura acting because 'there is a danger that that kind of stuff can mesmerise, can hypnotise an audience and render them unconscious, uncritical. They become no longer conscious of what they are and their responsibility for what they are experiencing'.[30] In *An Oak Tree*, the device is entirely laid bare for the audience's inspection; because we know that the second actor is making performance decisions on the spot, it is much easier to make critical judgements of their decisions. Yet the effect is the opposite of what Brecht predicted. In *An Oak Tree*, despite the non-illusionistic set, despite our knowing that the second actor is as new to the performance

134

as we are, the emotion appears to be heightened, actors become characters and a fictional landscape unfolds in our imaginations. The climactic scene of the play that I described at the very beginning of this chapter is, as Stephen Bottoms has said, 'harrowingly moving',[31] even though the confrontation between a grieving husband and wife over the death of their daughter is being shown to us by an actor who has never seen the script before arguing with a bald man in a silver waistcoat over a piano stool.

In part, the scene may move us because the vulnerability of the father, out in the cold night with a desperate belief in his daughter's continuing existence, overlaps with the vulnerability of the performer, clinging onto the fragments of script, and unsure of the next moment. In addition, there is what is sometimes called the Kuleshov effect, named after the experimental Russian film director who edited together images of an actor, Ivan Mozzhukin, gazing off screen with a shot of a bowl of soup, then of a coffin containing a child, finally of an attractive woman. Audiences reported that Mozzhukin could distinctly be seen looking hungrily at the soup, pitifully at the coffin, and lustfully at the woman. However, Kuleshov had cut in exactly the same piece of footage each time. The audience projected their own assumption of his emotional state into the impassive contours of the actor's face. Something of the same may happen in *An Oak Tree* where the relatively inexpressive performances, the non-illusionistic staging, are, in a sense, animated by the audience who get enough information about the story to supply the emotion themselves.

As such, *An Oak Tree* foregrounds some of the complexities of ordinary theatrical performance, in particular what is sometimes called the 'paradox of fiction'. Imagine waking in the night to hear unfamiliar voices downstairs, when you know you are supposed to be alone in the house. You will probably feel a mixture of fear, anger; your heart will pound, hairs stand up on the back of your neck, breath quicken. Creeping downstairs, armed with a rolled-up newspaper, you discover that you have left a radio on: your fear and anger and all the associated physical responses will disappear, almost immediately. This is because, in ordinary circumstances, our emotions seem to rest on beliefs about the world. We cannot meaningfully feel anger at a state of affairs if we do not believe that state of affairs exists; put another way, I cannot be angry that my best friend has stolen my money if I do not believe my best friend has stolen my money. But in our encounters with fiction, this rule seems to be suspended. I feel profound sympathy for King Lear when he discovers that Cordelia is dead, even though I do not believe either Lear or Cordelia exist or that anyone has actually been bereaved. The philosopher Colin Radford identified this paradox in an essay entitled 'How Can We Be Moved By the Fate of Anna Karenina?' (1975), in which he goes through several possible explanations for what happens when, as we appear to, we have genuine emotional responses to things that are not real and finds them all deeply unsatisfactory, concluding inconclusively that our responses to fiction involve a bewildering degree of 'inconsistency and incoherence'.[32]

I do not propose to pursue further the philosophical debate here, but *An Oak Tree* is evidently keen to push this paradox to breaking point. In one of the arguments between husband and wife, he suggests that she might try hypnotism to calm down. She retorts:

> It's like some abstract intellectual fucking concept for you, isn't it. Claire's death. She never existed for you in the first place. She was just some idea. The idea of a daughter, just as I'm the idea of a wife. Marcy's the idea of a child. We don't exist for you, do we, not in flesh and blood. So you haven't lost anything, have you. She's still there, in your head, where she was in the first fucking place. Well I have. I fucking have. Help me. (p. 98)

Dawn's accusation is that her husband is refusing to accept the reality of the situation, preferring to treat the world around him as a set of concepts and ideas. It is a despairingly sad moment of division between them. Yet it is finely balanced because, in reality, Dawn, Claire, Marcy, the father really *are* just ideas that exist in our heads. Claire really *did not* ever exist in the first place. We know so little about Dawn and Marcy that they really *are* just ideas of a 'wife' and a 'daughter'. In that sense, the moment pushes at the paradox of fiction very hard because, despite that, the scene appears to be able to evoke in an audience genuine emotion, even while the conversation is drawing attention to the absurdity of responding in that way.

This points towards the ethical and political dimensions of Crouch's work. Our ability to care about characters about whom we know little and who do not even exist is a signal of a broader mutual recognition of human value. In his next full-length play, *ENGLAND*, the central character is an art-lover with a heart condition – but this single character is played by two people: in the original production, Tim Crouch and Hannah Ringham, who alternate lines, both addressing us equally, no one having priority over the other. This indeterminate character directly addresses us for the first half of the performance to describe their beautiful life, the beautiful art that adorns their beautiful walls and the increasingly desperate search for a donor to replace their broken heart. Rather like the way we have to compose the image of the boy in *My Arm* out of both Tim Crouch and an Action Man, here we have to understand that the central character exists somewhere between the two performers. In fact, we will be familiar enough with the way theatre works to know that this is a script which could theoretically be performed by anyone, anywhere, so the characters necessarily exist independently of these individual performers. This does not make them wholly abstract: just as we do about the boy with the arm above his head, we learn a lot about *ENGLAND*'s art-lover: their passions, their relationship, their class, their location, their medical history and more. What we do not know is their gender. They are both or neither male and/or female. This creates a fascinatingly paradoxical stage character, someone who is rounded and vivid and individual, yet with a key marker of their identity suspended.

ENGLAND is a play about the value of art and human life, and the way that globalization distributes these values unequally around the world. In the final scene, the main character travels to a third-world country to meet the widow of the man whose heart was flown to the United Kingdom for the organ transplant. It is an awkward encounter, multiply complicated by the global inequalities that have structured their connection, and by the real suspicion that bribed surgeons allowed the man to die to get the precious heart. It asks a question: how much do we have to know about someone to care about them and value their human dignity? Would it affect the rights and wrongs of their case if we knew whether our art-lover was male or female? Should we feel more or less sympathy with the widow if we knew more about her background and history? Crouch's work shows just how little we need in order to value another person. This is significant in a world where we are connected across ever greater distances, where the numbers of people meaningfully involved in your own life – from the lover in your bed to the distant sweatshop worker who made your shoes – have multiplied. This presents an ethical challenge and those who argue that we can only have responsibilities towards people we know personally risk heightening those global inequalities.

An Oak Tree, like *ENGLAND*, allows these ethical concerns to flow through the performance. The fact that often audiences do sympathize with the father and mother, even with the incompetent, guilt-ridden hypnotist, underlines our persistent ability to sympathetically reach out across the distances to affirm the value of the human wherever it is found.

4. *The Author*

The critique of 'retinal art' initiated by *My Arm* and the exploration of human empathy in *An Oak Tree* are brought together in a different manner for Crouch's most controversial play of the decade: *The Author*. His previous play, *ENGLAND*, was new in its site-semi-specific character (Stephen Bottoms calls it 'site generic'[33]). The play toured specifically to art galleries, where its discussions of the value of art had particular resonance.[34] This new play was commissioned by the Royal Court Theatre in London and was written specifically for the Royal Court, to the extent that even when it subsequently toured, it was apparently set at the Royal Court. As part of Crouch's commitment to 'authorial acting' he brought the cast together early in the process. At the end of an early week of rehearsal, four months before opening, the cast held a read-through of the play for staff of the Royal Court,

138

in one of their light, airy rehearsal rooms, with a view to getting some feedback on a work-in-progress:

> as we met up outside, blinking, shaking and weeping in the sunshine, it became clear that discussion would not be possible. None of the audience members felt able to talk. Several were pole-axed by tears. Work meetings that had been planned were cancelled; one department took themselves off to the pub.[35]

During the run of the play in September–October 2009, several members of the audience walked out. Others heckled. On tour a member of the audience fainted. In the frenzied atmosphere of the Edinburgh Festival in 2010, the anger was even more vocal. It was, Crouch recalls, 'a fucking nightmare'.[36] What is it about *The Author* that provokes such strong reactions?

As the audience members enter the auditorium, they take up their places on a pair of seating units facing each other with perhaps a metre or two gap between them. There is no conventional stage space. As *The Author* unfolds, we meet two actors, Vic and Esther, an audience member, Adrian, and a writer-director, Tim Crouch, all of them sitting among us in the audience, who collectively tell us the story of a show they were all in at the Royal Court. The play emerges through fragments but we discover that it was called something like *Abused*.[37] It is about a father, Pavol, whose wife dies perhaps in a civil war (p. 191) and is left with his 16-year-old (p. 183) daughter Eshna who demands change (p. 191). Instead he begins to abuse his daughter (p. 175). We know there is an amount of blood (p. 178), there is sex and violence (p. 181); he punches her viciously in the face and claws his hand up her and pulls out her womb (p. 191). Audiences were known to faint or walk out (p. 194). There are flashing lights towards the end (p. 200). Although Tim calls it 'a poem, really. A personal lament' (p. 176), his aim is to create 'a shock . . . an amateur war zone on stage' (178).

If we know a bit about the Royal Court, we may know that plays a little like this have been performed here. In particular, *Abused* has some affinities with the work of Sarah Kane, particularly *Blasted* (1995) and *Cleansed* (1998), both performed at the Court. In the play Crouch

139

defends making his audience look at these images: 'How can we not? I replied. If we do not represent them then we are in danger of denying their existence' (p. 178). This has very strong echoes of Sarah Kane's famous defence of her work: 'If you are saying you can't represent something, you are saying you can't talk about it, you are denying its existence'.[38] More broadly, the play seems to be part of the movement described by Aleks Sierz as 'In Yer Face Theatre', also closely associated with the Court. Sierz's definition of this kind of theatre as 'experiential, not speculative [. . .] so powerful, so visceral, that it forces audiences to react'[39] is echoed as Crouch recalls the critical praise for 'the visceral, er, experiential quality of the writing' (p. 193). Adrian gleefully recalls the things he is seen on the Royal Court stage:

> bum sex and rimming and cock sucking and wankings and rapings and stabbings and shootings and bombings. Bombings and bummings!! I've seen someone shit on a table! I've seen a man have his eyes sucked out. I've seen so many blindings! And stonings. Um. I've seen a dead baby in a bag. A baby stoned to death. I've seen a dead baby get eaten! That was great! (p. 192)

Most of those acts can be found somewhere in the work of Kane, Ravenhill or Edward Bond.

Knowing a little about Tim Crouch, we may realize that he has never written or directed such a play. But it would be possible to go through much of the performance assuming these people were talking about a real event. However, towards the end of *The Author* we discover that the toll of performing the brutal part of Pavol changed Vic to the point that he viciously attacked Adrian, the audience member, in the street after the performance. We then hear Tim recount how, after a dinner party to celebrate the end of the show, he slipped up to a spare room and masturbated to some child pornography on the internet. When this is discovered in the morning, he goes to a flotation tank and cuts his throat. By this point, it should be clear that Tim Crouch is not identical with Tim Crouch.

Why did *The Author* cause some polarized responses? Attention focused on the climactic – in both senses – speech about child pornography. The subject, rightly, produces strong emotions and in the production, as Crouch started to speak, the lights began to dim and most of the speech was delivered in the dark; the result of that was to concentrate attention on the words, with no visual distractions in the way of forming strong mental images of the events described. We were, so to speak, directly confronting our own imaginations. With the actors sitting among us, the conventional distance between us and the theatrical apparatus had been broken down creating a further sense of vulnerability and openness. The speech itself is horrifying, as much for its naive self-justification ('Nobody was hurt' (p. 203)), as for the horrific details of the video: indeed, it is the juxtaposition of the two that make the speech horrifying. The specific description of the abusive act, the oral rape of a baby, is extremely complicated. We might feel that it is gratuitous: we could take it on trust that he is describing an act of child abuse without giving us the details. But then the whole play is asking questions about what counts as gratuitous, what counts as witnessing an act, how far we are complicit in images when we look at them. The speech is disorientating and daring. Finally, Tim Crouch has used his name for this character, as well as other details of his life such as his wife's name, and while we might come to understand that there is a witty distinction between Tim Crouch, the author of *The Author*, and 'Tim Crouch', the author of *Abused*, inevitably we wonder which Tim Crouch is confessing in that final speech. Ethically, the speech forces us to consider the various moral values of committing an act, making an image of that act, watching images of the act, describing that act, describing that fictional act and listening to a fictional description of that act. These are complicated distinctions and the discomfort of the speech derives from the way in which they collide and mingle.

However, as Crouch has pointed out, there is a much lengthier and more detailed description of a man being beheaded (pp. 193–5) yet no one complains about that. It is clear that there is a still deeper anxiety structured into *The Author* that makes audiences feel doubly implicated. Crouch once claimed that his 'dream preparation' for a show is 'to be with the audience, to be talking about something else' and then for the show to begin. I went to a preview performance of *The Author* at the Royal Court; I knew very little about the show. I took up a seat and when Tim Crouch came in I assumed he was not performing. Since we have met a couple of times, he sat in the seat next to mine and we chatted a little. When the play began, I realized, with all the horror of someone trenchantly averse to audience participation, that he was indeed part of the performance and would be chatting to the people around him as part of this play. Much of my work as an audience member in *The Author* was to figure out what my role was, the nature of the interaction expected of all of us, my responsibility for the performance, and the limits of my freedom. I was never wholly clear what the answers to these questions were. How far should we join in? Could we change the performance? Could we stop the performance? In theatrical terms, is this a piece of immersive, interactive theatre, or is this a piece of new writing in the conventional Royal Court mode? As Helen Freshwater writes, 'the anger amongst audience members, I think, is partly a product of the fact that they don't know which social script to follow'.[40] Claire Macdonald notes that the performance overlaid a live art and a new writing aesthetic which 'are signaling very conflicting things to us'.[41] Interactive theatre of various kinds had become increasingly mainstream in the 2000s (see pp. 48–60), and, in a sense, had created a new orthodoxy. *The Author* is not a wholly interactive performance. Whatever the responses elicited from the audience, the actors continue remorselessly performing the script as written. The show operates in a productively fuzzy area between Royal Court play and Punchdrunk, creating generic discomfort to ask difficult questions.

This makes *The Author* sound like a ceaselessly harrowing experience. In fact, Tim Crouch and the company went out of their way to put us at our ease. Adrian Howell began the show in an affable, rather camp way, talking to members of the audience, addressing them by name, and even handing out his Maltesers. There are various pauses for breath in the performance, during which the lights dimmed and theme tunes to television sitcoms were played, provoking comically Pavlovian feelings of pleasure. At one moment, when the show played at the Royal Court, there was a pause as the electronic moving lights performed a little dance of their own. In at least one performance, this was met with a delighted round of applause. The moments where the company ask the audience questions are initially non-threatening, simple, disarming and open. Early in the performance, there is a scripted walk-out (p. 168) which is intended to be, as Crouch says, a 'model of an action' available to any audience member.[42]

This changes gradually through the performance. Esther's question 'can you all see okay?' (p. 184) becomes ironic given how little there is to 'see' in this production. At one moment, Esther describes going to a refuge as part of the rehearsal process to talk to a woman, Karen, who had been abused by her father, then coming back to the rehearsal room to 'hot-seat' her character. They recreate the moment for us (which is, let us remember, Esther Smith, playing Esther Smith, performing Esther Smith playing Karen) but at one point, Esther (which Esther?) appears to be uncomfortable with Tim's questions (in the present or in the past? It's unclear). Tim presses on, disregarding her objections, opening it up to the audience: 'Would anyone else like to ask Karen any questions?' (p. 188). The moment lays bare the occasionally exploitative power dynamics of the rehearsal room, yet even so, in some performances, members of the audience did take up the offer to ask 'Karen' questions. Towards the end of the play, Tim asks 'Are you all okay? / Are you okay if I carry on?' (p. 194). It is a question that seems directly to implicate us in what follows; we have understood, perhaps, that the show will go on, even if we make interventions in it, *because we're still watching*. What we feel is what is usually latent in theatrical performance: the politics of looking, the force of theatrical convention, the contract between the image and the watcher.

The Author is a challenge to the politics of British theatre. In *ENGLAND*, the art-loving protagonist turns his or her experience of everything into banal art criticism: visiting Southwark Cathedral, regardless of its function, s/he admires 'the clean lines' of the architecture and sees the symbols carved into the stone as 'the works of an artist' (p. 126). Even visiting Guy's Hospital for a consultation s/he admires the 'clean lines' (p. 128). Aestheticizing seems to be a retreat from engaging with the world. The characters in *The Author* likewise turn everything into theatre. As part of their research, they took a trip to a country with a recent bloody history and 'We kept on saying "There's a Pavol!" and "There's Pavol"' (p. 183). When Esther goes to the women's refuge, she recounts 'I was really lucky. I met a woman who had been raped as a teenager by her father. That's just like my character, I said!' (p. 185). The antiseptic 'clean lines' of *ENGLAND* have their equivalent in Adrian's praise for the Theatre Upstairs, 'this is such a versatile space' (p. 165), as if the theatre is a neutral place where all things can and should be seen. But in a culture obsessed with images, believing in the right to see anything, we can forget that it is not the images that demand to be seen but our willingness to look that brings these images – violent YouTube videos, paparazzi photographs, pornography – into being. It is a logic in which the theatre is itself implicated and whose complexities have nowhere been more profoundly and challengingly explored than in *The Author*.

5. Conclusion

Tim Crouch has described the political impulse behind his work as springing from 'the old hippy in me, perceiving oppressive structures in traditional figurative theatre and wanting to confront them'.[43] In *The Author*, Adrian, a representation of the audience, recalls seeing 'a play last year. And I remember thinking, "that writer has imagined me". I've been imagined. Poorly imagined! The audience has been badly written' (p. 167). Crouch's work, while seeming to challenge and provoke an audience, seems to me to be an attempt to take the audience seriously. In Crouch's theatre, we are not talked down to, nor are we flattered.

Crouch's work makes the ordinary dynamics of theatre extraordinary and in doing so, in revealing the fault lines that jag through the most basic relations between actor and character, stage and fiction, author and text, theatre and audience, he paints a landscape of loss, brutality and redemption that is unique in contemporary theatre.

144

ROY WILLIAMS
Michael Pearce

1. Introduction

Since Williams' debut with *The No Boys Cricket Club* in 1996, he has maintained a prolific presence in British theatre. His plays have been performed in major venues in the United Kingdom and have garnered a number of awards.[1] Williams has also written dramas for radio and television as well as theatre for young people.

Although Williams' plays are populated by British working-class black and white men and women, his social commentary is not exclusively conducted through the dialogue of domestic politics. A number of plays take place against the backdrop of larger sociopolitical events: the Macpherson Report and the murder of Damilola Taylor in *Fallout* (2003); the Iraq war in *Days of Significance* (2007); the 1958 Notting Hill race riots in *Absolute Beginners* (2007); the race riots of the 1980s in *Sucker Punch* (2010). Other works draw on real-life events and current affairs as their inspiration: football hooliganism in *Sing Yer Heart Out for the Lads* (2002); gang culture and gun crime in *Little Sweet Thing* (2005); immigration in *Angel House* (2008); the penal system in *Category B* (2009). By tapping into events that circulate in the national consciousness, and by combining an ear acutely trained in authentic vernacular with a social realist style, the characters and issues in Williams' plays move beyond the confines of their social settings and become conduits for the larger debates that surround contemporary Britain.[2]

Williams' work does not slot easily into a particular generation of British playwrights. Suzanne Scafe criticizes Aleks Sierz's omission of Williams' work in his book *In Yer Face Theatre: British Drama Today*,[3] arguing that Williams' style aligns 'almost perfectly' with Sierz's template.[4] However, although explicit language and challenging subject

145

matter are features of Williams' plays, on the whole they avoid graphic representations of sex and violence. As Kritzer shows, writers such as Williams, of a minority race or culture, not only replied to the 1990s 'in-yer-face' generation of writers but by bringing their race, ethnicity and class to bear, 'revis[ed] its terms'.[5] Williams' interrogation of racism, belonging and cultural identity in Britain must be contextualized within the continuum of black playwriting in Britain which since the 1970s has persistently dealt with similar themes.[6] However, unlike many black British writers, Williams' plays do not draw upon the cultural traditions and history of Africa and the Caribbean.[7] Instead Williams' plays are rooted within a British social realist style and urban geography. Despite this apparent rejection of his diasporic roots, Williams' theatre neatly charts a diasporic trajectory as his focus shifted from the Jamaican 'homeland' of his parents in his early plays (*The No Boys Cricket Club*, *Starstruck* and *The Gift*) and settled in the 'hostland' of the United Kingdom where all of his plays of the 2000s have been set. Nevertheless, these plays still exhibit quintessential diasporic traits through their exploration of (un)belonging, identity and of the negotiation of the terrain inhabited by second- and third-generation black Britons and the 'indigenous' population. It is from this juncture that Williams draws his rich material.[8] Where Williams departs from his predecessors and some of his black British contemporaries is that he has virtually eliminated all first-generation black characters from his work and has severed his second- and third-generation characters from any sense of dual-belonging: his characters are rooted in Britain and unquestionably indigenous. Thus, identity, Williams demonstrates, is not fixed by racial and historical determinants but rather environmental and social factors.[9]

Williams' plays draw attention to the massive shifts that have resulted in Britain's increasingly multicultural and racial demographic. Peacock, defining multiculturalism as an ideal which 'refers to immigrants and the indigenous population preserving their cultures and interacting peacefully within one nation',[10] concludes in his analysis of Williams' plays that they contribute towards this ideal by underlining 'the cultural, social and political forces' that underlie 'inter- and intra-racial relations'.[11] Derbyshire, on the other hand, interprets multiculturalism as a sociopolitical policy rather than an ideal. He argues that Williams'

146

plays provide a critique of such policy 'that may disguise rather than address structurally perpetuated inequalities among racial groups'.[12] However, Williams' definition of multicultural is somewhat different to the ones expounded above, as demonstrated by the way many of Williams' characters speak, dress, act and imitate each other. Williams' representations suggest that for him, multiculturalism is less to do with discrete cultures struggling to co-exist in plural congruity and refers rather to what Gilroy identifies as 'the complex pluralism of Britain's inner-urban streets' which result in 'kaleidoscopic formations of "trans-racial" cultural syncretism'.[13] As Williams states: 'life in a multicultural society is one big grey area – and I want to see shades of grey when I go to the theatre',[14] Williams sees the conventional multicultural understanding of Britishness as unrealistically bounded and neat, and that in fact Britishness is hybrid and amorphous. In this way he identifies being black British as essentially British and vice versa. This is not to say that his plays are a celebration of 'optimism'.[15] On the contrary, the prevailing tragedy in Williams' dramas arise when these 'grey areas' of cultural miscegenation are contested, by whites and blacks alike, in the name of ethnic, racial and class purity.

Key aspects of Williams' theatre are his linguistic idiom, his challenging of social stereotypes and his theatrical use of space. The following chapter examines three of Williams' plays through each of these prisms. *Sing Yer Heart Out for the Lads* examines how space is used as a dramaturgical device to enhance Williams' investigation of British national belonging. Questions of black representation are explored in *Fallout*. Finally, Williams' linguistic idiom is examined in *Days of Significance* in order to demonstrate how culture, class and education are constructed and defined by language and how language is ultimately a means by which to both entrap and liberate.

2. *Sing Yer Heart Out for the Lads*[16]

Sing Yer Heart Out for the Lads was first performed at the National Theatre (NT) in 2002, and later restaged there in 2004.[17] The play is set in the King George pub in south-west London where the pub's football team assemble to watch the 2000 England versus Germany World Cup Qualifier. The lads are a stereotypical group of young, white, working-class football fans: they are big drinkers, violent, foul-mouthed, misogynist, patriotic, xenophobic, homophobic and racist. Complicating the stereotype of the English lad is Barry who, with St George's flags painted on his face, acts and behaves exactly like his fellow white, racist teammates, but is the only black member of the football team. In contrast, his brother Mark has come to extricate Barry and take him home to visit their sick father.

The screening of the live match in the pub and the reactions it evokes in the lads initiates a debate around national belonging and Britishness. Representing the far right is Alan, a member of a political group resembling the British National Party, and his protégé Lawrie. Lawrie wants to 'make a bomb or summin, go down Brixton and blow every one of them up' (p. 222), while Alan sources the arguments of Enoch Powell to demonstrate that 'the blacks, the non-whites, have absolutely nothing in common with the Anglo-Saxon Celtic culture' and that 'if they want to practice their black culture and heritage, then they should be allowed to do it in their own part of their world' (p. 188). Even the seemingly non-partisans like policeman Lee, who struggles with professional impartiality since being knifed by a black man, betrays a seam of racism. So too does the pub owner Gina who, on discovering that her son Glen's mobile phone and jacket have been stolen by the black teenager Bad T, refers to him as 'That fuckin little black kid' (p. 183). Above all, there is a general consensus between both blacks and whites that the worst thing you can be is a 'Paki'.

In *Sing Yer Heart Out for the Lads*, Williams interrogates the racial parameters of national belonging and identity in contemporary Britain: 'I very much wanted to write a bigger play, not just simply about race, but about British Nationalism: what does it mean to be British in the twenty-first century, who's more British now, the blacks or the whites?'[18] The dualist nature of competition, mirrored in the England versus Germany game, pervades the play's exploration of national belonging, which pits black against white in a tussle for the British title.[19] The dualisms in the play reveal how a sense of 'Britishness' operates through binaries of inclusion/exclusion and proffers a scathing critique of multicultural rhetoric that maintains cultures can live in harmony without taking into account the oppressive nature of the dominant ideology. Williams' play seems to support Gilroy's argument expounded in *There Ain't No Black in the Union Jack*, in which Gilroy demonstrates how discourses of national belonging in the post-war era were redefined in reaction to non-white immigrants. As a result, distinctions between race and ethnicity were collapsed. Culture became 'almost biologized by its proximity to "race"'[20] which effectively rendered Blackness and Britishness as 'mutually exclusive'.[21] This division is spatially represented in the play. The play's use of space not only underscores the themes of the work, but is also a key determinant of its action. Within the spaces, Williams replicates the complexities of 'nation'. In the play's pub setting, he establishes a territorial microcosm, complete with borders and ethnic affiliations and provides a glimpse into the operations of the 'imagined community' at work.[22] In doing so he exposes the way in which racial differences still patrol the borders of national belonging in the new millennium.[23]

The space of the play is divided between the interior of the pub and the outside estate, creating a literal and symbolic border. The King George pub, decorated in St George's flags, is the microcosmic representation of an historic England. It is in the traditional English pub that the disgruntled Alan and Lawrie seek refuge in old-fashioned values against the government's liberal policies which they believe work to marginalize the white working class and, as they see themselves, bedrock of the nation:

Lawrie There's nuttin that makes me wanna say I'm proud to be English.

Alan No one wants to speak up for you. It's not fashionable.

Lawrie Right.

Alan But they want to speak up for the blacks, queers, Pakis, that's fashionable. (p. 198)

The pub is both a home to three generations – Jimmy, Gina and Glen – and 'a home from home' (p. 160) for the lads. It is within the bosom of this (surrogate) family that a culture based on racial difference is nurtured and transmitted: 'Families are therefore not only the nation in microcosm, its key components, but act as the means to turn social processes into natural, instinctive ones'.[24] When Glen's mobile phone and jacket are taken by Bad T, Glen's grandfather Jimmy offers to teach Glen to fight so he 'can go back, sort 'em out' (p. 183) and Becks advises Glen to defend himself creating an all-white gang in retaliation: 'get yerself some white boys, Glen, stick together, show sum pride' (p. 212). The cycle of racism, perpetuated through the institution of the family/pub finds its apex when Glen stabs Mark and Glen succumbs to and echoes the racism that has been ricocheting around the pub all day with his final words: 'He's a black bastard, they all are' (p. 234).

The space of the estate outside, inhabited by the black youths Duane and Bad T, represents the space of the alien/other and is seen as a threat to the core English values of the King George. Glen's association with Duane and Bad T is framed in terms of cultural corruption. As Gina notes, it is because 'he's been hanging round with them black kids from the estate' (p. 135) that he now listens to rap music. Glen sucks his teeth, snubs the classic British rock bands (The Kinks, Pink Floyd) recommended by Jimmy, and speaks using patois-inspired slang:

Jimmy   I can't even understand half the things they're [the rap musicians] saying.

Glen   Ca you ain't wid it guy.

Gina   English, Glen, we speak English in here. (p. 135)

The influence of black street culture on Glen draws our attention to cultural shifts exemplified in British youth who are increasingly drawing upon a plurality of local and global influences in defining new and hybrid identities. However, such 'mixing' is viewed by Glen's family as a bastardization of his Englishness and affirms Errol Lawrence's observation that 'the "alien" cultures of the blacks are seen as either the cause or else the most visible symptom of the destruction of the "British way of life"'.[25] It is in fact Glen's 'mixing' with the wrong crowd that drives the action of the play. When Bad T takes Glen's mobile and jacket it not only precipitates the mob of angry protesters outside the pub, it also leads to Glen, thwarted in his plans to kill Bad T, murdering Mark. The crowd of black protestors that develops outside the pub is a stark illustration of the way in which the preservation of Britishness is defined along territorial and cultural lines. The 'army of black kids out there' (p. 226) is not only a threat to the site of the pub, but when they are referred to as 'a whole bleedin tribe' (p. 227) and 'those monkeys out there' (p. 230), the colonial imagery distils the 'battle' into a defence of white supremacy against the black 'savages'.

Through the characters of Mark and Barry, Williams explores the implications of such ethnic protectionism upon black Britons through the reactions of cultural retention and acculturation respectively. Mark's objective in the play is to extricate Barry from the pub and its white laddish culture and take him home to visit his sick father and 'his own people' (p. 209). The desire to reunite Barry with his roots reveals Mark's own retreat into cultural separatism as a result of his direct experiences of marginalization resulting in a profound sense of un-belonging:

Mark They don't want us here, Barry.

Barry We were born here.

Mark They don't care. (p. 210)

Despite the word 'nation' coming from the Latin 'nasci' meaning 'to be born', Mark's experiences reveal that birthright far from guarantees entry into cultural citizenship. He seems to have been defeated by the view, famously articulated by Enoch Powell, that 'the West Indian does not by being born in England become an Englishman. In law, he becomes a United Kingdom citizen by birth; in fact he is a West Indian or an Asian still'.[26] Mark's experience of racial abuse in the army where his CO 'was a racist wanker' (p. 214) has pushed him into a position of reactionary racism. As a result he has terminated his friendship with Lee who, although not exempt from displays of prejudice, struggles throughout the play to quash racist sentiment. Mark's heightened sensitivity to racism has to some extent coloured his judgement. He

151

accuses Gina of breaking up with him because he was black to which she retorts: 'I finished wid you cos you were boring [. . .] If you woke up tomorrow as white as I am, you'll still be boring' (p. 208). On the other hand Barry, desperate to be accepted by the dominant culture, is singing his heart out in support of England and ignores the casual racism of his friends.

In the same way that Glen is judged by his family, Barry's crossing of the imaginary border that separates white and black is seen as a betrayal of his roots by Mark. Where Britishness is defined by whiteness, the body becomes the site on which national belonging is first and foremost signified. Barry's allegiance is inscribed onto his skin in the form of a British Bulldog tattoo. The painted St George's flags on his cheeks are seen by Mark as a mask of his 'true'/black identity. He tells him to 'wipe that shit off your face' (p. 167). For Mark, Englishness is a contamination and something to be sloughed off: 'You think I'm here by choice? I feel ill juss bein here. I can't wait to go home so I can have a wash' (p. 167). Yet despite Barry's attempts to fit in, he is also ultimately rejected by his white football friends who, because of his blackness, perceive his cultural allegiance as being outside the pub and by extension the nation. Phil questions why Barry is not outside helping his brother Mark who is trying to placate the growing unrest:

Phil   . . . Barry, shouldn't you be out there?

Barry   ENGLAND!

Phil   Baz!

Barry   Wat?

Phil   He's your brother, you should be backing him up.

Barry   I'm watchin the game,

Becks   You ain't gonna miss anything.

Barry   So why are you still here then?

Jason   Cos we follow England.

Barry Wat you tryin to say, Jase?

Jason Nuttin.

Barry I'm not white enuff for England? (p. 194)

Williams does, however, point to the possibility of a more balanced model. Barry unsettles the play's stark dualities and it is his resolve that ultimately convinces Mark to make a stand for his belonging. Likewise it is Mark's sensitivity to racism which eventually leads Barry to stand up for himself against the covert racist comments of his friends. Mark and Barry, confronted with Alan's racist polemic, find a middle ground on which they assert their belonging. Mark tells Alan 'You won't win' (p. 220) and he and Barry begin to chant 'We shall not, we shall not be moved!' (p. 220). It is after this assertive outburst that Mark decides to stay and buy a round of drinks and begins to make amends with Lee.

The screening of the football match throughout the play provides a third symbolic space of the nation. The 'live' screening forges a bridge to the outside world, connecting the local space with the members of its wider 'imagined community'.[27] The televised match provides access to a reservoir of longstanding tradition and culture which have been expressly designed as instruments of nationalist propaganda, reliant upon the re-imagining of imperial Britain's former glory: for example, before the match begins 'God Save the Queen' is played. Significantly, the 2000 England versus Germany match was the last to be played at the old Wembley Stadium, home to English national football, and not only a symbol of national pride but the site where England won the World Cup against Germany in 1966. Its history is steeped in British imperialism; originally named the Empire Stadium, Wembley was built for the British Empire Exhibition of 1924–5 which was opened by King George V (hence the name of the pub) and showcased the power and might of the colonial empire. For the spectators, the game provides a forum in which they are encouraged to 'perform' their nationalism: the lads shout encouragement at the screen, they sing along to the national anthem, jeer when the German team enter and during the *Deutschlandlied* they sing 'Stand up, if you won the war!' (p. 166).

The broadcast literally 'wires' the lads into the football game in what Hobsbawn identifies as 'an expression of national struggle'.[28]

In the play's climax the borders between the localized spaces, pub/estate/Wembley, collapse. When England loses, the lad's support is displaced onto the growing tension between blacks and whites in the pub. Lawrie laments '. . . this whole country's lost its spine', 'We ruled the world' (p. 229) and determined to salvage England's dignity, he challenges Barry to fight saying '. . . Well, come on then, black boy, show us how English you are' (p. 230). Football's fundamental dualism resonates with the black versus white debate as the borders blur between the England versus Germany match and the pub versus the estate riot. The inside/outside space is traversed when two bricks are thrown through the pub window and open war is declared. For Lawrie, like a football match, there can only be one winner: 'Lass one standing at the final whistle, wins England' (p. 231). The chaos results in Mark's murder and Barry disowning England symbolized by wiping the painted flags from his cheeks. It appears that Alan's Powellist prophecy of 'rivers of blood' (p. 235) has come to pass.

Sing Yer Heart Out for the Lads is Williams' most pessimistic play. Despite commonality in class, environment and experiences, the play stresses that such local identity is subservient to the larger question of national belonging. Although Lee, Gina, Glen (initially) and eventually Barry and Mark attempt to navigate the complexity of fitting between rigid cultural and racial essentialist models, their actions and voices are all but drowned out by the din of Alan and Lawrie's 'England for whites' (p. 186) polemic, the riot outside and the stark imagery and spatial delineations which underscore Britishness as defined by cultural/racial separatism. Barry's reaction to his brother's death: 'I'll kill all of yer. Come on, come on! Who wants me, come on! Yer fuckin white cunts, all of yer!' (p. 235) renders Lee's advice to Barry and final words of the play: 'Don't lose yerself' (p. 235) an inaudible bleat. The play effectively undermines Anderson's assertion of the nation as a 'community' in which despite 'the actual inequality and exploitation that may prevail . . . the nation is always conceived as a deep, horizontal comradeship'.[29] Drawing similar conclusions to Gilroy, the play demonstrates that as long as Britishnesss is defined along such constructs that conflate race and ethnicity, there never will be any black in the Union Jack.

3. *Fallout*[30]

The critically acclaimed *Fallout* was staged in 2003 at the Royal Court.[31] The play explores the intersecting worlds of gang-culture and the police using two actual events as a starting point: first, the murder of Kwame and subsequent botched investigation is based on the 2000 Damilola Taylor case;[32] second, Williams examines the police as an institution in the wake of the 1999 Macpherson Report, published after the Stephen Lawrence murder, which concluded that the police were 'institutionally racist'.[33] In particular, the media frenzy surrounding the murder of Damilola rekindled a public fear of violent youth crime. Because of the murder in which a black Nigerian boy was killed by other black youths, 'black-on-black' violence became the new 'buzz' word and an 'underclass' of dangerous black youths was identified as the new malaise afflicting urban Britain.[34]

The play opens with the murder of Kwame, a boy of African origin, at the hands of gang leader Dwayne and his cronies, Perry, Clinton and Emile, who delivers the fatal kicks to Kwame's head. Because the audience is aware of the murderer's identity from the onset, the play is more a revelation of characters than a whodunit murder mystery. The play follows the police investigation led by Matt (white) and Joe (black). Despite their suspicion regarding the killers' identities, the police are unable to provide any incriminating evidence. In his desperation to arrest someone, Joe feeds Ronnie, a key witness, information. When the police Inspector discovers that Joe has led a witness during questioning, the investigation falls through.[35]

Whereas *Sing Yer Heart Out for the Lads* examines the roots of British racism, in *Fallout*, Williams presents us with its alienating effects on British society. Through his representation of the gang of youths Williams introduces us to a subculture that has severed itself from white British society. They speak using a combination of African-American and Jamaican-inspired patois and view Joe as a black man who has sold

155

himself in slavery to the white establishment. The absence of parental and community role models, failure of the educational system and the overriding poverty in the estate apprehends their future prospects. The character of Joe, who grew up on the estate but has since left, is also displaced. He is unable to reconcile the transformed non-racist Metropolitan Police with the same institution that he knew growing up in the 1980s. Joe's disorientation manifests in aggression towards the gang, who he feels are being treated with post-Macpherson kid gloves, and in provoking Matt with racial slurs in the hope that Matt will eventually let down his liberal guard and conform to Joe's stereotype of a racist policeman.

Although *Fallout* was a critical success, there were murmurs in the press regarding the negative issues surrounding representation of black people in the theatre.[36] This response to *Fallout* reflects a wider debate about black representation. While black theatre of the first decade of this millennium has enjoyed unprecedented prominence in the number of plays produced and the high-profile venues in which they have been presented,[37] this prominence has been accompanied by a proliferation of images of black hyper-masculinity, urban poor and themes of violence and male sexuality. Such representation, it has been argued, plays into the hands of dominant discourses, which stereotype black youths as violent, predatory and dysfunctional and ignore the diversity of the black experience.[38]

Williams, however, refuses to yield to what Mercer has defined as 'the burden of representation',[39] claiming that '[p]ositive role models, of whatever race, make dull characters, because they don't really exist',[40] that he is not writing about 'all' but only 'some black people,' and that he 'can't be a spokesman for a whole culture'.[41] In *Fallout* Williams presents us with complicated characters who occupy a position between victim and perpetrator and whose oppression is at once constructed by deeper social structures and perpetuated or transgressed by their own actions. In his representation of the gang he plays to and then undermines stereotypes in order to contextualize and then challenge dominant assumptions regarding black gang culture. Furthermore, in revealing the gang members as both victims and perpetrators, Williams highlights their agency which unsettles the debate around racism which perpetuates the placement of 'the white "us" of British society' at its centre.[42]

The group of youths under scrutiny is depicted under the stereotype that one might expect: Shanice and Ronnie were expelled from school for stealing; they hang out at the soulless fast-food cafe where Shanice works; the boys make a living from stealing; Emile and Dwayne pull knives and guns on each other in order to establish their gang hierarchy; and women become prizes in contests of machismo. As Derbyshire argues, the play draws our attention to structural inequalities, which have resulted in the youths' alienation from mainstream society.[43] However, Derbyshire also suggests, based on his reading of the work on subcultures undertaken by the Centre for Contemporary Cultural Studies (CCCS) in Birmingham, that the gang's violent subculture is predicated on resistance to deeply ingrained social racism.[44] Despite contextualizing their delinquency, Williams' primary aim is not absolution by finger-pointing at society's innate racism – although these are clearly factors that have shaped the youths' behaviour. Rather, through the black-on-black murder and the reaction of the gang in its aftermath, he highlights their agency. In doing so Williams provocatively challenges notions of black youth as victims.

The murder of Kwame confounds the notion that black gang culture can be entirely explained as a product of cultural resistance to white oppression. In his critique of subculture theory as developed in the 1970s and 1980s by the CCCS, Rupa Huq argues that because subculture was examined only in terms of its existence as a response to oppression, theorists tended to overlook the negative aspects of their case studies.[45] Furthermore, Huq notes, if subculture arises solely from resistance then it presupposes the inevitability of violence, 'rendering it excused as much as explained'.[46] In *Fallout*, Williams' portrayal of the youths and, for most of them, their apparently unfazed attitude towards the murder they have committed presents a challenge to a liberal audience well versed in the social causes that lie at the foundations of dysfunction. Had Williams' aim been merely to reveal the gang as a product of society's failings he may have followed David Wilson's argument in *Inventing Black-on-Black Violence* that if we are to 'supplant the meaning system of "black-on-black violence"' then the portrayal of violence needs to be not one of 'agency-infused kids rambunctiously roaming inner cities' but instead a depiction of 'hurt, hopeless, and searching youth in societally created settings'.[47] Instead, Williams balances the youth's victimization by demonstrating them equally as perpetrators, as agents in their own undoing and, crucially, in their tentative steps towards reformation at the end.

This sense of agency is carried through in the play's performance. Without an interval and with scenes that flow seamlessly into one other, the pace is relentless as the audience witnesses acts of un-premeditated violence and anger spontaneously erupt, allowing no time for reflection in scene changes. Reviews comment on Ian Rickson's direction as achieving a 'bruising, confrontational production' with a 'visceral impact'.[48] Countering this tone of seething aggression is the humour that Williams brings to the dialogue, especially through the clown-like banter between Perry and Clinton. The last line of the play is said in jest as Shanice tells Dwayne that they can go out but 'Yu ain't grindin me' (p. 117). The experience of high-octane acting and the often humorous dialogue between the youths highlights their individuality and underlines their independence. As a result, Williams ensures that the line between individual and social blame is kept taut.

The characters of Shanice and Dwayne also make important decisions that lead them to transformation at the end. Shanice's remorse guides her to confess to Emile that Kwame never tried to 'sex' her (p. 102) and that it was in fact she who made a pass at him, which he rejected. Her confession, beyond revealing that the murder was in part the result of adolescent jealousy, is seen as a brave act in a world where a bruised ego is enough motivation to kill. And it is Dwayne's feelings for Shanice that prevents him from shooting Emile:

Dwayne   Yu really think I woulda shot Emile?

Shanice   Yeah.

Dwayne   Believe. Yu know wat stopped me?

Shanice   Wat?

Dwayne   Yu, Shanice. (p. 116)

The play ends with Shanice and Dwayne having a rematch of a football game they played as children seven years before. This recreation of their childhood symbolizes a fresh start through a return to innocence. It is unlikely that their lot will change dramatically, nevertheless it underlines their desire to start anew and marks a moment of self-intervention. The social oppression experienced by the gang, the killing of Kwame and the accent on the characters' own decision-making all combine to present a gang of youths that are at once oppressors and products of their own oppression, disallowing any comfortable categorization of good/bad and victim/perpetrator.[49]

Through the character of Joe, Williams further blurs the line between hero and villain confronting intra-racism from a different angle. Williams presents us with a highly complex character, battered from all sides by what he perceives to be a racist society which negatively pigeonholes black people, yet now appears to be masking its fundamental prejudices with political correctness. The result is a deeply conflicted character. Joe despises the gang and is desperate to make an arrest and avenge Kwame with whom he identifies strongly as a high achiever and someone who was bullied for wanting to make a better life for himself. When the investigation falls through Joe takes justice into his own hands. He seeks out Emile and beats him up:

> **Joe** Niggers, Emile, can't play the game. You can't play the game, Kwame played the game, Kwame had a life. He was a decent kid. But you, you! (*Slaps him repeatedly*) You want a life, bwoi, get yer own. Why you have to tek his? You know what, it's fuckers like you, like that pisshead, is why I had to leave. Now it's fuckers like you that bring me back to where I started. You had to drag me down, innit? You had to drag Kwame down. (p. 112)

Joe's character challenges notions of assumed black solidarity that are blind to internal divisions, and presents us with a more complicated view of intra-racial relations. For the upwardly mobile Joe who has escaped from the estate, his hostile attitude towards the gang demonstrates the

159

negative impact of society's racial homogenizing which differentiates along racial as opposed to behavioural lines:

Matt   . . . They're your people, why do you hate them?

Joe   Listen, yeah, those boys are not my people. (p. 96)

Joe's anger expresses his struggle to be perceived as black and as an equal member of society. His use of the word 'nigger' is not evidence of his internalized racism. He applies the pejorative term to the gang to differentiate himself from them which exposes a frustration borne from living in a society in which all black people are perceived as the same. As Joe points out to Matt: 'if you're walking down the street at night, you see a bunch of black lads walking towards you . . . you know you're gonna cross that road, as fast as your legs can tek you' (p. 51). The notion that black strangers are prejudged by whites as threatening finds its roots in Matt's assumption that Joe should feel empathy because the gang are his 'people'. As Hall points out: 'after all, it is one of the predicates of racism that "you can't tell the difference because they all look the same"'.[50]

Joe's sense of displacement manifests in a nostalgia for the 1980s where racial boundaries were clearly demarcated:

Joe   Give me back the old school of police. Give them boys something to really cry about.

Matt   Not another word.

Joe   At least they'd know where they stand. That's all they want.

Matt   Is that what you want, Joe? (p. 97)

His projection of his own sense of displacement onto the gang results in Joe taking on the role of the 1980s police and replicating their treatment of young black offenders when he physically attacks Emile. When Shanice intervenes, he tells her:

Joe   I'm letting him know where he stands.

Shanice   Yu think dis is gonna change him?

Joe Bwoi drowning girl.

Shanice Wat else yu expect him to be? (p. 113)

Joe's action provides a startling inversion of the premise of the bad, white policeman.

At the end of the scene Shanice retorts to Joe: 'why should we be like yu?' (p. 113), underlining the fact that Williams does not provide role models and eschews notions of 'positive representation' in favour of 'realistic' depictions of characters which exhibit both positive and negative traits. In *Fallout* through his representation of black characters Williams presents and simultaneously undermines black and white stereotypes through complex characterizations, which fly in the face of representational expectation and complicate critical generalizations echoing Hall's declaration of 'the end of the innocent notion of the essential black subject'.[51]

4. *Days of Significance*[52]

Days of Significance was commissioned by the Royal Shakespeare Company (RSC) and premiered at the Swan Theatre in Stratford-upon-Avon in 2007. The play transferred to London where it played at the Tricycle Theatre in 2008.[53] It has toured both nationally and in the United States.

In *Days of Significance* Williams turns his hand to the Iraq war cementing further his role as social commentator and provocateur.[54] With the exception of the cameo role of a Sergeant Brookes whose honesty, integrity and courage make him arguably Williams' only black 'hero', it is an all-white play. As in *Sing Yer Heart Out for the Lads* and *Fallout*, Williams presents us with stereotypes, in this case, young working-class British youth from the south-east of England enmeshed in a culture of binge drinking, violence and sexual display and the 'squaddies' who are drafted from their community to fight in Iraq. The play is divided into three acts; the first and third parts are set in England, the second in Basra.[55]

The play takes its inspiration from Shakespeare's *Much Ado About Nothing*. The first act, entitled 'Much Noise' is loosely based on Shakespeare's plot while the final two acts are entirely Williams' creation. Unlike in *Much Ado*, the soldiers Ben (Benedick) and Jamie (Claudio) are not returning from war but preparing to leave. It is their last weekend in England and over the course of an alcohol-fuelled night they secure their romances: Ben with Trish (Beatrice) and Jamie with Hannah (Hero).[56] The second act, 'On the Side of the Angels', referencing Britain's alliance with the United States, is set in an alleyway in Basra where Ben, Jamie, another soldier Sean and their sergeant Brookes are under siege. We learn that Ben and Jamie have been involved in the torturing of Iraqi prisoners but it is clear that Ben was the instigator and most violent of the two. The final act, 'A Parting of the Ways' is set at a wedding reception in England. Ben has been killed in Iraq and has attained hero status with his friends. Meanwhile photographs of the torture of Iraqis have been published in the press. Jamie stands accused and is due to appear before a court-martial the following day.

The play, staged in promenade at the RSC, plunges the audience into the keenly observed world of small-town English 'chav' youth subculture.[57] Set against a booze-fuelled debauched night out complete with vomiting, fighting, urinating, genital-flashing, the characters communicate in a language driven by expletives, vulgar slang and popular culture. Once again we see Williams' desire to give 'the audience a slice of something they have not seen before'.[58] Susannah Clapp writing in *The Observer* commented that Williams was 'the first to bring a real beat of the street to the Royal Shakespeare Company'.[59] The 'Much Noise' of the first act could not provide a starker contrast to the refined, lyrical language in *Much Ado*. While Jamie and Hannah's attraction, mirroring Claudio and Hero, is tenderly romantic, Ben and Trish's sexually charged 'merry war' (1.1.59),[60] like Benedick and Beatrice's relationship, is fuelled by insults and put-downs. However, in this context the flirtatious banter between Ben and Trish is reduced to:

Ben   You want summin, Trish?

Trish   Yer head on a stick. So big, I can see it coming a mile away.

162

Ben   I can smell you coming a mile away. *The boys laugh.* (p. 180)

The vulgarity of the language, both what is said and the manner in which it is expressed, captures the verisimilitude of what Williams strives for in his writing. However, the play's language is more important than merely providing authenticity. Dominic Cavendish in the *Daily Telegraph* praised it for showing that 'all the ugly mayhem most of us bolt homewards to avoid is where you'll locate the sound, the song and the soul of England. A disturbing sound, a ranting song and a troubled soul – yes – but we shouldn't kid ourselves it's just background noise'.[61] As in *Much Ado*, *Days Of Significance*'s use of banter, overhearings, rumours, shared secrets and broken promises establishes language as Williams' primary point of interrogation. Through the character's use of language (and by implication education), Williams examines the ways in which language not only frames and constructs an individual's reality but also limits it as well.

The characters reveal their social and cultural intelligence through their inarticulate, base humour. Like the football fans in *Sing Yer Heart Out*, the characters in *Days of Significance* are misogynist, homophobic, xenophobic and racist. Education is ridiculed. Dan is a 'stinking student lamo' (p. 198), a man who stays at home 'wid the women' (p. 175). The play is divided by those who are 'for' and those who are 'against' the war. Implicit in this division is the level of education of the characters. Dan, the most vocal anti-war remonstrator is a university student. Hannah is about to start college and the poorly educated Jamie and Ben have opted for the army. It is Dan who exposes Ben and Jamie's complete lack of understanding of the war they are fighting in:

Dan   What do you believe, Ben? [. . .]

Ben   Saddam's a cunt, alright?

Jamie   He is a cunt.

Dan   Why is he a cunt?

Jamie   Cos he's got a big moustache.

Dan   Ben?

163

Jamie You grow a tache that big, yer up to summin.

Dan What was he arrested for? What are his crimes? How was he in breach of UN regulations? *(sighs.)* You don't even know. (p. 199)

Their responses reveal their puerility and Williams highlights the dark consequences of extricating these youths from their milieu and sending them to fight in a war they know little about. Here, Williams is careful not to blame Ben and Jamie but rather to reveal them as youths exploited by the army's recruitment process which preys upon young men of little education and means:

Dan [. . .] you wanna know why he signed up, truthfully? They had some woman soldier handing out leaflets on the high street, the only time him and J weren't looking at her arse is when they staring at her tits. (p. 193)

As Reinelt shows, 'the play's topicality derives from the now highly unpopular war and its disastrous and debilitating consequences for this underclass of young people, caught between some fleeting notion of British patriotism and an utter lack of comprehension'.[62] From their podium of poor education, this generation sings an 'anthem for doomed youth';[63] yet, Williams does not produce a polemic. Dan may be university-educated and his anti-war comments may resonate with the middle-class audience, however Dan's supercilious, manipulative character reveals him as someone who uses his intelligence to belittle, divide and disempower. It is Dan (following the Don John story-line in *Much Ado*) who tells Jamie that Hannah has been 'telling everyone how shit-scared you are about going . . . Bin telling Trish. Laughing their tits off' (p. 201), prompting Jamie and Hannah to briefly split up. When Hannah accuses Dan of blaming Jamie for Ben's death, he initially brushes her aside by demeaning her through her gender, 'Don't try and be clever, Hannah. Not when yer looking this sexy' (p. 258). When she persists, however, he proceeds to barrage her with complex facts about the war leaving her feeling intellectually squashed, against which her only recourse is to slap him and threaten further physical violence.

Williams expands upon the way in which language is used to establish dominance in the second act. Although set in Basra, the Iraqis are never seen. They are the faceless, silenced enemy, their identity refracted through English perceptions as: 'Ali Babas' (p. 219), 'sand-niggers' (p. 227), 'Fucking Arabs' (p. 238) and 'Fuckin' lowlifes' (p. 225). This racism, voiced heatedly in front of black sergeant Brookes, reveals deeply embedded racist attitudes in the fabric of Englishness when pitted against the 'other'. It also exposes post-9/11 and 7/7 Islamophobic discourses that corral all Arabs together as the enemy of the West. Ben's vitriol towards Iraqis who he sees as 'all the same' (p. 222) reveals a method of coping which constructs a reality through language that systematically dehumanizes the Iraqis and justifies killing Iraqi soldiers and civilians alike:

Ben Those kids, they're nothing but maggots. Their fucking dads are maggots. It was probably their same fucking maggot dads that jumped us. They're not people, they aren't human, they are the enemy, alright? I bin here six months, I ain't losing my life here, they can fuck off with that. (p. 228)

The way in which articulation plays a vital role in the construction of one's own reality and truth is demonstrated through the character of Jamie. Jamie's inability to voice his truth and to stand up for himself is his greatest impediment.[64] Despite voicing his disgust at Ben's behaviour towards the Iraqi prisoners and his flippant shooting of a child in private, Jamie is pressurized by Ben to corroborate his version of events when confronted by Brookes:

Ben *(presses)* J? Tell him.

Jamie *(cowers)* That kid was signalling to them. (p. 228)

Jamie's inability to assert his voice reaches critical stage when he returns from the war and stands accused of committing war crimes. He refuses to betray the army's unspoken code of loyalty:

Jamie Grass on my mates? Dishonour myself as well as my unit? You really don't know me, Hannah. (p. 265)

Ironically, he refuses to betray the same institution that is betraying him by using him as a scapegoat. When Jamie finally snaps and tells the truth about Ben's crime, his sense of release leads only to more suffering with Trish leaving '*heartbroken*' (p. 271) and his increased sense of isolation at having betrayed his silence.

In the third act Hannah becomes the focus of the play. Through Hannah Williams explores the notion that education and upward mobility exert their own threat when they loosen her sense of belonging in the community. She is caught between her new university friends' assumptions about the war and the role of British troops and her personal knowledge of Jamie and his limitations. As Hannah tries to reconcile these opposing arguments, she spirals out of control resulting in her drunkenly propositioning her step-father, Lenny. She reverts back to 'Hannah the slapper' because 'No one cares what that Hannah thinks. That Hannah does not have an opinion, on anything' (p. 263). She feels disassociated from the intellectual world, and it is Lenny who guides her to a decision to support Jamie. Ultimately, her ability for empathy demonstrates her intelligence beyond Dan's bookishness:

Dan   Did you see those pictures?

Hannah   He was following orders.

Dan   Bollocks.

Hannah   Now they're screwing him.

Dan   It was an illegal order.

Hannah   You really think Jamie knows the difference? (p. 257)

Williams may well be criticized for playing into the hands of dominant culture through a portrayal of the English 'yob' culture. However, while the larger environment may be stylized in stereotype, through the sensitive portrayal of Williams' protagonists he draws attention to a section of society failed by the education system and exploited by the state. Nevertheless, as he demonstrated through Joe in *Fallout*, escape is possible, albeit painful.

166

5. Conclusion

Williams' is a complex theatre that blurs binaries of victim/perpetrator, society/individual and ethnicity/race. Beneath the turbulence of his dramas Williams hints at a multicultural social ideal defined by creolization/inter-mixture rather than pluralism. He persistently draws our attention to the ruptures that result from the perversion of life's fundamental complexities to fit distinct and homogenous categorizations. In navigating these social ruptures, Williams inevitably exposes himself to criticism.[65] The urge to incite debate has been consistent throughout Williams' work since 2000 and is fostered by a belief that only through open dialogue can society arbitrate deep-seated prejudices and inequalities.[66] Similarly, since 2000 Williams' work has increasingly engaged with political issues in which the nation at large is implicated. By not resorting to easy solutions and by highlighting causes and possible areas of redress for the issues he explores, Williams' work is at once reflective of a dysfunctional society as it is hopeful of the possibility of its redemption.

Williams' *Sucker Punch* (2010) is set in the 1980s, a time when violent race riots expressed the shared experience of marginalization and racism among non-whites, leading them to unify in opposition to the dominant white social order under the shared term 'Black'. The play's retrospective glance elicited comparisons to contemporary Britain. Although many of the issues that fuelled the riots have been addressed, and the unifying category of 'Black British' has largely dissolved, new problems have surfaced which have led Williams to re-examine his personal identity and role as a playwright. In the past Williams stated about being identified as a 'black' playwright: 'I stopped worrying about labels long ago. Once there was a big thing about whether to be called a black playwright, and I thought, do what you like, just don't miss out the word playwright! If you want to worry about the label black, go ahead, but I'm not'.[67] However in a recent interview Williams stated that he now identifies with the label 'black British playwright'. In light of recent political and economic events and the prospect of funding cuts in Britain, Williams says, 'I think we need that [Black British] phrase more than ever' and 'we need to do whatever we can to jump up and say we're here'.[68] This anxiety belies Williams' belief that British society remains deeply prejudiced and indicates that there is much work to be done. His re-embracing of this title hints at a further engagement with issues of politics and race to come. Nevertheless, despite the label, Williams' plays address key concerns to both black and white Britons and in the process shed new light on what it means to be British.

DAVID GREIG
Nadine Holdsworth

When David Greig's (b. 1969) name is mentioned it is usually accompanied by the words 'Scottish', 'prolific' and 'intelligent'. In the past twenty years, since graduating from Bristol University with an English and Drama degree, Greig has had his work produced by many leading theatres in Britain including the Traverse Theatre in Edinburgh, Paines Plough, the Royal Court, Donmar Warehouse and the Royal Shakespeare Company (RSC) and from an early stage his work found an international audience. In 1990 he co-founded Suspect Culture with Graham Eatough and Nick Powell, a touring company based in Glasgow with whom he created a substantial body of work including *Timeless* (1997), *Casanova* (2001) and *8000m* (2004) between 1990 and 2009.[1] Indeed, running parallel to his work as a lone playwright, collaboration at home and abroad has been a hallmark of Greig's output. He is deeply invested in the possibilities of the collective imagination, pursuing ideas across different media as well as linguistic and stylistic boundaries.[2]

Critical attention on Greig has principally focused on his engagement with questions of the nation and national identity in post-devolution Scotland.[3] Greig has been vocal about his commitment to Scotland as a vital part of his personal identity – he was born there and returned after spending his early childhood in Nigeria – and his creative imagination and he has been pivotal to the emergence of new Scottish writing as a prominent force in the British theatre landscape alongside others such as David Harrower, Zinnie Harris and Anthony Neilson. He served as the National Theatre of Scotland's dramaturg for the first two years of its existence and several of his plays including *Caledonia Dreaming* (1997) and *Victoria* (2000) are specifically concerned with the particularities of the Scottish landscape as well as its history, politics and culture. He has even written *Dunsinane* (2010), a sequel to the 'Scottish play',

Macbeth. Nonetheless, a tendency to associate or limit Greig to his Scottish origins has resulted in a lack of sustained critical attention to the passionate internationalism of Greig's writing, something that this chapter seeks to redress.

Greig's refusal to restrict his imaginative terrain to his immediate locale is borne out by his decision to use settings as far and wide as Paris, the Pyrenees, America, Syria and outer space, alongside his perceptive critical reflections on contemporary global politics. In early works such as *Europe* (1994) and *One-Way Street* (1995), Greig was preoccupied by the political reorganization necessitated by the fall of the Berlin Wall and what character an emergent 'new Europe' might develop. The workings and implications of globalization is a persistent seam running through all his plays and in recent years Greig has become increasingly interested in the Middle East, the fraught relationship between the east and the west and American imperialism.

In all his works, Greig is acutely concerned with the markers of history and identity, but not in a sense of these being static and fixed. Identity is something that can be played with and reconstituted. His fixation with history is in terms of historical change and he is often drawn to acute periods of flux. For example, *The Speculator* (1999) is about the banker John Law and the period of economic speculation that modernized the global economy in the early eighteenth century and *Outlying Islands* (2002) takes place in the months prior to World War Two. In particular Greig is interested in human motivation, action and agency – how characters respond to the world in all its complexity and contradiction. As such, his work is often simultaneously tinged with a sense of optimism and pessimism. So, Greig has asserted the importance for him of the possibility of change, but this is tempered by a profound awareness of human, social and political failure, as he says 'we'll fuck up as much as we progress'.[4]

Greig persistently uses the metaphor of travel and journeys in his work. His characters are often lost in or exploring unfamiliar territory as in *One-Way Street* or *Pyrenees* (2005), which allows an exploration of personal history, memory and the qualities that mark individual human beings as unique, fallible, loveable. Travel is also seen as something that is enriching because it facilitates human interaction and exchange. Indeed the struggle for human connection, communication and intimacy is a recurring motif in plays including *The Architect* (1996) and *Mainstream* (1999). Equally, he applies the journey metaphor to his own creative processes saying, 'I see myself as sort of travelling along a road. It must be terribly annoying for an audience when I seem to veer wildly off it, but I never see it as veering. I just see the road as being incredibly wide, and I'm simply moving forward as best I can'.[5] The veering refers to the eclectic strands of Greig's work that encompasses experimental works created from workshops and open devising processes with Suspect Culture, main stage epic works for the RSC, plays for children and young people such as *Dr Korczak's Example* (2001) and *Yellow Moon* (2006), adaptations including *Tintin* for the Barbican in 2006 and *The Bacchae* for the Edinburgh International Festival in 2007, and the libretto for the musical *Charlie and the Chocolate Factory* (2013).

Believing that 'if the [ideological] battlefield is the imagination, then the theatre is a very appropriate weapon in the armoury of resistance', Greig has persistently asked himself 'how can I, as a theatre-maker explore, map and advance a progressive agenda?' without falling into the trap of dogmatic 'dialectical solutions in the old left-wing tradition'.[6] He cites Bertolt Brecht as his primary artistic inspiration and several of his plays exhibit epic structures and features, but he has equally experimented with different ways of constructing narratives informed by drawing, automatic writing or music as a way of allowing the pre-formed, unbidden, the deep unconscious to seep into his writing.[7] Greig has explained this in terms of his belief in the power of the imagination to intervene, to interrupt the narratives posed by the forces of global capital, media conglomerations and dominant political institutions – that the imagination, if invited to, can conjure with the impossible and, in so doing, suggest alternative narratives of power and emancipation. And, as such, the abstract interior landscape of the subconscious can be marshalled to evoke a sensory, metaphorical critique as opposed to a more literal socialist analysis. This formal experimentation reached an apotheosis in the first work under detailed discussion in this chapter, *San Diego* (2003).

1. *San Diego*

San Diego emerged out of a writers' retreat at Hawthornden Castle outside Edinburgh. Responding to an atmosphere that was 'quiet and ascetic, almost monastic', Greig decided to trust his instincts and to write whatever came into his head, allowing the work to be 'led emotionally rather than intellectually'.[8] He has spoken about how this 'bizarrely autobiographical' play took on a life of its own, generating resonances that grew out of his reading around globalization, concerns with migrant labour and a general atmosphere of anxiety around the September 11 attacks in New York.[9] From these origins a complex web of interconnected narratives emerged that broadly coalesce around the themes of migrancy, identity, belonging, home, a place of safety, human connection and intimacy, family, faith and rootlessness.

Inspired by Greig's first visit to America, the play opens with a character called David Greig, a young playwright who is on a plane to San Diego to see a production of one of his plays. He arrives in the city suffering the dislocating effects of consuming alcohol, sleep deprivation and travelling across different time zones. Clutching a hand-drawn map, the character is soon lost in the city. By inserting himself into the narrative Greig was interested in what tensions would emerge by generating 'a fictional character of the playwright, to whom you give your name and some of your characteristics'.[10] The character, played by Billy Boyd in the original production, wearing a t-shirt emblazoned with the name David Greig, is met off the plane by the entire cast also wearing David Greig t-shirts, a self-referential device that immediately raises questions around the status of the playwright, authorship and the blurring of fiction and reality. The result is strangely disconcerting, not least because the expectation that the Greig character will provide some form of stable authorial voice, guiding the spectator through the tangled narrative, is thwarted by his stabbing and death fairly early in the play. Yet, while the character of Greig is swiftly dispatched to a heavenly aircraft cabin hovering over proceedings, his presence acts as a constant reminder of Greig the playwright's function as the originator and driving force behind this intricate and multi-layered piece of theatre.

Refusing to adopt a causal, linear narrative, the characters and meaning collide and free-associate in *San Diego*'s kaleidoscopic form prompting Neil Cooper to describe it 'as if chaos theory had been dramatized, with Greig the butterfly wings beating from point to point'.[11] Greig leaves little solid ground for the audience as names, origins and identities continually slip and double and the audience is left to join the dots of this multi-perspectival work. This was not the first time Greig had experimented with a complicated, multi-faceted narrative. Dan Rebellato argues that *The Cosmonaut*'s (1999) bevy of 'characters, narratives and locations [. . .] is pulled together by a web of connections that transcend the logic of the plot' and Adrienne Scullion refers to *The Speculator* as 'an elaborate fantasy, huge and sprawling, telling many stories and filled with dozens of characters'.[12] But, largely because of the insertion of Greig as a character, the narrative structure seems far more wilfully experimental in *San Diego* than in these earlier plays.

The interconnected threads are loosely woven together through Kevin, the pilot of a Boeing 777. He brings Greig to San Diego, while unofficially an illegal immigrant, Daniel, with 'a head full of electricity' (p. 108)[13] risks his life clinging to the under-carriage of the plane in a quest to find his mother who abandoned him in Jos in Nigeria to become a backing singer for Paul McCartney's band Wings. Greig and Daniel have history, which culminates in Daniel stabbing Greig on a deserted roadside, a storyline that draws on Greig's biography as a Scottish white boy who spent his early childhood in Jos while playfully departing from it. It transpires that as a child, Greig may have thrown the acid that caused Daniel's distinctive blue scarring. When Daniel asks 'Why did you bring me here?' Greig responds 'I wanted to get to know you, I suppose' to which Daniel retorts 'I am utterly uninterested in what you want' (p. 102). So, in one complicated storyline, Greig offers a reflection on colonial guilt, fear of the *other*, and revenge, while simultaneously ruminating on the God-like role of the playwright in bringing characters into being. And this tangled thread is typical of the way Greig's self-reflexive experimental narrative circulates around big themes.

San Diego itself has multiple meanings in the play that depart significantly from the official narrative Greig reads on the plane.

173

Quoting a guidebook, he notes that it 'has the highest quality of life in any city in the United States' (p. 5), but as Neil Campbell and Alasdair Kean stress, the meaning of any city varies depending on the interpreter's outlook, whether they are reading from 'skyscraper or street level, uptown or the ghetto, inside or out, feminine or masculine, rich or poor' and Greig captures this quality in his play.[14] For the pilot, San Diego is an exemplar of Marc Augé's concept of the non-place,[15] an anonymous complex of freeways and apartment blocks whose only distinguishing marker is a Hilton International hotel that can be found in any major city across the world. It is a place where the forward march of commerce ensures that nobody stops on the freeway to help a man, Greig, bleeding to death.

The underbelly of the city is revealed through the homeless and destitute illegal immigrants Pious and Innocent. Originally from Nigeria, Innocent and Pious are chasing the 'America Dream' that John Hartley refers to as a weapon extending 'American supremacy beyond its own hemisphere'.[16] Lost figures with limited possessions who argue over their respective pasts, future and potential legacy, for them the city is a place of menial toil and violence. A place where police officers unlawfully shoot the unarmed Innocent in the back with no fear of reprisal because they are expendable shadowy figures inhabiting the dark recesses of the city and its economy. Yet, Greig also gives an example of the migrant 'American Dream' working, albeit at a price. Daniel's mother, who changed her name from Patience to Amy, has made the journey from a drug-addled backing-singer to a successful real estate dealer, but at the expense of any meaningful relationship with her son, family or cultural heritage.

All the characters in *San Diego* are desperate for human connection and meaningful intimacy, but their relationships are characterized by failed attempts to communicate, misunderstandings and paranoia. In particular, the traditional family unit is broken and in crisis. Children are suffering from allergies, are lost or abandoned, a situation Greig underlines with repeated reference to the television show *America's Missing Children.* The pilot fails to develop a meaningful relationship with his children and is inept at anything close to intimacy. His disturbed daughter, Laura, is desperate to communicate with her emotionally and geographically remote father from the confines of a mental institution in England. When she fails to reach him her sense of inadequacy manifests itself in the brutal extremes of self-harm. Even though he is in the same city as his actor son, Andrew, who is playing a pilot in a lame post-9/11 film about hijackers, he is unable to advise or to communicate. Andrew, in turn, is dealing with the collapse of his own small family unit under the weight of his wife's paranoia over the welfare of their nine-month-old son and her retreat into fanatical religious observance as a way of coping with the world's ills. Yet, Greig pulls other possibilities for familial-style relationships into the frame. Daniel rejects his biological mother and finds a protective mother substitute in Pious and the audience learns about a Quebecois biologist playing the role of mother to a group of orphaned goslings.

In a pivotal speech at the end of Act One, Greig informs the audience that ironically the limbo transit time of air travel is the only real time of secure identity and belonging:

The cabin of the aircraft is the only space where we can be certain that we belong – we have a ticket with our name on it

On the seat in front of us there is a map which shows us clearly where we are going

And we are going forwards. (p. 78)

In the same speech Greig notes that 'the average child born this century will spend more of its lifetime on an aircraft than it will with its grandparents' (p. 78). A sobering thought highlighting the threat to local and familial networks posed by globalization and the increasing internationalism of many affluent Westerners. For instance, when the pilot visits his daughter she expresses her desire to go home, but as her father offers her the *gite* in France, her mother's place in Hong Kong, his flat in Surrey, the cottage in Fife or a new house that he would buy for her, it is clear that these are part of a property portfolio but not homes. Unsure where to go, Laura remains in stasis, locked in a cycle of abuse and institutionalization. This theme is underscored by the repeated metaphor of the mystery of how geese have the instinctive urge to migrate together in the 'Great big beautiful V' (p. 74). This symbol of unison in flight is an echo of the Boeing 777, 'a community of two hundred and fifty-six people' (p. 78) but whereas the geese leave, travel and live together, the inhabitants of the aircraft are isolated strangers temporarily inhabiting the same air space with no shared purpose or design, a fact that is gloriously sent up in Greig's satire on the 'conceptual consultancy' that attempts to rebrand the aircraft as a temporary village.

In different ways all the characters are yearning for a sense of self worth and – meaning that they try to fulfil through therapy, their careers or religious faith. Yet, it is the budding romance between self-harmer Laura and David, who suffers from chronic attention deficit disorder, which provides the play's emotional centre. David's manic energy and incessant wise-cracking contrasts with Laura's laboured existence of silent bodily examination, cutting and fainting. Starved of attention Laura finds solace and a sense of connection in sharing her flesh with David. As their relationship matures they reach beyond a deeply troubled masochism to find comfort and redemption in their shared love; a love that enables David to concentrate long enough to save Laura's life after she has taken an overdose. Their discovery of each other and their ability to support each other's needs provides a cautious sense of optimism and reconciliation at the end of the play.

Much of the play's theatrical impact relies on the collision of elements: aural, visual and textual. The sound of a baby breathing close to a monitor is intercut with a cockpit alarm, a phone ringing and 'the huge sound of the plane' (p. 11). In one particularly telling silent moment Laura examines her naked body while holding a kitchen knife; Innocent plucks a goose; Pious sharpens a knife and Greig dies on the street from stab wounds (p. 32). The images are at once unconnected and totally connected by the threat and reality of violence, the cutting of flesh. In this moment several different narratives cohere before spinning off into their own internal logic, an enigmatic quality that prompted Ian Shuttleworth to refer to it as 'a beautiful music of a play'.[17]

The play's first production was presented by the Tron Theatre for the Edinburgh International Festival at the Lyceum Theatre in Edinburgh during August 2003. Simon Vincenzi's design emphasized the anodyne sterility of an airport with a potted palm tree, vending machine and banks of suitcases, a mood enhanced by Graeme Miller's neutral score of muzak. The aesthetic of the waiting room and the play's self-reflexivity was equally underscored by the words David Greig and the play's title flickering incessantly across an LCD display screen. Coupled with the Greig character and Greig's decision to co-direct his show with the choreographer Marisa Zanotti, this resulted in accusations of narcissism. Several critics also found the play's unwieldy formal experimentation and the tenuous integration of theme and character frustrating. Others praised Greig's ambition, his thoughtfulness and willingness to experiment with theatrical form and representation. In the next play under discussion, *The American Pilot* (2005), Greig returns to a more easily decipherable Brechtian parable structure.

2. *The American Pilot*

The American Pilot revolves around the aftermath of a crash during which an American pilot is lost in the hills of an unnamed country in the midst of civil war. Greig does not pinpoint a specific country, but in production the dress, music and hookahs confirmed the setting as the Middle East – somewhere. Injured, the pilot is rescued by a kind local sheep farmer who brings him to shelter in his barn. Representing the ordinary citizen, the farmer and his wife respond to the pilot's material presence – his cold emaciated and injured body. Their sense of common humanity drives them to care for the man as best they can with food for his hungry belly and painkillers for his discomfort. But this simple act of hospitality is complicated by the broader political situation. The pilot has landed in the middle of rebel territory populated by angry dissidents intent on fighting a corrupt political regime, which is funded by the United States. The pilot's fate is therefore left in the hands of the Captain, the leader of the rebel faction who cannot decide whether the pilot should be held to ransom, be used as a hostage to draw the attention of the world's media or whether he should adhere to his translator's logic that the pilot's monetary value could be dwarfed by his symbolic propaganda value if they filmed his execution for global distribution.

Written before the 2003 invasion of Iraq, but after the launch of Operation Enduring Freedom that saw American and British troops entering Afghanistan, Greig's play reflects on America's relationship with the rest of the world in the aftermath of 9/11, the 'war on terror' and in the run-up to the second Iraq War. More than this, it is about the social imaginary of America, its iconicity and mythological status. Greig has admitted that *The American Pilot* has a very clear genesis in Heiner Müller's play *The Road of Tanks*, which is written from the perspective of a Russian soldier at the Front during World War One. Struck by the lines

THE GERMAN have you seen HIM How does HE
Fight THE GERMAN have you seen HIM seen HIM
A horizon of tanks HE is THE GERMAN.[18]

Greig was inspired by how the idea could be translated for a new political moment:

I just saw the whole play – I saw the whole thing: a pilot lands – the villager sees him – he is "THE AMERICAN" in capital letters – we saw him coming – the American – he was beautiful, the American.[19]

A largely one-dimensional, overly aggressive action-man figure who, despite his precarious position, exudes confidence and complete faith in his compatriots to launch a successful rescue mission, the pilot serves as a theatrical device for Greig to explore how America's economic and military power has led it to dominate the international political agenda by demanding the application of American versions of democracy and economic liberalism throughout the world. As Michael Billington observed, 'what Greig captures excellently is the idea of the world as a shrinking global village dominated by US values', a point comically born out by the instant recognition of the cartoon character Daffy Duck by locals in a remote hilltop village.[20] Yet, Greig has admitted that the play is 'quite ambivalent about America', a position captured through the different responses the pilot elicits.[21]

American cultural critics have written about the two key aspects of imperialism and liberation that, although seemingly contradictory, underpin the global phenomenon of Americanization. As John Hartley summarizes:

One pole saw Americanization as imperialism – the imposition of global mass culture on a previously highly differentiated patchwork of indigenous cultures, in the service of the commercial and military expansionism of the US military-industrial complex. The other pole saw Americanization as Liberation.[22]

Some inhabitants of Greig's remote, imagined Middle Eastern community regard the pilot as a symbol of American imperialism. As such the pilot provides an opportunity for them to degrade his – or, more importantly, his country's – iconic status. Against his better nature, the Captain relishes the sight of the pilot's bound, wounded body encased in a dirty, blood encrusted jumpsuit and tries to humiliate him further by making him lick the dust from his boots. Meanwhile the Captain's translator, a lapsed Marxist, wants to kill the pilot to avenge the death of his beloved Belle, the Captain's daughter, who died at the hands of an American built missile. Admitting his 'mind is a desert of fear and grief' (p. 55),[23] the usually deep-thinking, sensitive translator stabs a knife into the pilot's broken leg and makes preparations for his execution. But, rather than simplistically adhering to the image of barbaric avengers, both these characters feel demeaned by their behaviour. The translator's bodily revulsion at his action makes him vomit, while the Captain regrets his loss of control and refocuses on his role as a principled soldier fighting for an ideological cause.

Other members of the community think that America represents liberation or pleasure via popular culture as demonstrated by the locals partying to the music emanating from the American pilot's stolen iPod. As Andrew Hammond acknowledges, 'while the Arabs suffer America's policies, they are also listening to its music, following its fashion, watching its TV shows, lapping up its gadgetry and inventions, and asking themselves how they can emulate all manner of American success'.[24] The relationship of the Arab world to the United States is far from simple, a fact epitomized by the translator, whose experience of America has left him with a contradictory mixture of longing and loathing.

Embodying Greig's faith in the endless possibility of the imagination epitomized by her first line, 'I had a dream once where the sky was torn open and there was a different world behind it' (p. 12), Evie, the farmer's Western-influenced independently minded daughter, sees the golden skinned, blue-eyed pilot as a fallen angel to be idolized as a glowing symbol of an alternative world. Evie embraces the liberator narrative, convincing herself that 'America sent him to save us' (p. 59). She believes the pilot will secure her community access to a global media platform where they will be able to make their hardships known.

Jaded by 35 years of fighting, the Captain is seduced by Evie's liberation narrative. Believing she can be a talismanic figure, he imagines Evie leading an army and recruiting followers with her vision and oratory powers. Under her influence, he decides to keep the pilot alive and to symbolically return him to his country as a gesture of their desire to negotiate and be accepted as civilized people. Unfortunately, neither the Captain nor Evie banked on the self-interested local trader, whose loyalty to his profit margin wreaks havoc. The trader is a familiar character in Greig's work, and evokes earlier incarnations such as Morocco in *Europe* (1994) and Euan in *Victoria* (2000), who enable Greig to critique the ethics of the unfettered free market. Having embarked on secret negotiations with the Americans, the trader succeeds in bringing the rampaging army to the heart of the local community in a 'shock and awe' assault that ends in brutal tragedy. As the American military arrives to rescue one of their own, chaos reigns amid the apocalyptic auditory onslaught of military helicopters, rapid gunfire and explosions that lead to the deaths of the Farmer, the Trader, the Captain and the Translator. As Benedict Nightingale observed, 'We're left with an impression of a world where some lives matter far less than others'.[25] Evie gets the fulfilment of her liberation narrative as the pilot protects her and winches her to safety and, by implication, to a new life, but at the expense of all she has known – clearly there is a high price to pay for liberation.

The American Pilot premiered at the RSC, which was in the process of reinvigorating its new writing agenda following the arrival of Michael Boyd as Artistic Director. Directed by Ramin Gray and staged as part of the 'New Works' festival (2004–7), an initiative to mount a festival of new plays after the end of the official season, the production premiered at The Other Place on 27 April 2005. By this point the play had garnered significant topicality following not only the 2003 invasion of Iraq by a United States led coalition but also the shocking accounts of physical, psychological and sexual abuse of prisoners by American forces emanating from Abu Ghraib prison in Iraq and the death of Nicholas Berg, an American businessman abducted and beheaded in Iraq on 7 May 2004 by Islamic militants who filmed his execution to post on the internet. In recognition of its timeliness, the production was revived at the Soho Theatre in London a year later, by which time the play appeared even more apposite given the heightened political tensions and increasingly violent insurgency against the coalition forces in Iraq.

Theatrically, Gray's production emphasized symbolism and a story-telling idiom. To open the production, the American pilot was splayed across the stage in cruciform while all the inhabitants of the remote civil, war-torn country looked on. This simple image of the American military and Christian iconography in a Middle Eastern setting captured the potent presence of difference, a quality also suggested through the use of translation. Set in an unnamed country where the indigenous population does not speak English, all the characters deliver their lines in English. This familiar theatrical device, made famous by Brian Friel's *Translations* (1981), emphasizes cultural difference as excruciating attempts to communicate across invisible language barriers ensue. Equally, the hip-hop on the pilot's iPod contrasted sharply with the gentle melodies of the indigenous music played on a cimbalom-type instrument. These theatrical strategies served to make the moments of genuine exchange when the farmer and pilot laugh over a cigarette, when the pilot shows Sarah a photograph of his family and when Evie sings her rendition of Jamelia's pop song 'Superstar' to the pilot, all the more poignant.

181

Notably, in Gray's production, all the characters stayed on the stage and visible throughout, emphasizing the significance of the community but also revealing the heterogeneity of its inhabitants. Individual confessional monologues directly addressed to the audience invited them to appreciate the multi-perspectival quality of the script. These personal insights also served to make the final scene all the more shocking as Gray exploited the theatrical potential of an attack that Greig describes as 'overwhelmingly massive and violent' (p. 71).

Unsurprisingly, *The American Pilot* garnered significant attention in the United States where it received several productions and it is interesting to compare the different critical receptions. Whereas British reviewers applauded the RSC's production for its effective stagecraft and its insightful, compassionate assessment of a complex situation, Lynne Meadow's production at the Manhattan Theatre Club, New York in 2006, David Gassner's production at Theatre Schmeater in Seattle in April 2008 and Amy Rummenie's May 2008 production for the Walking Shadow Theatre Company in Minneapolis, all faced significant criticism by American critics. Rohan Preston dismissed Rummenie's production as a 'slim, one-note drama' and equally, Joe Adcock resented 'a cynically stereotyped American shoot-'em up finale worthy of a video game but not of much use to a self-respecting drama' when he reviewed Gassner's production.[26] Notably, a lot had happened in the 18 months that had passed from the play's premiere at the RSC to its New York production in November 2006, when the situation in Iraq was grave and deteriorating as the American death toll continued to rise. The frustration with the situation was clearly evident in Charles Isherwood's review for *The New York Times*,

A generic play about an American soldier held captive and possibly primed for execution can hardly be expected to rivet our attention – or perhaps even escape our dismay – when real soldiers (and real civilians) are mired in predicaments of a similar kind on the other side of the globe, day after brutal, bruising day.[27]

There is no doubt that real-life events that had initially given Greig's play gravitas and political significance, within a couple of years had the capacity to make the play seem naïve and potentially opportunistic depending on the cultural context and the presiding political zeitgeist. Nonetheless, Greig continued directing his attention to the politics of the Middle Eastern region in the next play under discussion, *Damascus* (2007) which proved equally controversial when it travelled beyond its origins in the United Kingdom.

3. *Damascus*

Damascus originated in the artistic exchanges Greig has maintained over a number of years with young theatre artists in the Middle East. This work began as part of an extensive international programme of work pioneered by Elyse Dodgson at the Royal Court that saw Greig helping to devise a comedy, *Mish Alla Ruman (Not About Pomegranates)* with the director Rufus Norris and the Al Kasabah Theatre in Ramalla in 2001. Since this formative contact with the Middle East, Greig has run numerous playwriting workshops there with a view to encouraging and disseminating theatre material from the region. Greig has admitted learning an enormous amount about the complexities of relations between the West and the Arab world through these workshops and *Damascus* articulates these complexities in a theatrical format.[28]

Initially Greig resisted his drive to write about the politics of the Arab world because he was concerned about appropriating somebody else's experience and troubled by the difficulties of representation. As he says, 'I was just tremendously nervous of trying to represent people in the Middle East, because of that old Western thing of misrepresenting other cultures'.[29] After realizing he would be intrigued by the prospect of a play called 'Edinburgh' written by a Syrian writer, he allowed himself to enter this imaginative terrain and reflected his trepidation in a play 'obsessed with the anxiety around the representation of the *other*'.[30]

The play explores the relationship between the liberal English West and the secular outward-looking Arab world. The central character, a Scotsman called Paul, arrives in Damascus to sell his 'integrated English language learning system' (p. 14),[31] which provides an

183

introduction to the intricacies of spoken and written English, to the Syrian education authority. Replete with a cast of politically correct multicultural characters who are designed to showcase Paul's sensitivity to cultural difference, his textbooks comes under close scrutiny by the sharp, progressive and intellectually switched on Muna and are roundly dismissed by her boss, the cynical disenchanted Wasim, who is more interested in having a good time and rekindling his prior relationship with Muna.

Adopting a familiar Greig trope of a character disorientated by travel, jet-lag and sleep deprivation, Paul is worried about being in a 'war zone' (p. 10) and of losing his sense of smell, which Greig exploits throughout the play for its comic potential when it transpires that the stench of urinals temporarily reactivate his olfactory senses. Intending to make only a brief over-night stop, a security alert at Beirut airport delays Paul's return to England and his family. Having initially rejected sightseeing in favour of sleep, with unexpected time on his hands he embarks on a journey of discovery, exploring the old city and becoming intoxicated by its history, sites and people. Despite seeing himself as a culturally sensitive liberal, Paul is seduced by the possibility of exotic otherness – Muna, the Souk and the narrow alleys of the old city.

Inevitably the play draws on the iconicity of Damascus itself. Widely reported as one of the world's oldest continuously inhabited cities with a rich commercial, intellectual and cultural life, it carries the architectural and cultural markers of a multilayered genealogy having been variously controlled by Persia, Greece, the Ottoman Empire and France before becoming part of independent Syria in 1946. Controlled by both the East and the West during its history, Greig makes use of the contested site and its complex demographic that consists of a majority Arab Sunni Muslim population, alongside Palestinian, Christian and Jewish communities, to highlight the shifts of time and cultural change. Importantly, as a country dominated by the Arab nationalist, secular, socialist regime of the Bath party Syria also holds many similarities with Iraq. According to Greig, 'Iraq is the shadow that every audience member will have in their head when they watch the play'.[32]

Indeed *Damascus* is set against a backdrop of simmering tensions in the Middle East. A repeated stage direction indicates that a television screen in the hotel lobby of the mediocre hotel serving as Paul's temporary home 'shows news images of the current situation' which in the premiere production at the Traverse Theatre in Edinburgh begun on 27 July 2007, included images from Iraq, Palestine and the release of Alan Johnston, the former BBC Gaza correspondent held hostage for 114 days. With the sound permanently down, this visual device insistently brings to mind the myriad troubles in the region that regularly play out on television screens in the West, but that can never capture the reality of life for ordinary citizens living in the region.

The hotel lobby serves as the play's meeting, eating and entertaining space. Elena, a Ukrainian Christian Marxist transsexual, plays the piano in the lobby and successfully breaks up the play's 'elegant naturalism'.[33] Representing the fluidity of Damascus in human form, Elena serves as an on-stage witness, a one-woman chorus commenting wryly and directly to the audience on what she sees as she adapts songs to work for every occasion: high octane versions of Arabic pop classics for the disco, lush romantic film music for the meetings of clandestine lovers and hymns to drive the guests out of the dining room. In performance, her presence and soundtrack provides a funny, and often disorientating, element to this otherwise largely naturalistic play. Zakaria, the hotel's multi-purpose receptionist, porter and waiter feels 'dead inside', unfulfilled intellectually and emotionally, as well as sexually (p. 38). For him the west signifies freedom, liberation and the possibility of casual sex and he sees Paul as his potential liberator. Around these characters 'Greig spins a dazzling, sometimes dizzying, extended metaphor about a relationship between the West and the Arab world that is built upon mutual fantasy and projection'.[34]

Through Paul and Muna's discussion of his textbooks various cultural assumptions are revealed and Muna's requests for revisions raises the thorny question of censorship. Muna is liberal and outward looking but wholly conscious of the constraints of her national context. Evidently navigating difficult territory, Muna stresses the importance of generating citizens who are capable of participating in the 'global marketplace' (p. 25) at the same time as promoting a 'strong respect for Arabic values' (p. 25). Hence, while finding the process uncomfortable, she is alert to aspects of the text such as individualism, materialism,

185

disrespectful children and physical intimacy before marriage that would be unacceptable in her culture.

Greig complicates this narrative by ensuring that there are also revisions to do with respecting progressive aspects of Syrian culture. So, Muna dismisses the depiction of Mrs Mohammed in full niqab as inappropriate for a secular state working to right the wrongs of regressive patriarchy, whereas Paul was aiming to show values of religious tolerance in Britain. When Paul broaches the subject of censorship being an assault on democracy, their exchange becomes increasingly heated at Muna questions how Paul, standing in for the West, can dare to lecture the Arab world on democracy and human rights following the second Iraq War and the torture of suspected terrorists following illegal extradition to countries like Syria. With evident unease, Paul is left floundering. Unfortunately, this is theatrically a bit clunky because as Muna takes Paul to task for his cultural assumptions, she is equally lecturing the audience.

The intricate processes of communication, crosscultural translation and understanding drive the play. All of the characters fancy themselves to be writers: Paul writes his textbooks, Zakaria has ambitions of becoming a scriptwriter in Hollywood and Wasim fancies himself a poet, but they all fail. Paul is crippled by political correctness, Zakaria lacks sufficient skill and while Wasim longs for writing that captures the urgency of the street, his concern with politics and imperialism has long since been replaced by second rate erotic fiction. Above all, this is a play about language – what it says, what it cannot say, what it can teach, what it cannot, what can be translated, what cannot. It looks at how language is determined by its wider political context and its different manifestations in everyday conversation, on the streets and in poetry. Rather than telling the truth, language is used to construct fictitious communities or to placate as when Wasim tempers Muna's irate language during a meeting with the education minister. In fact, language is at its most revealing in the repeated outbursts of 'Fuck. Piss. Cock' (p. 28) that accompany the moments when things do not go Paul's way.

Greig also successfully deploys language as a potent theatrical device. Wasim and Paul's inadequacy in French leaves them at the mercy of Muna who comically and selectively translates for them. Paul and Muna's mutual attraction is creatively expressed through a tentatively teasing and playful use of verbs and tenses that is delightful to watch in performance. In an interview with Dominic Cavendish, Greig stressed that 'it's a play about unsaid things, the power of unsaid things'.[35] On one level this concern comes to the fore through Greig's exposure of the revelatory potential of body language. Equally, Greig reveals the tragic consequences that arise from the avoidance of speech because it is too painful or awkward when Paul fails to be honest with Zakaria about his chance with American girls, who mock him for their amusement, or his skills as a writer. After seeing the film script of his life unceremoniously dumped in the bin, Zakaria shoots himself and dies as Paul holds his hand, a lasting image of the liberal west and the secular, ambitious east failing to communicate in any meaningful way.

First performed by the Traverse Theatre Company on 27 July 2007, there was a general feeling that the production misfired particularly because, as Lyn Gardner found, 'the veneer of witty comedy has suffocated the play's emotional and political reverberations'.[36] Nonetheless, almost all reviewers noted Greig's capacity for intelligent debate and the need to facilitate the kind of crosscultural exchange represented in *Damascus*. In March and April 2009 the British Council organized a tour of *Damascus* to Egypt, Lebanon, Syria, Jordan, Tunisia and the Palestinian territories. The tour involved performances of the play followed by discussion forums and dialogues between theatre-makers, critics and journalists from Britain and the Arab region in order to facilitate productive dialogue. From Britain, participants included the journalist Sarfraz Manzoor, theatre critic Joyce McMillan and Greig himself, alongside Arab counterparts such as the Lebanese director Paul Matar, the Egyptian critic Nehad Seleiha and the researcher and novelist Adaneya Al Shebly from Palestine.

It was always going to be a risky strategy, taking a play about the Middle East by a Scottish playwright written for a British audience to the Middle East. As one cultural commentator from Beirut commented, 'High-cultural dialogue is a fine idea, one that's fiendishly difficult to embody within a single work – regardless how talented, high-minded, and sensitive the artists involved'.[37] And so it proved to be. Critical opinion was sharply divided and the company faced ferocious criticism from those who regarded the play and its tour as 'patronizing colonialism' or resented the resources directed at this production that could have been spent facilitating work by Arab playwrights.[38]

Ironically, although Greig was intent on revealing the casual racism, cultural prejudices and neocolonial attitudes that come to the surface in Paul's textbooks, he ended up being accused of just the same pitfalls. Whereas British critics and audiences largely homed in on the way *Damascus* lampoons the Scotsman abroad and his cultural naivety, McMillan acknowledged that to the Arab World the play 'looks like a thumbnail sketch of their entire culture, summed up in three troubled characters'.[39] On the other side of the divide sat critics who admired Greig's commitment to the Middle East and those such as the Egyptian commentator Mehna Al-Badawi who argued that the play articulated 'the situation of many who are struggling for self-expression in societies full of cultural tension and political uncertainty'.[40]

4. Conclusion

The thing that unites all three of these plays is the desire for communication whether it is between individuals or across cultural barriers. The tenuous, fragile moments of connection between Laura and David in *San Diego*, the pilot and farmer in *The American Pilot* and Muna and Paul in *Damascus* are examples of communication against all the odds, when love, desire and a core sense of humanity enable humans to interact with other human beings. In these touching moments, political, cultural and personal differences temporarily dissolve and there is a glimpse of possibility for change – in attitudes, circumstance and outcome. Indeed, it is in these small acts of individual agency rather than the metanarratives of socialism that Greig's politics reside – put simply, Greig invites his audiences, as well as his characters, to see the world from different perspectives in order to promote heightened understanding rather than answers. He is not arrogant enough to presume that his plays have the capacity to change the world, but they are profoundly political, as he argues,

> Theatre can play an essential role in helping to sustain and build a more human-centred, human-valued society in which what it means to be human can be provisionally articulated.[41]

This concern with what it means to be human raises the question of citizenship and civilization that lurks in the background of Greig's plays – what roles and responsibility does being human entail? What does it mean to be civilized? How can people contribute to local economies, improved environmental awareness and offset the impact of the forces of neoliberalism and global capital? How might we privilege and act upon conceptions of global citizenship and understanding rather than profit, self-interest and prejudice at the beginning of the twenty-first century?

Still relatively young, Greig has a long career yet ahead of him. As dramaturg for the National Theatre of Scotland he has played a pivotal role in nurturing and developing the dramatic landscape in Scotland through his own and other's work, but there can be no doubt that Greig's interests exceed the boundaries of national borders. He is an internationalist, someone willing to address global concerns in his work, as well as to travel and produce his work on the international stage. As we have seen, when plays travel through time and geographical contexts their meanings can alter significantly, but this is part of the dialogue that Greig is keen to foster. He is not just interested in setting his plays in foreign lands and cultures, but of opening up conversations about what it means to engage across cultural boundaries and how questions of ethical accountability, human rights and global citizenship make demands on us all – these conversations may falter and provoke intense debate but the significant thing is that they take place at all. One of Greig's greatest skills as a dramatist is to take risks, to experiment, to try new ideas, structures, ways of telling a good story and through these stories he will continue to contribute to a necessary probing of human behaviour.

DEBBIE TUCKER GREEN
Lynette Goddard

1. Introduction

debbie tucker green is the leading black British woman playwright of the first decade of the twenty-first century. She made her main London debut in 2003 when *dirty butterfly* was staged at the Soho Theatre in February, and critically received as a 'promisingly forthright piece of work' (Shore, *Time Out*, 5 March 2003)[1] that signalled her as 'decidedly a talent to watch' (Marlowe, *What's On*, 5 March 2003).[2] A production of *born bad* (2003) followed soon after in April at the Hampstead Theatre, winning her the Laurence Olivier Award for Most Promising Newcomer, and Kate Bassett's acknowledgement as 'one of the most assured and extraordinary new voices we've heard in a long while' (Bassett, *Independent on Sunday*, 11 May 2003). Regular productions of tucker green's plays have since been staged at London's eminent theatre venues. *stoning mary* (2005) and *random* (2008) premiered at the Royal Court Theatre Downstairs, the Royal Shakespeare Company commissioned *trade* (2005) as part of its new work season at the Swan in Stratford-upon-Avon before transferring to London's Soho Theatre, and a vibrant production of *generations* (2005) and a revival of *dirty butterfly* were produced at the Young Vic in 2007.[3]

tucker green's place within the milieu of early twenty-first-century British playwrights is secured by the critical attention and acclaim that is paid to her work as a legacy of in-yer-face theatre.[4] Her portrayal of difficult subjects, concern with 'dislocation [. . .] alienation [. . . and] nihilistic despair'[5] and careful attention to theatrical form and language are likened to Sarah Kane and a host of other well-respected European and American playwrights including Caryl Churchill, Samuel Beckett, Henrik Ibsen, David Mamet and Harold Pinter. However, it

190

is also imperative to situate her within black literary and performance traditions, particularly as she cites her main influences as coming from black playwright and poet Ntozake Shange, Jamaican poet Louise Bennett and the 'urban' music of singers such as Lauryn Hill and Jill Scott. tucker green describes her plays as starting from 'a voice in her head that won't go away, and grow into scraps of writing that she then fits together'[6] (Gardner, *Guardian*, 30 March 2005), an organic fluidity that underpins a style of writing that collapses the boundaries between music, poetry and theatre. As she explains to Lyn Gardner, 'I never set out to write plays [. . .] I was just messing about writing stuff down [. . .] I didn't know whether it was a poem, the lyrics to a song or a play. It is all much of a muchness to me. It's all words, ain't it?'[7]

This chapter explores how three of tucker green's plays (*dirty butterfly*, *stoning mary* and *random*) provide new directions for a politicized black British playwriting practice that experiments with form to provoke audience consciousness about some of the atrocities of contemporary life. Linguistic experimentation and a distinctive use of theatrical form underpin provocative dramatizations of the impact of disturbingly traumatic and violent situations in the world today. This chapter also aims to respond to the two main repeated criticisms of tucker green's work, first that her plays would work better as radio dramas than staged pieces, and secondly, that the careful attention to style pretentiously displays her own writing virtuosity in a way that outweighs the engagement with the issues at the heart of each play. I argue for the importance of tucker green's work as theatre plays that bring audiences together in a shared space as witnesses to the effects of trauma, violence and loss and raise important questions about human rights.

The 2000s was a breakthrough decade in which black British playwrights achieved an unprecedented mainstream presence and were recognized as writing 'state-of-the-nation' plays. The West End transfer of Kwame Kwei-Armah's *Elmina's Kitchen* (National Theatre, 2003) to the Garrick Theatre in 2005 marks a key moment in the recognition of the wider appeal of black British plays to predominately white, middle-class, theatre-going audiences, while continuing to hold the promise of attracting new (young, black, working class) audiences to the theatre.

191

The increased visibility of black theatre during the 2000s resulted partly from Arts Council policies and initiatives, such as the Eclipse conference and subsequent report, the Sustained Theatre initiative and the Decibel project, which aimed to address continued institutional racism and enhance cultural diversity in the British theatre sector.[8] However, it is also imperative to see the rising profile of early twenty-first-century black British playwrights as a reflection of their increasing engagement with some of the urgent topical social issues of the times, particularly those relating to urban teenage violence, which expanded the concerns with identity and diaspora of their 1980s and 1990s predecessors.

debbie tucker green's playwriting is easily comparable to contemporary British new writing traditions, but remains unique within a black British theatrical context in bucking the trend for socially realist plays about black masculinity in crisis that made a resurgence during the 2000s.[9] She does not foreground identity politics or concerns with the intersection of race, class and ethnicity in a diversifying Britain, instead focusing on a range of local and global issues, including domestic violence, incest, female sex tourism, poverty in the developing world, AIDS, genocide, child soldiers, death by stoning, urban violence and teenage knife murder. A particular trope of her writing is a concern with highlighting how selfish individualism, apathy and inaction are complicit in continued violence and trauma.

tucker green keeps her age, background and details of her life private and does not make explicit links between her race, gender and playwriting. However, although she has not identified her work as feminist, the breakdown of naturalist form in stories that prioritize women's experiences present alternatives to the predominantly male discourse of black playwriting in the 2000s. Unlike the prominent black male dramatists of this era, such as Roy Williams and Kwame Kwei-Armah, her plays foreground female perspectives on trauma, violence and abuse, while at the same time questioning some of the limits of contemporary feminism. Although men are often depicted as the perpetrators of abuse in her plays (a man domestically abuses his partner in *dirty butterfly*, and a father sexually abuses his 'dawta' in *born bad*), tucker green seems to be more concerned with examining how a lack of solidarity between women is complicit in allowing these instances to continue. *dirty butterfly* depicts two neighbours who do nothing to intervene on hearing a third being domestically abused, and culminates in a showdown in which the victim takes her female neighbour to task for refusing to help. Similarly, in *born bad* tucker green was interested in 'betrayal, in women betraying women'[10] and she shows the fallout as female family members (Mum, Sister 1 and Sister 2) are confronted for being complicit in Dad's incestuous abuse of his Dawta by ignoring what was happening to protect their own position in the family. An Older Sister avoids dealing with the fact that her younger sibling is about to be stoned to death for murder in *stoning mary*, and on hearing that she received only 12 of the 6,000 signatures needed on a petition to earn a reprieve the Younger Sister verbally rebukes the various communities of women who failed to rally to her cause. An exploration of female sex tourism in the Caribbean in *trade* depicts a lack of solidarity between three women who argue over the permutations of their sexual relations with the same man.[11] *random* shows how a Mum and Sister's immediate grief on receiving the news that their teenage Brother/Son has been stabbed to death results in feelings of isolation and distance from each other.

tucker green's unique contribution to styles of black British theatre lies in her formal experimentation with rhythm and language as a way of breaking away from black playwrights' usual concerns with identity politics depicted through social realism. She resists the authority of the English language by rejecting the use of upper-case characters to spell her own name and the titles of her plays, further disrupting conventions of form by writing sparse, phonetic and rhythmic dialogue that is simultaneously stylized and yet eminently realistic in capturing the sound of how people really speak through overlapping speech and often fragmented and incomplete sentences. In response to Aleks Sierz's description of her writing style as obsessive she says 'That's how people speak [. . .] Listen to a group of kids: just repeat and repeat and repeat'.[12] Musical influences are apparent in the distinctive use of poetic dialogue where the rhythm is punctuated by beats, pauses and active silences (where character names are listed without speech) and repetition is used as a key dramatic strategy that circles around an argument to gradually reveal the issue at the heart of the dramatic conflict. Director Sacha Wares has directed three of tucker green's plays, and describes how the rehearsal process for *random* was attentive to the instructions in the writing. She sees the language and punctuation as a code where everything is deliberately placed for the actors to decode the rhythm of the speech in order to create the impact of emotion in the plays.[13] Full stops, commas, hyphens, slashes, ellipsis, brackets and italics, all indicate something about the rhythm of the text and the meaning these create for the characters, whether it is a rapid speech, a moment of interruption and overlap, emphasizing a particular word, sarcasm, a long pause, a short momentary pause and so on. Wares states,

> All of this is a bit like musical notation – instructions on the page that tell the performer when to pause, when to slow down, when to speed up, what to give an accent and so on. It's quite technical – but the performer's job is to follow the writer's instructions and to discover for themselves the emotional or psychological reasons behind the rhythm changes.[14]

Further nuances are added to the carefully arranged dialogue, which is fleshed-out by actors who fill '*beats*' and '*active silences*' with gestures and looks that bring the characters and the stories to life.

2. *dirty butterfly*

dirty butterfly was first produced at the Soho Theatre on 26 February 2003, directed by Rufus Norris, announcing tucker green's arrival on the London theatre scene and introducing standards of style and content that have remained central to her oeuvre – a concern with the unpleasant sides of human behaviour, dysfunctional relationships and complex interpersonal dynamics. *dirty butterfly* is one of two tucker green plays to deal with personal, domestic and sexual abuse, marking out new terrain within black British (women's) theatre by tackling the issue of domestic violence without making race an explicit aspect of the story. The play examines how the lives of three neighbours have become interwoven by a case of repeated domestic abuse. A white

194

woman, Jo, is routinely subjected to beatings and sexual violence from her husband, but he is not seen in the play, which focuses on the effect that the situation is having on the interpersonal dynamics between her and her two black neighbours, Amelia and Jason, who overhear what is happening but do nothing to intervene. Although the race of each character is specified, their racial and cultural identity is not a focus of the play, which explores their subjective responses to witnessing abuse. Amelia is more concerned about the impact of noise on her own life, while Jason stays in to listen and appears to be secretly aroused. Robert Shore cynically sums up that such a portrayal might problematically tempt spectators to conclude that '[t]here's no such thing as sisterhood and all men get off on violence' (Shore, *Time Out*, 5 March 2003).

The first section of *dirty butterfly* is a three-way scene in which internal monologues and dialogues between the characters are used to dissect the implications of the nightly happenings as 'each of the three tries to retain his or her dignity in the face of half-articulated accusations that they collude in this abusive relationship by doing nothing to stop it' (Shuttleworth, *Financial Times*, 4 March 2003). The writing is left open for decisions to be made about 'who is talking to who and when, with varying implications for the characters'.[15] Such decisions can determine whether audiences see Jason and Amelia as a couple or exes, living separately or in the same house, place a greater emphasis on Jason's sexual voyeurism or on his fear and on Amelia as either 'frighteningly hard-nosed or maybe deeply frightened' (Bassett, *Independent on Sunday*, 16 March 2003). tucker green's trademark rhythmic and poetical dialogue of overlapping and fragmented speech establishes a shifting power dynamic that circles around a discussion of how they are each affected by the abuse. Amelia blames Jo for sleepless nights and takes desperate measures to avoid being disturbed – playing her music loudly, sleeping downstairs on the living room sofa, washing and brushing her teeth in the downstairs sink and leaving home for work earlier than she needs to so she has left in the mornings before Jo awakes and another day of violence is set in motion. Amelia does not want to hear, so she will not feel bad, and argues that Jo should remain quiet in the face of mistreatment. She refuses to understand why Jo remains in an abusive relationship and does not leave her tormentor, but she is most upset by the feeling that her relationship with Jason has been disrupted because he would rather stay in to voyeuristically listen to the events in Jo's flat than spend time with her. Amelia feels that Jason is neglecting his relationship with her, and she is envious of the attention that he is giving Jo. Amelia lacks the understanding that we might associate with solidarity between women that could help to counter violence against women, raising the typical objections that allow the abuse of women to go unchecked, such as blaming the woman herself for the abuse and condemning Jo for hitting back.

> **Amelia** *You* made it extra – see! You make it different, Jo, you let it get worse'n what it needs to be. You wanna hit back you make sure you win. You wanna play contender – you stay in the ring.[16]

tucker green does not show actual instances of violence in her plays, focusing instead on the impact of the traumatic and disturbing situations on her characters. Butterflies in Jo's stomach are not an anticipation of excitement, but rather represent a foreboding feeling that today will be her last. Her fear is evocatively captured in an account of being desperate to 'piss' first thing in the morning, but being too scared to move in case she wakes the tormentor lying next to her. Jason finishes Jo's sentences in this account, sharing the telling of her story of trying to sneak out of bed in a way that illustrates the extent to which his existence has become intertwined with hers.

> **Jo** you ever wanted – to piss?
>
> [. . .]
>
> Hold it in for the longest time convincin yourself you don't really wanna – butcha got no choice an/ haveta –
>
> [. . .]
>
> Haveta go before it makes its own route outta me body.
>
> [. . .]
>
> know I shouldn't go but I have to get up to – this mornin/ I have to

196

[. . .]

And I look beside me to/ check –

[. . .]

I sneak a peep, shift a touch, ease up –

Jason   from under.

Jo   Ease out

Jason   from beside him

Jo   and creep out

Jason   of their bed.[17]

Jo's account establishes 'pissing oneself' as a fear response, highlighting her disempowerment and limited capacity to do an everyday action that most people would not think twice about. Thus, Jason's later description of wetting himself might also be read as an indication of his fear of being too scared to move, an anxiety that is underlined by his increasingly stammered speech.

Jason   You ever pissed yourself and not known it.

You ever had to piss and not know it, done it and not realised and f-f-found out too late.

[. . .]

I'd never pissed like that till t-t . . . today.[18]

tucker green critiques a culture in which a lack of community ethics, social responsibility or direct action allows unacceptable situations of violence and harassment to continue. The dynamic between Jo, Jason and Amelia on the one hand highlights just how closely they are living to each other and yet how individualized and distant they are in terms of fulfilling any neighbourly responsibility. tucker green's stage direction that 'the audience should surround the actors'[19] adds a further claustrophobic element that traps the characters in their troubling dynamic, while bringing spectators in close as complicit witnesses. As

Peacock observes, this device is a way of 'conveying immediacy by not establishing a realistic location for the first scene'.[20] The Soho Theatre production accentuated their isolation and disconnection from each other by perching them precariously at different heights on a steeply sloping roof, and the Young Vic revival underlined their verbal jousting by staging the first scene on a raised square stage that was reminiscent of a boxing ring.

The consequences of inaction are made apparent in a naturalistic epilogue in which Jo turns up at a café where Amelia works as a cleaner with blood dripping from between her legs. But Amelia remains angry with Jo and is more concerned about the mess that the blood is making on her pristinely cleaned floor than with helping someone potentially bleeding to death in front of her, which is part of a recurring dynamic in which Amelia refuses to help Jo:

Amelia   look what you're doin – where you're drippin – look at my floor!

Jo   Look at me.

Amelia   No.

Jo   Look at me.

Amelia   Wha' for?

Jo   Look what he/done –

Amelia   why? Jo?

Jo   Let me show you *Amelia* –

[. . .]

Amelia   I don't wanna see. I don't need to see. I don't have to see – you. Yeh.
So no.[21]

The café scene brings *dirty butterfly* within visceral in-yer-face traditions that demand attention through shock tactics and explicit displays of offensive or troubling vulgarities designed to push audiences out of their comfort zones and question moral norms. Kate Bassett's reflection 'I left this play feeling, emotionally, as if I'd been punched in the throat' (Bassett, *Independent on Sunday*, 16 March 2003) echoes Sierz's original coinage of in-yer-face theatre as a genre that 'takes the audience by the scruff of the neck and shakes it until it gets the message'.[22]

dirty butterfly presents an alternative to dramas and films that focus on the healing and survival of abuse victims, raising a number of moral questions about domestic abuse. Jo is a difficult character who resists empathy, and although audiences may well be troubled by the unacceptable violence and her neighbour's lack of help, they also see her selfishness towards them and the inherent frustration of close modern living as her life impinges on theirs. Ian Shuttleworth points out that Jo is 'clearly the victim and yet paradoxically defiant' (Shuttleworth, *Financial Times*, 4 March 2003). She is aggressive, belligerent, obnoxious and antagonistic towards her neighbours, reprimanding and belittling Jason for his obsessive listening, while seemingly enjoying his attentions and the jealousy his actions induce in Amelia, thus herself somehow complicit in fostering the situation. Robert Shore welcomes the fact that Jo 'does not behave as sympathetic victims in well-meaning socially conscious drama are wont to do', claiming 'it's curiously reassuring that plays about "real people" and "real issues" don't always have to be upbeat or too obviously well meaning' (Shore, *Time Out*, 5 March 2003). Sam Marlowe also finds Jo 'a refreshingly unsympathetic figure, who refuses to accept her victim status even when she's vomiting up blood in front of [. . . a] horrified Amelia' (Marlowe, *What's On*, 5 March 2003).

tucker green's complex portrayal of the characters' responses to Jo's situation contributes to debates about attitudes and assumptions about domestic violence, but critics' opinions were divided, with many claiming that the stylistic elements undermined the play's provocative potential about the issues raised. Dominic Cavendish complains that 'their Ali G-style patois [. . .] teeters the weighty subject matter on the brink of ridiculousness' (Cavendish, *Daily Telegraph*, 4 March 2003) and Robert Shore felt 'The poetic-demotic language can become a bit mannered, and there are some rather overheated passages [. . .] that, despite the seriousness of the subject matter, invite parody'

199

(Shore, *Time Out*, 5 March 2003). Ian Johns also suggests that 'her mannered poetic-demotic style risks making the audience feel equally disconnected with what's happening on stage' (Johns, *The Times*, 6 March 2003). Such criticisms that style overweighs substance recur in reviews of tucker green's plays, but, as Deirdre Osborne argues, these comments reflect how (predominantly white male) critics are measuring in relation to a range of assumptions about standards of 'good theatre' and 'thus ignoring the emotional throb that this pared down language pounds out in delivery'.[23] tucker green's stylistic flourishes are fundamental to her innovative stamp on models of contemporary (black) British playwriting that 'uncompromisingly jar (both in content and rhythm) against the familiarity of social realism'.[24] Thus, although audiences do not witness the actual domestic abuse in *dirty butterfly*, they are left with an overwhelming sense of feeling its effect.

3. *stoning mary*

stoning mary was first produced at the Royal Court Jerwood Theatre Downstairs on 1 April 2005, directed by Marianne Elliot, making tucker green the first black British woman playwright to have a play première on the main stage at London's key new writing venue. The production furthers tucker green's experiments with theatre realism by casting white British actors to perform three interconnecting stories that are usually associated with black people in various parts of Sub-Saharan Africa – 'The AIDS Genocide. The Prescription', 'The Child Soldier' and 'Stoning Mary'. The play shifts rapidly between the three scenes, each accompanied by a bright white projected scene title that provides 'a headline you cannot look away from' (Segal, *Sunday Times*, 10 April 2005), and the links between the narratives becomes clearer as the stories unfold. A Husband and Wife are arguing about which one of them should have the single prescription that they can afford for AIDS medication, a Mum and Dad bicker about the memory of their son who has been taken away to become a threatening Child Soldier, and Younger Sister (the eponymous Mary) is in a corrections institution awaiting death by stoning for the revenge murder of the Child Soldier who killed her parents (the AIDS couple).

Audience expectations about these issues as reported in the British news media are unsettled by the stage directions that 'The play is set in the country it is performed in. All characters are white'.[25] It is tucker green's contention that not enough is being done to address these issues, and the use of white actors is a particular strategy to challenge the usual perspectives and invite audiences to consider how they might feel if these things were happening to white people in their own country. tucker green is thus echoing then Prime Minister Tony Blair's speech to the World Economic Forum in January 2005 in which he states 'If what was happening in Africa today was happening in any other part of the world, there would be such a scandal and clamour that governments would be falling over themselves to act in response' (27 January 2005). In a rare interview with tucker green published in the Royal Court production's education pack for *stoning mary* she explains her intentions for the play:

There are certain things that are happening in the world and I'm intrigued by what isn't being talked about, what falls out of the news, what isn't in the news. [. . .] It seems a bit blatant to me that some things are off the radar, there's an invisible news agenda. [. . .] I'm not going to dictate what the audience should think, but the play is flipped for a reason, the people are white for a reason, it's set over here for a reason. I'm just asking 'what if'?[26]

The use of white actors unsettles familiar associations with these stories as specifically African issues by situating them within the context of a wider/(global) world and asking audiences to consider what they might do if these things were happening here. The labelling of white characters by their function (Older Sister, Younger Sister, Mum, Dad, Husband, Wife, Corrections Officer, Wife Ego and so on) and the typically Christian name 'Mary' underlines a 'universalizing' characteristic that implicates us all. D. Keith Peacock likens tucker green's aim to

> a Brechtian *Verfremdungseffeckt* (alienation effect) through which the audience experience the characters and their concerns from a viewpoint other than that prescribed by the British media. The intention is not to distance the audience, but by altering their perspective and thereby forcing them to read the situations portrayed in terms of their own environment, to generate empathy.[27]

According to Peacock, the alienation effect is enhanced by the use of ego characters wherein four actors simultaneously play the roles of Husband and Wife and their respective egos who describe inner thoughts and motivations (and again in a later scene between Older Sister and Boyfriend, which repeats the same AIDS medication conflict). The egos draw attention to body language and other tactics that are used to avoid dealing with a situation, or to assert power over another, laying bare the nuances of the relationship dynamic in the unfolding argument between Husband and Wife. Given tucker green's concern that not enough is being done to address these urgent African issues, the egos might also be read as a way of prodding audience consciences by highlighting defence mechanisms, and diversionary or defiant behaviours used to avoid signing petitions or to 'stalk past charity collectors in the street before they can catch your eye' (Victoria Segal, *Sunday Times*, 10 April 2005).

Husband Ego   Eyes to the skies it.

[. . .]

She eyes to the skies it – focus on the floors it

[. . .]

Wife Ego   Shows me his hands

[. . .]

Husband Ego Hands in pocket

[. . .]

Wife Ego Hands in pocket then –

[. . .]

hands in pockets doing defiant – doin defiant badly.[28]

Each of the three stories depicts characters avoiding dealing with (or responding insensitively to) an urgent matter, and audiences have to read between the lines to see how the dynamics of the characters' interpersonal relationships are metaphors for how avoidance amounts to complicity in global violence. A Husband and Wife refuse to concede the prescription, each pointing out how their own survival should be valued over the other's. When Older Sister visits Younger Sister in prison, she initially avoids discussing the imminent death sentence by criticizing the heavy-rimmed prescription glasses that her sibling has been issued with and complaining about being called to visit. A Mum and Dad argue about who their son loved most, recalling fond memories of his innocence, of playing and laughing with him before he was kidnapped to become a child soldier who Mum then feared on his brief return home. But his absence reveals holes in an antagonistic relationship in which Dad expresses his grief through angry recriminations towards the woman he blames for losing their son. Dad attacks Mum by likening the smell of her perfume to a smothering love of their son.

> Dad he did – he smelt of you – [. . .] there was no smell of him left – he had no smell of his own [. . .] the only linger left on him was *yourn* – was from *you*.
>
> The smell of whatever you smothered
>
> yourself with – of whatever you
>
> drowned yourself in.
>
> [. . .]
>
> The smell of your not-quite-right.
>
> The smell of the didn't-cost-much.

203

The smell of the two-for-one.

The smell a the been-on-a-bit-too-long –

[. . .]

the smell a the nuthin-natural-about-it,

the nuthin-nice-about-it. He smelt like

that – [29]

stoning mary epitomizes how tucker green portrays difficult domestic and family relationships and dynamics to highlight wider concerns about the repercussions of ignoring important global issues. Older Sister appears to be insensitive towards the urgency of her younger sibling's situation, and although a moral question surrounds Mary's decision to seek retribution for her parents' murder, the sight of the slightly built actress anxious about whether she will be saved from a brutal death herself provokes empathy. Younger Sister defiantly defends her murder of the Child Soldier by stating 'Least I done somethin. I done somethin – / I did'[30] and on hearing the news that only 12 people (of the 6,000 needed) signed a petition that could earn her a reprieve from the death penalty she launches an almost two-page long, angry, yet eloquent, verbal attack against the 'bitches' (women) that failed to intervene on her behalf:

So what happened to the womanist bitches?

. . . The feminist bitches?

. . . The professional bitches.

What happened to them?

What about the burn their bra bitches?

[. . .] The black [. . .] white [. . .] brown [. . .] underclass [. . .] overclass [. . .] political [. . .] bitches that love to march [. . .] study [. . .] debate [. . .] curse [. . .] the educated bitches [. . .] that can read [. . .] count [. . .] Pretty bitches.[31]

The diversity of women's communities named in this rant suggests a fragmented and individualistic society that limits intervention and communal activism, and is particularly critical of the lack of feminist unity and sisterhood. When viewed in the context of a Royal Court production, using white actors, Younger Sister's speech might also be said to implicitly carry a broader message to white middle-class audiences about Western culpability in African devastation, paramount in the British public's complacency towards political intervention to aid the crises. Spectators were implicated further by removing the seating from the front stalls of the downstairs theatre and placing some audience members to stand around the front of the stage, as though witnesses to the public stoning and thus raising the possibility that they could intervene to stop it. Older Sister breaks her promise to attend her younger sibling's stoning, and as 'MUM *picks up her first stone*',[32] audiences are left with a final example of a lack of solidarity between women as the lights fade at the end of the play.

stoning mary comes from tucker green's personal disillusionment about Western complacency (and thus culpability) towards developing world crises. Aleks Sierz describes the play as 'a passionate political outburst' and commends tucker green's use of poetic language, which 'describes the chilling reality of barbarism with a text that sings off the page'. However, Sierz's view that 'this is the most cutting-edge new writing experience in London' (Sierz, *What's On*, 13 April 2005) is not shared by the many other critics who felt that the form detracted from the seriousness of the issues under consideration. Ian Johns states, 'It's a neat chic style but feels at odds with the horror and desperation of the stories before us', and concludes that 'The style and staging of *Stoning Mary* ultimately makes its concerns easier, not harder, to ignore' (Johns, *The Times*, 7 April 2005). Charles Spencer states 'It is undoubtedly a jolt to hear such issues debated by white actors in estuary English', but complains that he 'tired of Green's showy stylistic flourishes. [. . .] The effect is of a writer drawing attention to her own virtuosity rather than her subject' (Spencer, *Daily Telegraph*, 7 April 2005). Ultz's set design supports the non-specific location by placing the actors on an empty horseshoe shaped expanse covered in blue clay with stones around the edges, but some critics complained that the design distanced the actors and prevented emotional engagement with the play. Michael Billington's complaint that 'it still feels more like an acted poem than a fleshed-out play [. . .] because the action appears to happen in some abstract no-man's land' (Billington, *Guardian*, 6 April 2005) and Quentin Letts' observation that props, scenery and 'a few stage reminders of modern Britain [. . .] would have made the play less inaccessible and elite, and might have accentuated Tucker Green's central point' (*Daily Mail*, 6 April 2005) are further indications of how expectations of social realism continue to govern the reception of contemporary British theatre.

4. *random*

random was first produced at the Royal Court Jerwood Theatre Downstairs on 7 March 2008, directed by Sacha Wares, and revived as part of the Royal Court's 'Theatre Local' season of plays in a disused shop in the Elephant and Castle Shopping Centre in March 2010. The original production must be seen in the context of the sharp rise in the number of teenagers being stabbed to death in London during 2007 and 2008, which became an issue of concern to the national government and was regularly reported in the news.[33] *random* is a poignant response to the issue of teenage murder, which narrates an ordinary day in the life of a black family – Sister, Brother, Mum, Dad – that becomes tragic when they receive the news that their Brother has been randomly stabbed to death on the street in a random altercation during his school lunch hour. By not showing the stabbing itself or focusing on its causes, tucker green departs from black playwriting conventions that focus on the (mostly male) victims and perpetrators of urban teenage violence and explicitly show disturbing images of violence on stage.[34] Instead, *random* focuses on (black) female perspectives of the impact of knife crime, resonating with tucker green's primary concern with the effect of traumatic and violent occurrences rather than their causes. Audiences familiar with the many prominent media reports of teenage murder are given an alternative insight into one family's immediate response and grief at the loss of their youngest member and are forced to witness the impact close up as Sister narrates precisely how the day unfolds. Claire Allfree's review highlights that tucker green 'makes no concessions to the liberal conscience eager to understand black teenage violence. Her interest is in giving voice to the people left behind' (Allfree, *Metro*, 12 March 2008).

tucker green foregrounds a black family's experience in *random*, while at the same time deploying a number of theatrical strategies to render the tale wider than the specifics of 'black' experience. The story is told as a monologue performed by one black actress who plays the four main family roles and other minor parts as Brother's teacher and Sister's work colleagues. Using generic character titles rather than culturally specific names that would locate them within a particular social context adds a 'universal' quality that moves beyond a purely racialized appreciation of the play. Sister is the main narrator, who opens and ends the play, thus all of the other characters might be seen as refracted through her perspective, each signalled by an individual accent and speech rhythm – Mum's warm Caribbean lilt, Brother's laid back tones and Dad's monosyllables capturing the soft personality of 'the kinda dad who . . ./ don't say much./ Unless he have to'.[35] The virtuosity of actress Nadine Marshall (and Seroca Davis in the 2010 revival) is highlighted as she stands almost still in a harsh white spotlight on a completely bare Royal Court stage, wearing an ordinary tracksuit top and jeans and addressing the audience as though they have come into her home.[36] Character changes are marked with subtle shifts in body stance, accent and rhythm, and the lack of a realistic set enables fluid transitions to imagine the different settings in which the play occurs – bedrooms, kitchen and the front room of the family home, Sister's office, the street, the classroom, the back of a police car, the police morgue and the street shrine.

The narrative structure moves from humour to pathos, underlining tucker green's focus on the effect of trauma, violence and loss. The day starts off with humorous observations of the routines of a normal family day as Sister wakes up in a bad mood, listens to the 'Birds bitchin their birdsong outside',[37] wonders why her boyfriend has not been in touch and argues with her Brother when he refuses to lend her his mobile. In contrast, Brother takes an extra five minutes in bed to enjoy the sounds of the 'Birds sweetin their birdsong outside'.[38] Mum burns the porridge, and worries about whether her children have eaten enough breakfast and are wearing enough clothes for the weather –

'still tink bein young – is bein invincible'.[39] Sister leaves to attend an office job that she resents, Brother arrives at school late and Mum settles down to watch daytime television. But the 'banal normality' (Sierz, *Tribune*, 21 March 2008) of their morning is shattered when the police arrive on the doorstep with the news that Brother has been murdered. Thereafter, the mood changes as the second half of the play takes audiences into the less familiar terrain of post-murder routines. tucker green homes in on female perspectives as Dad becomes even quieter in the second part of the play and we witness Sister and Mum trying to come to terms with their loss – the unfamiliarity of Victim Support Officers consoling a shell-shocked Mum, Sister viewing the body in the police morgue and her opinion of shared public mourning as friends and acquaintances lay flowers at the make-shift street shrine erected where her Brother was killed.

The humorous account of the family's morning is replaced with disdain for the police whose invasion is epitomized by wearing their 'Dark boots and heavy shoes'[40] into mum's pristine front room and offering the family cups of tea in their own home, for the media brigade of 'blue-eyed reporters/shieldin their zeal/for a – 'good', 'urban' story'[41] and for the silent witnesses who respectfully grieve quietly for Brother in public, yet refuse to come forward and speak out about what they saw.

> Whole heap a witness
> Polices say.
> Whole heap a somebodies
> on street.
> Saw.
> Whole heap a peeps
> on road
> was present.
> But I lissen –
> hard –
> an' still I hear . . .

(*Silence.*)

Silence shoutin the loudest.

Cos it seem that

now no one wanna witness

what happened

to my Brother.[42]

Marissia Fragkou argues that tucker green's concern with fragmented communities 'invites the audience to consider issues of vulnerability, collective responsibility and dependency'.[43] The narrative arc accentuates these themes by creating an overwhelming sense of grief for a young human life needlessly cut short. Unlike Kwei-Armah's *Elmina's Kitchen* (2003) or Williams' *Little Sweet Thing* (2005) where audiences watch the story build towards a tragic denouement in which a teenager is killed, the murder in *random* occurs in the middle of the play and audiences are made to endure its aftermath. The murder itself is not shown, but its brutality is made explicit in Sister's description of Brother's body in the morgue, his face and arms covered in slashes, a missing eye, and the smallest 'killer cut'[44] barely visible in his back. Paul Taylor notes 'the delighted laughter of recognition' (Taylor, *Independent*, 12 March 2008) of young audiences to the close-knit family's morning routine, which gave way to a stunned silence as the reality of Brother's plight became clear. Charles Spencer recognizes that 'the writing seemed to penetrate the very heart of grief' (Spencer, *The Daily Telegraph*, 12 March 2008), and Aleks Sierz commends tucker green for 'dar[ing] to give us a brief glimpse of the emotional truth behind the depressingly familiar headlines about knife crime' (Sierz, *Tribune*, 21 March 2008).

Although some critics found the West Indian accents 'hard for a white-middle class ear to follow' and were uncomfortable with 'a couple of lines which are pretty sharply prejudicial about white people' (Letts, *Daily Mail*, 11 March 2008), the play was generally well received and their comments highlight how tucker green's focus on the family's grief generates empathy in audience members irrespective of their own race, class or gender. Aleks Sierz draws a commonality between the audience and the grieving family when he states that 'Although the family is black and the parents have been written as if they were migrants rather than British born, it is interesting that their grieving is so typically English. Heads down, and made dumb by shock and despair, both Mum and Dad prefer silence and solitude to cussing and company' (Sierz, *Tribune*, 21 March 2008). While we might wonder about Sierz' underlying assumption that black British people would express their grief any differently from 'English' people, his statement also highlights how tucker green emphasizes the experience of grief as a 'universal' response to loss.

Furthermore, the use of a singular black actress playing multiple roles across race, age and gender infers a wider focus on an ordinary or 'universal' British family that accentuates the issue as a teenage concern rather than a specifically black one. Joe Kelleher's analysis, for example, demonstrates that the family's helplessness 'appear[s] to put the politics of the situation outside the reach of those most affected by it and with the greatest interest in doing something about it',[45] while pinpointing how political messages in the play are heightened by the 'ordinariness' of the actress on a bare stage, in 'ordinary' clothes, addressing an 'ordinary' audience as though they were her invited friends brought together to listen to her testimony.

tucker green counters stereotypical perceptions of black fathers as either absent or feckless by presenting Dad as a firm but kind and fundamentally important member of the 'universal' nuclear family who takes control when the police visit and identifies Brother's body. Several moments in the play also challenge the predominant media portrayals of young black masculinity and 'black on black' violence, unsettling controversial views such as then Prime Minister Tony Blair's that 'the spate of knife and gun murders in London was not being caused by poverty, but a distinctive black culture . . . the recent violence should not be treated as part of a general crime wave, but as specific to black youth'.[46] Blair claimed in a widely-reported speech, 'We won't stop this by pretending it isn't young black kids doing it'.[47] Brother is killed during his school lunch hour, not while skipping lessons, and he is portrayed as an innocent victim of a random assault and not typically a member of a gang. The revelation that he has been murdered counteracts assumptions that the police have come to the

210

house because he has broken the law, which several reviewers admitted to thinking. Sister's visit to the street shrine highlights alternatives to media portrayals images of urban youth by emphasizing 'Black on Black love'[48] as his school friends pay their respects 'In a heavy silence. / With their – / MP3 wires dangling / their / mobile phones / on silent',[49] and drawing attention to 'a hard-lookin 'hoodie' . . ./ under the cloak of Adidas / is a brotha / whose eyes don't stop flowin. Wet raw with weeping./ But . . . they don't show that bit tho'.[50]

random makes an important intervention into the representation of teenage murder, highlighting 'this cycle of shit'[51] as an all too often experience in contemporary urban communities. Critics observed the appropriateness of *random* playing at the Elephant and Castle Shopping Centre and aiming to reach the young urban audiences about whom the play speaks. However, as much as the transfer signals a success of the Royal Court's outreach endeavours, tucker green's strategic narrative organization reminds audiences that this is a human story of concern to us all. Alone in her deceased Brother's empty room at the end of the play, Sister savours the same 'stink' of his body odour that she had condemned in their early morning encounter, and ponders the arbitrariness of his premature death:

> Random don't happen to everybody.
> So.
> How come
> 'random' haveta happen to him?
> This shit ent fair.[52]

5. Conclusion

debbie tucker green's playwriting exemplifies the use of linguistic and formal experiments as the basis of a politicized playwriting that raises awareness about some of the urgent topical issues of our times. One of the main repeated criticisms of tucker green's plays is that the poetic form and lack of realistic sets or conventional stage action would make them work better on radio rather than as theatre pieces. Michael Billington's review of *stoning mary* states 'Words alone do not make drama: what one craves is a marriage between action and language' (Billington, *Guardian*, 6 April 2005) and several critics felt that the direct address storytelling in *random* would work better as a radio play, or in the more intimate setting of the Royal Court Theatre Upstairs. However, such views ignore the impact that tucker green's plays make by confronting live audiences with troubling aspects of contemporary human life. Part of their effectiveness comes from audiences being together in a shared space as witnesses to the intense emotional effects of violence and loss. Her portrayal of cruelty and indifference towards family and neighbours in crisis imply wider connotations of community responsibility in which live audience members are firmly implicated. The liveness of performance forces audiences to engage and the stylistic aspects encourage them to 'hang on every word' (Gardner, *Guardian*, 21 March 2006). The vivid portrayal of characters and the virtuosity of a solo actress to make seamless transitions between them were lost in the radio broadcast of *random*, and *stoning mary* requires a visual element to endorse the effect of white actors playing 'black' stories. In a live performance, audiences experience the sheer skill required to bring a tucker green play to fruition, where ensemble acting is required to convey the meaning of the carefully arranged words, and make sense of overlaps, interruptions and active silences to achieve an emotional impact.

tucker green's importance as a contemporary political British playwright is manifest in her use of an interconnection between form and content to provoke audience sensibilities about important social issues, while using a style of writing that foregrounds a new approach to tackling issues through theatre that focuses on affect. Rendering her characters' experiences as both specific (e.g. giving a voice to women or black people) and 'universal' (e.g. emotions of grief, fear, loss) is fundamental to her success as a contemporary (black) British playwright. Her 'human stories' articulate some of the urgent and immediate world concerns of the world today.

212

CHAPTER 3
DOCUMENTS

This section of the book presents a series of largely unseen original documents that shed new light on the work of the playwrights featured in this book. They contain unpublished alternative sections of plays, new interviews, letters and emails, writing notes and other materials.

1. Simon Stephens[1]

Patrick and Declan and Trish
In 2010, the Lyric Hammersmith presented *A Thousand Stars Explode in the Sky*, a play Stephens started writing six years earlier with fellow playwrights David Eldridge and Robert Holman, and he credits the experience of working on that play for influencing the shifts in his writing thereafter. In particular, one exercise that the three writers carried out was specifically important in unlocking a new kind of writing.

> One of the things we did very early on was we wrote a series of scenes which were never intended to be connected. Which operated as provocations to one another. We brought them to the workshop to see what we made of these things. And there was a scene I wrote very early on in the workshop, I remember showing it to them and reading it with the actors and it really freaked the fuck out of them all. It really frightened them. It's a genuinely frightening and unsettling scene that I wrote to frighten and unsettle Robert and David. For other reasons as well, but that was certainly one of the agendas in the writing of the scene. And that absolutely sits in the spirit of *Motortown*. If you read that scene

and then read *Motortown* you can see that *Motortown* was born out of that spark. I really enjoyed how much it frightened David and Robert. Especially Robert! I really enjoyed how much it freaked him out and I thought 'fuck, I'm going to do this again!'[2]

This is the scene that he wrote.

* * *

The front room of a flat in Dagenham Essex. Patrick and Declan, two brothers and Trisha their friend have a fourteen year old boy tied to a chair. 'How Deep Is Your Love' by The Bee Gees is playing.

PATRICK   He looks like you.

DECLAN   Fuck off.

PATRICK   I reckon he does. Little monkey eyes. Look at him. Hm Hm Hm Hm Hm. Int he Dec? Int he a monkey? Fucking gibbon.

DECLAN   Pat.

PATRICK   I like this song. All their voices and that. 'It's seventies night at Raquels!'

DECLAN   Patrick.

PATRICK   'Come on girls. Get up on the dance floor. Its time for a slow number. This is the Bee Gees.'

DECLAN   Where did you find him?

Pause.

PATRICK   On the Chase.

DECLAN   How old is he?

PATRICK   I didn't ask him.

DECLAN   He looks about fourteen Patrick.

PATRICK I can never tell anymore.

DECLAN He's a fucking child.

PATRICK You ever get that? If you asked me to guess somebody's age. Nowadays. Seriously. I never have a fucking clue about anything.

DECLAN You can't just get a, take, a fucking, a child and just bring him. Patrick. You can't that's fucking bang out of order. Look at him. He's been fucking crying and everything.

TRISH You seen his skin?

DECLAN What?

TRISH He's got beautiful skin. Look.

They look. The boy watches them.

DECLAN What you gonna do?

PATRICK What?

DECLAN Patrick what are you gonna do with him?

PATRICK I don't know. I think he's quite funny.

DECLAN He stinks.

PATRICK He did a piss. Filthy cunt.

DECLAN You wanna take him back.

PATRICK Fuck off.

DECLAN You do Patrick. I think you need to take him back, seriously.

PATRICK Fuck off Dec. Always going on.

DECLAN I'm serious Patrick.

PATRICK I'n't he? Trish? Always fucking going on. Always fucking giving it. Watch this.

215

Patrick punches the boy hard in the face.
The boy closes his eyes tight. He is shaking.

PATRICK (*nursing his fist*) Ow. That fucking hurt actually. You think he's all right?

DECLAN Patrick.

PATRICK Yeah.

Beat.

What?

Beat.

You want a cup of tea?

DECLAN What?

PATRICK I could fucking murder a cup as it goes. Should we put the kettle on. Trish. Put the kettle on.

TRISH Fuck off.

PATRICK Go on sweetheart.

TRISH Put it on yourself.

PATRICK Fucking listen to it.

DECLAN Patrick.

PATRICK The gob on her.

DECLAN Serious.

PATRICK All right. All right. I'm going. I'm fucking going.

Patrick leaves.

DECLAN That wasn't what I was talking about. The tea.

TRISH He's all right.

DECLAN   Trish. What are we gonna do?

TRISH   be all right.

DECLAN   I think we should take him back.

TRISH   Don't be silly.

DECLAN   I think we should though. Look at him. I'm going to.

TRISH   Declan.

DECLAN   I am. I'm going to. I. Fucksake.

TRISH   Declan don't.

DECLAN   Here. Have you got some fucking. Shit. This is tight.

He tries to remove the gag but can't.
The boy opens his eyes. Watches him. Pleads.

DECLAN   Have you got any scissors?

TRISH   No. I don't.

DECLAN   We should cut it. Get some scissors and cut it.

TRISH   I don't Declan. Seriously I don't think you should touch him.

DECLAN   Look at him.

TRISH   Think about the fingerprints, babes. They'll be all over the place. They'll know it's you.

DECLAN   No.

TRISH   They will Dec. You know they will. And if they identify you, sweetheart, what will they do then? I think I'd go completely mental if you got sent down again.

DECLAN   Trish.

TRISH   Seriously babes, I really think I would.

DECLAN Fuck.

TRISH Declan.

DECLAN Fuck. Fuck. Fuck. Fuck. Fuck.

Patrick comes back with three cups of tea.
The boy stays watching Declan.

PATRICK Here we are. Lovely jubbly.

They drink their tea.

PATRICK You want a fag Dec?

DECLAN Ta.

PATRICK Trish?

TRISH Thank you.

They smoke their cigarettes.

PATRICK You think he'll tell?

DECLAN You what?

PATRICK If we let him loose do you think he'll tell on us.

DECLAN I don't know.

PATRICK I was just thinking about that. I was in there making the, with the, making the tea and I was just thinking what if he fucking goes and tells on us. Eh? What then? What the fuck would we do then? We'd be completely.

DECLAN I don't think he knows us, does he?

PATRICK But he'd recognise us.

DECLAN Not necessarily.

PATRICK He'd recognise the address though.

218

DECLAN   He might not.

PATRICK   He fucking would. I would. If somebody did to me what I did to him I'd definitely recognise the address. I don't know what to do about it. (*Pause.*) We need some more milk. Here.

He puts his fag out on the boy's face.
The boy winces. Shakes. Squeezes his eyes tight in terror.

DECLAN   Patrick stop it.

PATRICK   Fuck off.

DECLAN   I'm fucking warning you.

PATRICK   Don't be silly.

DECLAN   I fucking am. You can't do. You're completely. This is completely.

PATRICK   What?

DECLAN   It –

PATRICK   Completely what, Declan? Are you going to finish one of your sentences or what? It's a bit, fucking, does your fucking. I never know what you're thinking or anything.

He kicks the boy's shins. And then harder, kicks his arms.
Becomes exhausted. Gathers his breath. Notices Declan staring at him.

PATRICK   Remember Gascoyne Estate? You remember that? Living there. That was great that. I used to fucking love it. Used to. (*Pause.*) I'm all sad now. Cause I'm gonna have to kill him probably. To stop him. Telling and that. Aren't I? I fucking am and I really didn't want to. (*Pause. The boy is staring transfixed at Declan.*) Do you really think his skin's beautiful?

TRISH   Yeah.

PATRICK   You're not gonna tell anybody are you?

TRISH   No.

PATRICK   Good girl. (*Slurps his tea.*) Are you Dec?

DECLAN   What?

PATRICK   Are you gonna tell anybody about this?

DECLAN   I don't know. I don't. I.

PATRICK   Come on Dec. You're not, are you? Course you're not. You're my fucking. You're my fucking brother Dec. Eh? I'n't yer? Me and you Dec! Fucking Gascoyne estate? Eh? Fucking hell.

He smiles at him. Ruffles his hair.

You wanna have a go?

DECLAN   What?

PATRICK   I think you should. I think you should have a go.

DECLAN   No.

PATRICK   Give him a kick or summink.

DECLAN   No.

PATRICK   Go on. Just a little nudge. Little rabbit punch. Go on Dec. Go on. Go on Dec. Trish will. Won't yer? Trish? She will.

DECLAN   I think he's lovely.

She stands up. Goes to him. Strokes his cheek.
The boy winces at the touch. He stares at Declan.

TRISH   Feel that.

PATRICK   What?

TRISH   Go on. Feel his cheek, Patrick. Stroke it.

Patrick goes over. Strokes his cheek.
The boy winces. Stares at Declan.

PATRICK   Oh yeah!

TRISH   Soft innit?

PATRICK   It is, yeah.

She kisses it.

PATRICK   Here, Dec. You wanna watch her.

TRISH   Shut up.

PATRICK   You do. She's being right rude.

TRISH   Poor thing. He's only little. He's been crying.

She dries his tears. Kisses his cheek. The boy winces.

TRISH   He looks like Thierry Henry a bit. Don't he?

She lifts her top up and shows him her bra. The boy stares at Declan.

PATRICK   Fucking hell.

She pours her hot tea on him. The boy doesn't respond any more. His eyes are closed. His breathing slows.

DECLAN   Trish!

TRISH   Does feel funny. Doesn't it?

PATRICK   It feels fucking great!

TRISH   I quite like it.

PATRICK   You should try it Dec.

TRISH   You should you know?

PATRICK   Here. Has your phone got a camera.

TRISH   What?

221

PATRICK   We could film it. Put it on the Internet.

DECLAN   Fucking hell.

PATRICK   Couldn't we. Film me kicking him. (*Kicks him hard.*) Bouff. Like that.

The boy doesn't respond.

TRISH   I don't know if it'll work. We could try it.

PATRICK   I might set him on fire. Burn him a bit. Could you film that do you think?

DECLAN   I'm going.

PATRICK   Don't.

DECLAN   I fucking am. This is doing my head in. This is completely fucking horrible.

TRISH   Spoilsport.

The boy starts to smile.

DECLAN   I'm going and I'm going the cops.

PATRICK   You are not.

DECLAN   I fucking am.

TRISH   Dec, don't.

DECLAN   This is completely. You've completely lost it. This is completely insane.

TRISH   It's not really.

DECLAN   I'm. I'm. I'm. I'm.

PATRICK   Nobody'll believe you.

DECLAN   What?

PATRICK   If you go. Tell the cops. They won't believe you. What are you? Some scuz junky cunt. They'll think it's a fucking, just a fucking, just some kind of joke. Won't they? Won't they Dec. Won't they really though eh? They will Dec. I think they will.

Turns and does a spinning kick on the boy in the chest.
The only reaction from the boy is to gather himself and smile.

PATRICK   Hi- Ya!

Singing

I feel you touch me in the morning rain! And the further that you walk away from me I wanna hold you in my arms again. Oh you come to me on a Southern Breeze . . . da da da da da da da da . . . oh it's me who you need to show: how deep is your love?

He bursts out laughing. He doesn't notice that the boy has an almost beatific smile now.

Hey, Dec. If you do go. If you do tell them. I will find you. I'll only do the same to you. I don't care if you are my brother. I don't care about any of that. You know that don't you?

No response.

Dec?

No response.

You do don't you?

No response.

He won't tell. Look at him. How would he tell. Bless him. He's fucking smiling! Look at that! What's he fucking smiling about? Hey! Monkey face! What are you fucking smiling about? Go on then Dec! Away you go! Off you go! Go on Declan! I'll see you yeah! See yer mate. You have a good night, you fucking chickenshit cunt grass. You have one on me yer cunt! Go on!

The two brothers stand looking at each other.

223

Kelly and Edward

The following scene was written in a playwrights' workshop when Stephens was Writing Tutor on the Royal Court's 2004 US tour of *4.48 Psychosis*.

I gave the students a writing exercise, where I ask writers to think of two characters and a location. I have a bag or a box or an envelope and in this envelope is a collection of transitive verbs, normally about a hundred. I go round and each writer has to chose one. This verb dictates the action of the scene. So, for example, their first character has to 'seduce', or 'belittle' or 'inspire' their second. They write this for ten minutes. Then I repeat [the exercise] and the writer continues the scene with a new, random, change of behaviour. They do this for ten minutes, then I repeat [the exercise again].

For some reason, in Columbus, Ohio, I decided to do the exercise myself – I normally don't. Edward and Kelly is the scene I wrote when I pulled out Torture, Interrogate, Impress.

It is surprising to me how much of it remains in that central scene in *Motortown*.[3]

*   *   *

Kelly is fifteen.
She is sat on a chair in the middle of the stage. She is very frightened.
There is a small table to the left of the chair.
Edward is forty-two. He wears a shirt and tie.
There is a door, open, stage right.
Edward points to the small table.

EDWARD   Put your hand there.

KELLY   No.

EDWARD   Put it there.

KELLY   Don't.

EDWARD Kelly. Now.

She puts one hand on the table.

Now keep it there.

KELLY Dad.

EDWARD I'm going to leave the room now. I'm not going to tell you when I'm coming back. But when I come back I want your hand to be there.

KELLY Please don't.

He smiles at her briefly then leaves.
She keeps her hand on the table.
He comes back in with a cigarette.
He lights the cigarette.
He smokes it for a while, watching her.
He puts it out on her hand.
She screams. Starts crying.

EDWARD Don't cry. I said don't cry.

KELLY You're –

EDWARD What? (*No response.*) What Kelly?

KELLY You're horrible. You're being horrible to me.

EDWARD Did I say that you could move your hand?

KELLY No.

EDWARD No, I didn't. I didn't tell you you could move your hand. So why, Kelly, Kelly, look at me, why did you move your hand Kelly?

KELLY Because you burnt me you fucking monster.

He bursts into a giggle. Then stops. Gathers himself.

EDWARD   Take your top off. Kelly. Take your top off. Do it Kelly. Move your hand to take your top off.

She does. She is terrified. Trying to stop herself from sobbing.
He kneels to kiss her chest above her right breast.
He moves away.

It's horrible. You taste horrible.

She shrinks back from him.

Don't put it back on. Don't.

He lights another cigarette.
Smokes two thirds of it grinning.
Holds it to her face.
Pulls it back. Smiles.

Don't cry Kelly. Sweetheart. Baby. You cry all the time.

KELLY   Dad, I want to go now.

EDWARD   I know love. I know you do.

He moves away from her.
There is a long pause.

I don't want you to be my daughter anymore.

A long pause.

KELLY   Well, I am.

EDWARD   I'm sorry?

KELLY   You can't decide. People can't decide.

EDWARD   I see you in the morning. Making your breakfast. Putting blueberries into your yoghurt. And you're maybe drinking an orange juice. Or an Apple and Mango juice. (*Beat.*) Shivering. (*Beat.*) This is what I always dreamt would happen.

KELLY   No.

EDWARD   From when you were about five.

KELLY   No.

He turns back to her. Grins again.

EDWARD   Do you know how many words I can spell? Do you? Kelly? Thousands of words. I can spell thousands of words Kelly. More than anybody I know. Do you know how many press ups I can do? Kelly, look at me. I can do a hundred press ups. Here. Feel my muscles. Kelly. Feel them.

He flexes his bicep.
She refuses to move her arm to touch it.

FEEL MY MUSCLES KELLY!

She does.

They're hard aren't they? Aren't my muscles hard Kelly?

KELLY   Yes.

EDWARD   I know. Here. Watch this!

He moves to the door frame and lifts his weight up on it. Pulls himself up ten times.
Counts every one. Turns back to her.

Isn't that great?!? Not many people can do that Kelly. Not many people can.

She barely dares look at him.

Ask me a question.

No response.

Ask me a question, Kelly. Ask me a question.

KELLY   I don't know any questions.

EDWARD   Capital cities! Ask me a capital cities question Kelly. Go on. Ask me 'What's the capital of . . .?' Kelly. You ask me. 'What's the capital of . . .?' Go on. Kelly.

227

KELLY I don't know.

EDWARD You say 'What's the capital of . . .?' Say that Kelly! Say it! Please!

KELLY 'What's the capital of . . .?'

EDWARD And then you think of a country. Say it again Kelly and think of a country.

KELLY What's the capital of . . .?

EDWARD Go on Kelly.

KELLY Bulgaria?

EDWARD Sofia! See! Sofia!!! How fucking brilliant is that?!? How many men could do that Kelly?!? Not fucking many, that's how many! Not. Fucking. Many!

SHE NEEDS TO BITE BACK MORE.
HE QUIETENS
REALISES THE IMPOSSIBILITY
ASKS HER WHAT THAT MEANS FOR THE BOTH OF
THEM?
SHE DOESN'T KNOW.
THE QUESTION REMAINS UNANSWERED

I Like Gap Jeans

This short play was written for the Royal Court Young Writers' Programme – on which Stephens was a tutor – as part of their contribution to a pop-up anti-globalization theatre event.

There was this one night [in October 2004?] when all the different theatres all over London were given a pod in the Millennium Dome and audiences could go into these theatre pods. The Royal Court commissioned me to write a two minute play and it was my first exploration into political theatre, which is dramatizing political ideas by having characters articulate the antithesis of what I know is the right thing to feel. Which really sits under the writing of Paul in *Motortown*.[4]

* * *

I like Gap jeans. I fucking like Starbucks. I like a blueberry muffin and an iced fucking latte in the morning. I love, I love, I love, there is nothing I love more than my fucking trainers. Walking through the city in my trainers. With their soles so light you could feel like yer flying. And you walk down the river on a morning like this with the sky like that and the sunshine and yer trainers and you feel like you could conquer the world. So don't fucking come here. With your piss-arsed fear about fucking war for oil. I'd like to see you ride yer fucking bike without it. I'd like to see you drive your car. I don't give one fiddler's fuck. I don't give a jap's-eye. I don't give a fucking wank. I like Nescafe Gold Blend. And a Kit Kat.

You're bleeding.

Because at least I could be bothered to get up for fucking work. And at least my fucking ancestors could. And at least we don't fucking shoot each other. And there is no fucking genocide in Hackney. Not like there is out there. And our leaders don't spend my country's money on fucking gold-plated Rolls Royces and prostitutes and Veuve Cliquot and cocaine.

Your eye.

At least there's that. Look out there! Breathe it in! Fucking breathe it in! Gulp it! Look at that! Seven hundred fucking years of not fucking lying on our arse and begging for a fucking favour. Seven hundred years of fucking pushing forward. I'll give you one word. One fucking word. Brunel. Isambard Kingdom Brunel. The Clifton Suspension Bridge. The Manchester Liverpool Railway. I'll give you another one. Big Mac. I like Big Macs. You know why?

In the corner, it's all –

Cause they taste good. For lunch.

It'll get everywhere.

2. Tim Crouch

Notes on An Oak Tree
This document was written for Karl James, Andy Smith and Chris Dorley-Brown prior to a workshop in September 2004 at the National Theatre's Education space (which was a portakabin behind the National on Upper Ground). It reflects a number of conversations with various people, particular Andy Smith, who had a crucial role in helping think through how the 'Second Actor' device would work. It also reflects a lot of research, reading and thinking about hypnotism. Following this workshop, Crouch wrote a draft of An Oak Tree. *I have annotated some of the references in the notes but preserved as far as possible the format and stylistic idiosyncrasies of the original.*

an   oak tree
fears   and   theories
themes   and   fancies

A formless hunch

Peter Brook talks about 'a deep, formless hunch, which is like a smell, a colour, a shadow. . . .'[5]

So, this is my present relationship to an oak tree. And this is where I'll be on Monday morning when we meet.

I welcome your hunches, your questions.

I thought it would be good for all of us if we had some pieces of paper to hold in our hands at the start of the process. So here are some fairly undergraduate thoughts and associations on the subject. They're not particularly ordered and they're not particularly insightful. We're making a piece of theatre, not writing a text book. . . .

As I've said, feel free to bring anything along to encourage the sense of show and tell. I'll try and make sure we have some big paper, pens, a CD player and a video recorder.

Nothing is confirmed about this show other than the funding . . . and I will bring the ACE[6] form along so we can see what we're working with.

As I've said to some, My Arm just happened. This, on the other hand, feels a bit like procreational sex. It's scary – I hope we conceive . . .

I also hope that by the end of Tuesday we will feel a consensus on what we want to do with this piece. A consensus that will guide me into writing.

The story
At present, I have no suggested alteration to the main story of the play as publicized. (repeat, however, that nothing is confirmed . . .)

A man's daughter is accidentally killed by a car. (loss)

The man's response to his loss is to turn a tree next to the site of her death into his daughter. (creation)

The driver of the car is a hypnotist who, since the accident, has been unable to hypnotise. (loss)

The grieving father seeks out the hypnotist and, together, they manage to momentarily re-materialise the girl. (creation)

genius will be in the detail and I don't know the detail of this story. I don't know what the characters will say to each other. I don't know how it starts. I don't know how the girl will be invoked.

but I have a hunch about the story.

This story must contain the play, not vice versa

We must trust the story to do its work. Like My Arm, if nothing else, this is a story. We must test the story to confirm that when it is told simply that it will contain all the other stuff . . . And then we must tell the story simply.

Simple . . .

what might it be about? What is the 'other stuff'?

interrogate the hunch . . .

To present and examine the life of the imagination after monumental loss.

This theme seems full of timeless pre-occupation; accentuated by the current proximity the world seems to have to death and loss.

A metaphor with regard to the relationship of art to calamitous everyday events.

But a story about two men who have no idea they're in a metaphor . . . Two men to whom shit has happened.

Depth, I hope, to be found in considering the hypnotist as artist who, as a consequence of what happens, loses his ability to create.

Also to consider the father as 'artist' who, as a consequence of what happens, has no choice BUT to create. What he does to the tree is an unreflexive human response to an incident.

Neither men are articulate about their larger meaning, but both responses coming from an 'obliteraion of self' – a crisis which has knocked them out of themselves.

'What has happened is that the commonplace has entered the sphere of art . . . physical presence and behaviour have become art . . .' (with reference to the Arte Povera movement – using commonplace materials in its making. A man called Kounellis exhibiting 12 live horses in a gallery in Rome . . .⁷)

which brings us on to . . .

art

'For art to be, the idea of one thing must be given by another thing.' etienne decroux

Is this the North Star for the whole oak tree experience?
The idea of one thing being given by another?

It's there in the act of suggestion; it's there in the glass of water; it's there in the dead girl in the tree.
It's there in a word, an image, a photograph.
It's there in the David Knight Hypnotic Experience.[8]
It's there in the second actor.

If art is a response to something, then most often it is a response to loss. Without 'loss' (however that may be defined) there is no need to 'create' (however that may be defined). In the figure of the father then, there is a clear metaphorical/metaphysical analysis of the human impulse towards art – and, in this instance, conceptual art . . . But the father is unaware; he just responds the way he responds. In a sense the play is testing a notion of art (that the (conceptual) artistic impulse is authenticated in/by reality) – but at no time is it doing so explicitly. All must be inside the story.

The story of two characters with problems to overcome. (Just like The Archers,[9] really . . .)

Two grandmothers meet in a park. One is pushing a pram. 'What a beautiful grandchild,' says one. 'That's nothing,' says the other, reaching for her purse. 'I'll show you her picture!'

why think about art for this story?

What questions are asked by art?

Where is the consolation in art? Can loss be eased by art?

Can a painting be what it depicts?

A lady visited Matisse in his studio. Inspecting one of his latest works she unwisely said: 'But, surely the arm of this woman is much too long.' 'Madame,' the artist politely replied, 'you are mistaken. This is not a woman, this is a picture.'[10]

'Take an object. Do something to it. Do something else to it.' Jasper Johns[11]

'Reality authenticates art, art in turn introduces order and gives a metaphysical dimension to reality.'

Jaroslaw Kozlowski (?)[12]

Art vs Hypnotism

**To see the world in a grain of sand
And a heaven in a wild flower**[13]

Is the art/hypnosis analogy sound? We need to waterproof this idea . . .

What questions are asked by this parallel?

'The gateway to the invisible must be visible.' René Daumal[14]

So something needs to be put in place as a substitute/representative for something else. (This is easier than just 'imagining' from nothing.) A physical support for transubstantiation. For christ's body we have bread; for Craig martin's oak tree we have a glass of water.[15] Communion wafer is as much like flesh as water is to wood . . .

The father uses the tree as the supporting idea of his daughter. If he wants his daughter back, he is as likely to achieve this in the tree as in a photograph. A photograph looks like other photographs. ('a painting announces "I am art because I look like other paintings"'.) Also, a photograph is an analogue of the real. Also, a photograph captures an historical moment. Because the tree does not purport to be his daughter, and it is alive, then it is easier for him to see his daughter in it. This is the act of suggestion.

He could have chosen a cigarette butt by the kerb where she died, a piece of litter. With the tree there is a sense of permanence – it does less and therefore allows him to bring more to it. The flowers wrapped around the tree rapidly become insignificant.

Also, all the father wants to do is to hold his daughter again. He misses her materiality, as everything else about her still exists. He can't hold a memory, a photograph is materially insufficent. The tree, however, is nothing if not MATERIAL.

Materiality is the message . . .

The Hypnotists say:

When the imagination and the will go into conflict, then the imagination always wins.

Examples of skin blistering when the subject is told they are being touched by a hot poker. Imagine attempting to climb a glass of water.

'Hypnotists make members of the audience lose their inhibitions by accessing the creative areas of the brain.'

Stages of stage hypnotism:

1. Belief and Expectancy
2. Disorientation and confusion
3. Suggestion and repetition
4. Relaxation and Sleep

I don't think this is far off from a description of how theatre works – particularly considering that 'sleep' has double meaning – as an hypnotic trance where the subject operates through their subconscious and also, as SLEEP, where the subject is so bored out of their mind that they fall asleep . . . and we've all done that.

The architecture of theatre is conducive to hypnosis – disorientating, sounds, dim lights, etc.

Also, the focus on voice, language, confusion. Things happening without explanation.

All hypnosis is self-hypnosis.

Language

The power and precision of words – able to transport, transform.

Ourselves as products of a dominant linguistic programming . . .

Left or standing, 1971

His precision and accuracy
suggesting clean cuts, leaving
a vacancy, a slight physical
depression as though I had been

in a vaguely uncomfortable place
for a not long but indeterminable
period; not waiting.
Bruce Nauman[16]

Language being central to both theatre and hypnosis.
Using language to represent and organize our experience – to communicate with others.

'Hypnotic WORDS:

The keys to all hypnotic inductions are the Hypnotic WORDS, and the soothing, positive, reassuring manner in which they are executed. They have a specific energy and can be a very powerful influence on people, affecting their truths. Hypnotic WORDS delivered in the right rhythm and tones have an astonishing impact consciously. But when bypassed by the conscious mind, which restricts and edits, they become even more profound in the altered, subconscious state. Since you have been mesmerized through advertising, commercials, social interactions, and other means, negative messages have become imprinted within your subconscious.

Transforming these self-defeating messages is the task of the hypnotist. The objective is to alter, reverse, or eradicate the condition so that you, the subject, will become free of the psychologically damaging influences. While the mind, through repetitious bombardment, has accepted the notion that it may be prone to failure in all endeavors, the hypnotist can induce suggestions and, virtually, reverse the infliction. Through the hypnotist's voice, the Hypnotic WORDS can be delivered with such an infiltrating impact, the subconscious mind could literally enable you to change the course of your life for the best. Practice speaking aloud, discovering the right timbre and cadence of your voice, and you will have discovered the foundation of a good hypnotist.'[17]

Trees

Buckthorn	Blackwood	Cedar	Ash	Oak
Alder	Oak	Hawthorn	Cypress	Elder
Oak	Spruce	Poplar	Rowan	Larch
Birch	Maple	Oak	Plane	Sycamore
Elm	Oak	Whitebeam	Beech	Chestnut

grief/loss

Grief fills the room up of my absent child,
Lies in his bed, walks up and down with me,
Puts on his pretty looks, repeats his words,
Remembers me of all his gracious parts,
Stuffs out his vacant garments with his form;
Then have I reason to be fond of grief.

King John Act 4 Scene 1[18]

**It may be necessary
to recognize that
there is such a thing
as being inconsolable . . .**

'I watched from the living room window as the two young police officers walked towards my front door. When they removed their hats I knew Stephen was dead.'

'Caitlin's death on that night has a touch, a sound and a colour.'

'I was alone, unable to communicate the unimaginable, entirely diminished, a dancing shadow without my dancer.'

'What do I do now, with all this love?'[19]

'There was another physical phenomenon that I could never have anticipated. It's that pair of invisible cement blocks that someone ties together and loops over your shoulders . . . the ropes come to rest on your two shoulders and the lengths of the ropes is perfectly measured to assure that the two blocks will press in . . . from front to back . . . on your lungs. It is possible to breathe with the blocks on your shoulders, but not to breathe deeply.'[20]

'The loss of meaning that comes with the death of our child is greater than any we could imagine, but we will have to invent new meanings.'

'Death – which most of us now only encounter in any intimate way in our 40s, through the death of a parent – has become something that we overwhelmingly learn about and consume through the media. But as such it is shorn of any pain, any real understanding, wedged between stories about celebrity or the weather, instantly forgotten, the mind detained for little more than a minute, the grief of those bereaved utterly inconceivable, the idea that their lives have been destroyed forever not even imaginable in out gratification society: pain is for the professionals, not something to detain the ordinary mortals.' (Martin Jacques, Guardian)[21]

I WILL SHOW YOU FEAR IN A HANDFUL OF DUST[22]

[. . .]

---

drama/conflict/action/etc

**TWO CHARACTERS
WITH CLEARLY-
DEFINED EXTERNALLY
DRIVEN NEEDS.**
there

[. . .]

the second actor

a knotty one. I've mentioned the idea to some people and they've raised their eyebrows and seemed to suggest it was crass intellectual posturing

. . .

excellent

I've also sat in theatres recently and imagined it working in a thrilling way.

But would we be overloading a simple story that needs to be told?

There's lots to talk about.

The subject not being the master of its own house.

It does seem to connect absolutely with the themes of the play – the idea of one thing being given by another, the notion of projection, suggestion, entrancement. I like the idea of the de-materialized actor . . .

Also, we are visibly working the dynamic of a hypnotist and his subject – watch the david knight videos, and that relationship is there – people giving themselves over to being something else.

I presume people will either love it or hate it – and are we being brave or stupid to pursue it?

We always have the opt out clause . . .

it must feel integral

It must never be a distraction.

Is it just a gimmick?

Very excited about the international potential of such an idea – travelling to other countries and bringing actors from those countries into the piece – even letting them speak in their own language.

aesthetic precedents

Think about:

Bruce Nauman

I saw his Violent Incident at Tate Modern. His commission for the Turbine Hall starts in october.[23]

I bought a book called Please Pay Attention Please: Bruce Nauman's Words.

He cites inspiration from Beckett and Wittgenstein . . .

I am struck by pieces that incorporate text – the strength of his language – and also those pieces that are PROPOSALS. The proposals feel to be in a similar area to what we're proposing with oak tree. He was doing them in the late sixties, Craig martin's oak tree was in '73. Am I terminally behind the times?

His proposal work is performative.

Here are some things from the book I bought:

'Mostly produced in 1968–69, these pieces consist simply of written (or dictated) texts that outline a set of conditions for another to follow, in some cases leading to fabricated objects or executed performances. For example, *Untitled* (1969), Nauman's submission to the exhibition "Art by telephone" states the following':

> 'Hire a dancer and have him phone me from the museum. (Female dancer is satisfactory.)'

239

'The dancer is to carry out or perform the following instructions: the dancer should stand with his arms held straight like a T, with his legs crossed. He should hold the telephone between his legs. He should then jump up and down following the cadence I give him, for as long as he can until becoming too tired.'[24]

. . .

'While the *Untitled* proposal actually yielded an executed performance, others made by nauman at the same time are far more ambiguous, some even flouting the feasibility of any physical elaboration due to the extreme or outright impossible conditions outlined within. For example, one *Untitled* piece from 1969 begins "A person enters and lives in a room for a long time – a period of years or a lifetime."'[25]

I love this impossibility. And also this humour. It chimes completely with the tree and the girl. I am also excited by giving impossible and poetic instructions to the second actor that can encompass different dimensions of meaning and story-telling. But to have the potentiality of those instructions materialized/glimpsed at through a human form. I'm excited about giving the minutiae of descriptive detail to moments of theatre.

Also:

INSTRUCTIONS FOR A MENTAL EXERCISE, 1969

A. Lie down on the floor near the centre of the space, face down, and slowly allow yourself to sink down into the floor.

B. Lie on your back on the floor near the centre of the space and slowly allow the floor to rise up around you.

This is a mental exercise.

Practice each day for one hour.

1/2 hour for A, then a sufficient break to clear the mind and body, then 1/2 hour practice B.[26]

and for the spectator:

> Press as much of the front surface of
> your body (palms in or out, left or right cheek)
> against the wall as possible.

> Press hard and concentrate.

> Form an image of yourself (suppose you
> had just stepped forward) on the
> opposite side of the wall pressing
> back against the wall very hard.[27]

And things to do with trees!!!

The second one was carried out and the tree died . . .

Amplified tree piece, 1970

"Drill a hole into the heart of a large tree and insert a microphone.

Seal the hole with cement.

Mount the amplifier and speaker in an empty room and adjust the volume to make audible any sounds that might come from the tree.'

Microphone/tree piece, 1971

'Select a large solid tree away from loud noises.

Wrap the microphone in a layer of 1/4 or 1/8 inch foam rubber and seal it in a plastic sack.

Drill a hole of large enough diameter to accept the encased microphone to the centre of the tree at a (convenient) height, and slip the microphone to within an inch of the end of the hole.

Plug the hole with cement or other waterproof sealant.
Extend the microphone wire inside to the pre-amp, amp and speaker.'[28]

INSTRUCTIONS

The same tone of instruction operates in hypnotism.

This is from a book on hypnosis:

'You need to have another person present to guide you into hypnosis . . . For instance, the hypnosis script as it is called, may suggest "Tighten the muscles in your feet." The instructions thus occupy the conscious while relaxing the mind, allowing the suggestion to be accepted. . . .'[29]

The links between the proposals of nauman, the mechanics of hypnosis – both encouraging an ALTERED STATE. Both requiring one person to lead and one person to suspend their conscious self.

BUT I DON'T KNOW.

ANDY?

Technicalities

How do we encorporate real life onto the stage?
How does our blank actor operate? How do they read the lines?
What technology is required for this play?
What images are required that cannot be created by words and bodies?
How important is sound?
Who operates this show?

Fears

What's to be scared of?

that writing about this subject will bring me bad luck. Jinx me. I have a daughter.

That we have good ideas, but they won't make good theatre.

That I will be accused of manipulating ideas and emotion.

That the story will never rise about the ideas of the story.

That we will try and control everything.

That the second actor idea will never lift itself – that it will impede the story-telling.

That, by my nature, I am too pedagogic – that I want to educate/ explain. And therefore am in danger of losing the mystery at the centre of this story.

You know, all the usual ones.

Questions to be explored

what do we want to have happen?

what do we want to have heard?

what do we want to have seen?

why this play? why this way?

why this story?

imagine something more perfect than this

Original ending to *The Author*

By the end of The Author, *Vic and Esther have already left the auditorium/stage. This ending begins with Tim's last words and Tim leaving. Then someone who has not previously spoken begins to speak. As Tim Crouch explains it, 'We are introduced to a fifth actor – in my mind, the "Reader"'.*[30]

TIM . . . . You won't forgive me, anyway. I know you. Look at you. You won't. You won't forgive me.

Anyway.
Nobody was hurt.
Anyway.
I continue.
The writing is leaving the writer.

the death of the author.
music and lights!
Tim leaves the auditorium.
space.
more space.
an elderly woman stands up.

WOMAN I would like to say something. Now that we're on our own. I would like to say a few words.

Adrian, you asked where am I with hope? I hope you were really asking me about those things. About hope and safety. Do you remember?

ADRIAN   Of course.

WOMAN   Watching this play, I was reminded by something I read in a *Reader's Digest* in a hospital waiting room. I was there with my husband last summer. It was the day we all of us dread with our hearts, when the doctor tells you how it is and you go home and curl up on the bed and hold each other. And if you're wise, you say your sorries for letting each other down.

My husband had gone in to have another scan. The third of the day and the final proof of something we both knew anyway. I was in the waiting room. The consultant brought me in and showed us the image on the screen – the dark shadow clinging to the side of my husband's lungs. I half expected that he would offer to print it out for us, as if we were proud young parents of this new life growing inside him.

And in the *Reader's Digest* in the waiting room there was an article by a famous author, Stephen King, not him but someone like him. Someone whose work I didn't know but whose article made me determined to get to know. I love to read, now I have more time on my hands. I'd read all day. I can't watch telly any more. Read and come to the theatre. I'm also a Friend, Adrian.

The article was about stories, telling stories, story-telling. It talked about the early days when the story-teller would stand behind the audience. The audience would face a wall or an empty space, and the story teller would stand behind them and tell the story without anyone looking at them. The audience would then see their own pictures, project their own vision of the story into thin air. This struck me. This gave me hope.

I was reminded of that during the play we saw tonight.

I enjoyed the play. I hope you did too, but it doesn't really matter whether you did or not. Not to me.

space

Well. There. Now.

I assume we're all right to stay, but I'd like to catch a 10.19 train which I can do if I leave now. So. Please. I don't want to stop anything, but I'm off. It's been lovely to meet you. Lovely to meet you, Adrian.

ADRIAN Lovely to meet you.

WOMAN I'm seeing *The 39 Steps* next week. We go as a group. Looking forward to that.

ADRIAN I've seen it. You'll have a great time!

WOMAN Bye bye.

the elderly woman leaves.
space
end

3. Roy Williams

Interview

This interview with Roy Williams took place in early September 2012 in the kitchen of his house in Greenwich, South London, shortly before the opening of his adaptation of Alan Sillitoe's story The Loneliness of the Long Distance Runner *for Pilot Theatre in York.*

I started as an actor, mainly in Theatre-in-Education, young's people's theatre. Theatre Centre, and a company up in Leicester called Action Transport. I did a TIE show up in Scotland, in St Andrews. That was pretty much my theatre experience, doing shows for young people. Would have been late eighties/early nineties. Then in 1992 I decided to take my writing seriously so I applied for a place at Rose Bruford.[31] The acting work was sort of drying up but also I was losing the love for it. First I thought I'd give it a rest for a couple of years while I'm studying, but as I got into being back at college, things changed. I never formally gave up acting; I just stopped going to auditions. I signed off from my agency. I just sort of eased off from it.

I was one of those kids who had a real love of books and literature. My mum read a lot, still does. I don't know where it came from; I was just that kid; that's what piqued my interest, storytelling. So it was always there; it was always in my psyche. It just took me a while to propel myself into doing something about it.

The Rose Bruford course was a new thing. We were guinea pigs and there were a lot of flaws in the whole set up of it, which came apparent very quickly. So it was quite rocky but we got through and despite that it was a good experience. I'm not sure whether you really can teach someone playwriting for three years and you could say the same about acting; it comes down to the individual and what they need. I needed three years in that environment where I'd be encouraged to read more plays than I ever had, so I stuck at it. A few writers came out of that course: Leo Butler, Darren Rapier, Grant Buchanan Marshall did that course too.

And my first play, *The No-Boys Cricket Club*, which was done at Stratford East in 1996, was my exam play for my degree. We all had to write a full-length play for the degree and that was my one. It got me noticed. It was timing as well. Stephen Daldry had been praised for re-igniting the Theatre Upstairs at the Royal Court and there was this whole new wave of playwrights coming through – you know, Nick Grosso, David Eldridge, Rebecca Prichard, Joe Penhall – they were the new faces. So my name kind of got caught up in all that which was great for me. Once I'd graduated, I sent it to more than one theatre and Stratford East gave me a call and the Royal Court too; in fact it was the same week, I remember that. The Court didn't want to put it on but they liked enough about the writing that they took an interest. A few months later they gave me a commission.

In fact the first play that got done at the Court wasn't the play they commissioned. They rejected that one and they were right to reject it, because it was awful. But it's funny how these things work out; Jack Bradley [literary manager of the National Theatre] came to see the play at Stratford East and off the back of that gave me a residency at the Studio and in that eight-weeks, I wrote *Lift Off* and when I delivered that to Jack, he then gave it to the Royal Court and said let's do a co-production, which then became my first Court play.

That was a very big deal. When I was at Rose Bruford, we went to the Court to see Max Stafford-Clark's production of *King Lear*.[32] In fact we had a pre-show talk with Max. We all went up in the dress circle and he came in and answered our questions. (I remember I asked him a question but to this day I can't remember what.) So I was very aware of the Court and its history but it was a pipe dream to think I'd ever get a play on there. So when eleven years later I had a play on that main stage, it was incredible. I'm kind of glad that the first play I wrote for the Court I didn't actually write for the Court, because you don't have that pressure. It's kind of how my career's gone; it's never been, okay let's throw Roy right in the spotlight. Nothing like Polly Stenham, you know the way her first play was taken up.[33] That didn't happen to me and I'm kind of relieved. I don't know if I could have handled that. I don't know if I'd still be here talking to you.

Sing Yer Heart Out for the Lads

Sing Yer Heart Out for the Lads started in that Transformation season at the National Theatre.[34] I remember being disappointed that it wasn't going to be in the Cottesloe, which is where I always imagined it would be, but I got over that pretty quickly; I mean, it was the National Theatre. And it was the show that opened that season so I was very flattered that they chose it.

It was Jack Bradley who got me to write it. It was not long after *Lift Off* and I told him this story about watching a football match in Birmingham and he leapt on it and said, you should write that play. I was watching this game in a pub; it was quite relaxed, quite civil and then about five minutes before it started this rush of young guys came in and completely changed the atmosphere. It was very unsettling, uncomfortable, all that jingoistic stuff: 'Engerland! Engerland!', 'stand up if you won the war' . . . I remember there was another black guy in the pub and as the game was playing it was all 'German' this and 'German' that. I mean I giggled at some of the comments but when that sort of thing happens I always think, okay, what if one of the black players makes a mistake, what are they going to say? Are they going to be able to stop themselves? Is it going to be the black person next? Where's that going to place me and this other bloke, whose eye I kept catching, as if he's thinking the same thing as me. It's funny because I've been in pubs to watch football matches and experienced that before but it was the first time that 'Writer' Roy had experienced it.

The minute that experience was over in the pub I was writing ideas and scenes down on a napkin. It's one of the very few plays I've written that really hasn't changed much from the very first draft (which no one sees) to the final version. The structure and the story was dependent on a particular game; the game I based the play on isn't the one I saw in Birmingham. I knew – this is how anal I am about football – that England were going to play Germany again in the World Cup qualifiers in October 2000 and I had this light bulb moment when I thought, okay, I'm going to go and watch this game and whatever happens in it, I'm going to write the entire play around it. Whatever happens happens. Also it was going to be the last game played in the old Wembley Stadium, because after that they were going to knock it down and rebuild it. (And I'm glad they did because the last time I'd been was 1982 and even then it was a shithole. . . .) And it was against Germany, so the play was just asking to be written. And it was a dull, boring game, not a classic at all, but what made it so special was Keegan resigning at the end. So perfect, so symbolic. I was like, oh he's practically *telling* me to write this play . . .[35]

I watched the match and recorded it at home. I had to watch that match over and over, making notes. In the first production you never saw the match, you just watched them watching the match. But when Paul [Miller] directed the revival he wanted a big screen and that actual match to be played; they slightly cheated the timing on it, but it was absolutely dependent on the technical people getting it right every night or it could have been embarrassing.

The Monsterists came about at the Studio.[36] I think the ringleaders were Colin Teevan and Richard Bean but it wasn't a general call out to playwrights; it was just the people who were around the Studio at that time. In the very first meeting we came up with the word Monsterists and we just thought we'd push for theatres to let us write big plays. And it was surprisingly successful; we've all been able to write big plays – Moira [Buffini] had *Welcome to Thebes*, David [Eldridge] had *Market Boy*, Richard [Bean] did *England People Very Nice*, Rebecca [Lenkiewicz] had *Her Naked Skin*[37] – and we'd like to think that helped other playwrights think they could write big plays; like Mike Bartlett – I mean, you'd have to ask him, but I wonder if *Earthquakes in London* was made possible by the Monsterists on some level.[38] We were quite smart about it and honest about it, because we didn't want to come across as a bunch of whinging playwrights; we made it clear that it was our thing and we knew it only had a certain shelf life. But we made our case and we stated it and it seemed to have an effect.

All of these plays are ensemble pieces. When I was acting, the plays I most enjoyed had ensemble casts. Right from back then, I always thought that was an exciting way to tell a story, to put the world on the stage rather than being too intimate – not that I have a problem with those plays, I think they're great, but at the time I just felt I wanted to challenge myself, push myself, and put a world on the stage. With *Sing Yer Heart Out,* in the pub, even though it was unsettling, I still thought, the energy, wow, if I could bottle that . . . And I had artistic directors who encouraged me to think that way.

Fallout

Fallout was my first [Royal Court] Downstairs play and I didn't want to let the Court down, let myself down, because I was very excited when Ian Rickson[39] said to me, 'okay, I think you're ready to write a play for the big stage'. And after we had a meeting he took me downstairs to the main theatre. I think it was dark at the time. And he left me alone; he just said, 'stay here for a while – long as you like, soak it up'. And I just sat there for an hour, looking at it, thinking, what can I do, what can I do? And I came back a year and a half later with *Fallout*.

Of course when they did it they totally changed the auditorium.[40] I wasn't expecting that! But it was good. It was Ian's vision for the play; once he'd expressed an interest in directing it and it was all agreed, he told me what he was going to do and it really lit my fire. Like me, he really wanted to see that world on stage. These young people I was writing about, he wanted them to take over that space, as if to say to the audience, okay, you normally cross the road to avoid us, but for ninety minutes you have to listen to us. So he thought we should change the space, make the audience more complicit. You avoid these streets but now the street is running through your theatre.

You can never reproduce how people speak because the way people speak is boring, but I tried to capture the energy in the way those kids speak. In a way they did half the job for me. And like *Sing Yer Heart Out*, I thought I've never seen a play like this yet, especially not on a big stage. Again it was about bottling that energy and putting it on the stage. There weren't any real models for that, for putting those big groups on the stage, keeping that energy going, except maybe Shakespeare. When I wrote it I thought a lot about Shakespeare; so I didn't have a particular set in mind. I thought big stage directions would slow the pace down; I thought, no no, you don't need that. People enter, people leave, and their dialogue tells you where they are, and I just trusted that the audience would be able to keep up and say, oh, they're in a police station now. The kids are the guides; they know where they're going even if we don't.

The story of Damilola Taylor was obviously the inspiration.[41] And what I decided was to follow the original story as closely as possible and to have no fear about that. And I did. In a way, I looked at the real story and broke it down in the way I would a play. And then I borrowed that structure to write the play – but the more I got into writing it, the more I chipped away the original story and let the play breathe. Though I kept a lot of what actually happened, to the point that the lawyers got concerned! There was one reference in the play which was so close to what happened, they said this could lead to trouble for you, so I changed that – and actually it made the piece better by detaching it even more from the real events. But early drafts, certainly, were very heavily following that story; because basically – forgive this crude word – you pillage it to help you tell the story *you* want to write.

Joe was my mouthpiece for some of the debates that were going on at the time. He's not based on a real detective but he is based on the psyche I've seen in so many black people – including myself: you know, I got away from the estate and sometimes, you know, I hate being black! I hate those stupid black kids because they make themselves look bad and they make us all look bad. But to write a serious play, you have to take everyone seriously, and I also wanted to show their potential; and even if you kind of hate them, you're laughing at their jokes! I like that. I want to be conflicted when I write, when I'm in an audience. A key ingredient of a good play for me is seeing a good character do a bad thing or a bad character doing a good thing. Like when Shanice and Ronnie follow the teacher home, I wanted to shake things up a bit. I didn't want them to be totally innocent and blameless, they're also culpable. Particularly Shanice because the play is kind of about her admitting her role in the boy's death.

Putting a gang on stage is a challenge because they're a gang, they're one big thing, but they're also individual. I don't plan how those individual characters develop; I just find it in the writing. But even in *Fallout* there were two characters I thought were too similar and when I did the TV version[42] I was able to rectify that by just making one of the characters much younger than they were in the play.

Days of Significance

Writing *Days of Significance*, which was another large-cast play, the way I approached it was to say to each character, right, what's your purpose in this story? What do you *want*? What also helped me with that piece was that I was encouraged to think big; it was Paul Sirett[43] who commissioned me and he said, we're doing this Complete Works season[44] and we're commissioning four playwrights to write new plays, inspired by Shakespeare. And because it's the RSC, they have these big companies of actors, so you can think big.

I had two ideas for plays at the time. One was that I knew I wanted to write something that responded to the Iraq War. And that's as far as my thinking took me; I just knew I wanted to do that. And the other idea was that I wanted to write about these young people going out on the piss in market towns, binge drinking. And then I realized they were the same play. And I think the Kenneth Branagh version of *Much Ado About Nothing*[45] was on TV around that time. I thought, hello, this is about soldiers, coming back from war. And then there was the sparring between Beatrice and Benedick and that's when I knew how to put both those plays together in one. And that solved things for me because how do you respond to the Iraq War? What, Blair and

Bush lied? No shit. What's dramatic about that? And that had all been said and dramatized by then, so when I got the binge-drinking idea, I thought, now I know what I can say about it. It's about our arrogance as a nation, going over to fight this war; we want to impose our way of life on yours but we can't even look after our own. And this generation that goes out on the piss: that's the generation we're sending to die.

And in some of Shakespeare's comedies there's this structure: Act I normality, Act II in the magic forest, Act III back to normality. But really I took the structure from *The Deer Hunter*,[46] and for all I know the screenwriter took his structure from Shakespeare. (I did it backwards, because he has the wedding in the first act.) One of the actors, when he read it, said, 'This is the Essex *Deer Hunter!*' I thought, funny you should say that . . .

The fun thing about writing is that you have to inhabit positions opposite to your own. I have my own wanky liberal beliefs about the War – and I'm proud to have them – but I wanted to dare myself to think the opposite: maybe the Iraq War was a good thing, so the characters really test my views.

The first version of the play in Stratford was very different from the second one that we brought to London. The first two scenes are very similar but the third scene is very different. Because when I wrote it, I knew I wanted it to be in three acts and I wanted each act to be sort of self-contained and in as close to real time as possible. But also I wanted to write a very different theatre form in each act; so the first act was very big, Shakespearean, the world; the second would be much more intimate, black-box theatre, like the Royal Court Upstairs, very naturalistic; and the third one would be more abstract, surreal. So in the third act the main character is Hannah who was in the first scene, but she comes back, and it's like it's taking place in her head. She's in the middle of the stage having four real-time conversations in her head but they're coming in and out like they're memories.

And two massive problems arose from that. The first is that the audience was so settled with what they'd seen in the first two acts that the third one jarred with them. And I'm the sort of writer, when I go see my play I watch the audience and I could just tell by the way people are sitting that they were losing it. And the other development – which

I can admit now didn't work – was that Hannah is in crisis and the person who pulls her out of it is her step-father; but in the version in Stratford he does that by declaring his love for her. And the director had a problem with it, the actors had a problem with it, audiences had a problem with it. I think they all felt that when he says that, you lose all sympathy for him. They couldn't understand: I think they just felt he's just a dirty old man. So it didn't quite work.

It never got heated. But Maria [Aberg, the director] had a problem and the actors Clare [-Louise Cordwell] and Nigel [Cooke] didn't like it. I mean, they were totally professional and just got on with it, but when the play finished in Stratford and we knew it was going to go on the following year in London, that was one of the first things that Michael Boyd discussed with me: 'that last scene – I'm not feeling it, Roy . . .' But he was just the last of a long line of people who told me. As I said, it never got heated. It was at an interesting point in my career because I'd never encountered that before and I sort of dug my heels in and said, I really believe it works. I'm not a playwright who cuts off his nose to spite his face; I hear people out and if I think their way is better then we'll try it. But in this case, I was absolutely adamant that my way was right.

I still thought I was right but when I watched the audience, listened to the audience, I had to acknowledge that people were struggling and you have to pay attention to that. So Maria and I sat down because we both knew we had to resolve it though I said, I haven't got a bloody clue how to do it. I knew it was all about that character, her being in a crisis. And I was a working holiday in France – I had my laptop with me – and I had this lightbulb moment where I thought about advice I give out when I do workshops for young writers (which, usually, I never follow myself!). Flip it over. Do it the other way round. If you don't know how a character gets from a to b to c, start at c and work backwards. And I thought about it and I thought, that's it. *He's* not in love with *her, she's* in love with *him.* The next thought was of course, no, she's not really in love with him, but what if she makes a pass at him? It was always about her growing up, her growing maturity. The War is a kind of backdrop to that. The War happens to her and she's supposed to have a view about that but in the first act she says, the war doesn't matter to me; she goes out and gets drunk. She doesn't want to be smart. And then she is in crisis; I always thought of her at the edge of a cliff, ready to fall off. And I'd been thinking, what can she do to jump off? And that was it; she has a close relationship with her stepfather and she makes a pass at him. That's the way she can really lower herself; make a drunken pass at her stepfather. And he still does declare his love for her but in a totally different way, as her father.

And the other thing is that I got on so well with that cast and some of them had very little parts in my play because they had much bigger parts in *Pericles* but when we went to the Tricycle I wanted to bring them all back from the first act into the third. Though in the first act the drunkenness is chaotic and funny but in the third act it's much less so because you know what some of them have been through. Of course it was also me putting my Shakespeare hat on again: even though the War creeps into it unsettling everything, let's end the play with a wedding.

Selections from Days of Significance, *Act III*

Days of Significance *changed considerably between Stratford and London. In the original third act, Hannah seems to be imagining or remembering a series of conversations that swirl fluidly across the stage. In the first of two extracts presented here, Hannah imagines confronting Jamie about the accusations of prisoner abuse. In the second, very near the end of the play, Hannah discovers that her stepfather, Lenny, has sexual feelings for her.*

A.

Jamie   Do you think I'm a monster?

Hannah   I don't want to think about any of this. This fucking war!

Jamie   So what you want?

Hannah   Come back to me.

Jamie   You don't know me.

Hannah   So, tell me, make me understand.

Jamie We used dogs on them.

Hannah No.

Jamie We'd drag them out of their cells.

Hannah Stop it.

Jamie We'd have the dogs straining at their leashes, snarling at them. They'd be lying on the ground, stark naked, heads covered with bin liners, crawling around in pain, bite marks, down the sides of their bodies. We'd a right laugh when the dogs would go for their bollocks first, every time. We'd take turns sitting on top of them. Our knees pressed into their backs. Blood pouring down their legs. That's when we had the pictures taken.

Hannah You musta known it weren't right.

Jamie It was an order! What am I supposed to do, say no? Don't turn against me as well Hannah. Don't look at me like some monster.

Hannah How should I look at you J?

Jamie I was following orders.

B.

[Lenny is comforting a distraught Hannah]

Lenny I say it, cos you're special.

Hannah Special? Special how Len? What is so special about me?

Lenny You care.

Hannah Care? I told my boyfriend and best mate to go fuck themselves.

Lenny You didn't mean it

Hannah I did mean it.

Lenny You're confused.

Hannah   You're the one who confused Len.

Lenny   Stop it, stop it now, I won't let you do this to yourself.

Hannah   Do what? I mean, what you got me down as Len, some sort of crusading angel, whose gonna make the world, alright?

Lenny   Why not? (*Hannah laughs*) Why not, the whole bleeding world's crying out for one.

Hannah   The words Cuckoo, land and cloud spring to mind.

Lenny   Just care Hannah, That's all I want, its what we all want.

Hannah   To care?

Lenny   Is that so bad?

Hannah   So lame.

Lenny   My old man would say sometimes, the worth of our lives comes not in what we do or who we know, or what we say, but by who we are. (*Hannah scoffs*) Oi, I'm serious.

Hannah   Ain't so simple.

Lenny   But what if it is though? What if it is that simple?

Hannah   (*cringes*) Oh, Lenny, stop it.

Lenny   Please Hannah, don't do this to yourself.

Hannah   Do what?

Lenny   You're not throwing away your life.

Hannah   You wanna lay off the strongbow, mate.

Lenny   You make me feel that I matter. All the time.

Hannah   Oh Len . . .

Lenny   (*snaps*) And I love you for it.

Hannah   Love you as well, but . . .

Lenny Jesus, Hannah!

Hannah What?

Lenny Can't you see?

[. . .]

Hannah Len?

Lenny You know what, I shouldn't have said what I said, forget it, please?

Hannah Lenny?

Lenny It's nothing, alright?

Hannah So where you going?

Lenny Upstairs.

Hannah Turn around.

Lenny No.

Hannah Look at me, Lenny.

Lenny I'm so tired too, sweetheart.

Hannah I said look at me.

Lenny I can't. Please!

Hannah Look at me! (*Hannah pulls him to face her*)

Lenny Say something.

Hannah Oh, God.

Lenny I'm sorry Hannah.

Hannah You're sick.

Lenny No, don't say that.

Hannah You fucking pervert!

Lenny Hannah?

Hannah   No.

Lenny   Please!

Hannah   What's the matter with you? Oh, God!

Lenny   Listen . . .

Hannah   Get away from me! Don't touch me! Get away from me.

Lenny   Oh darling.

Hannah   Don't call me that, don't call me anything, just get away from me.

Lenny   I'm so sorry.

Hannah   (*screams*) Get away! My skin is crawling.

Lenny   Hannah?

Hannah   Pervert! You are a fucking pervert! You're like a dad to me. You brought me up.

Lenny   Sweetheart

Hannah   But you couldn't resist!

Lenny   Please don't.

Hannah   What were you thinking?

Lenny   Nothing.

Hannah   'Hannah, the slapper!'

Lenny   Don't think so little of yourself.

Hannah   You do of me.

Lenny   No, babe

Hannah   All those cuddles and kisses, all that time you just wanted to . . . .

Lenny   No!

[. . .][47]

Hannah Don't touch me.

Lenny You think I'm disgusting.

Hannah Yes!

Lenny I ain't no perv Hannah. I ain't some dirty old man. Don't ever think of me like that please, don't ever! It would kill me if you did sweetheart, it would kill me. Please understand what I'm saying to you. I am so, in love with you.

Hannah squirms

Lenny Trish, Lauren, your mates. They don't hold a candle to you my darling, they don't come anywhere near. You're different, you know you are. You see things from all sides. You understand everybody, you want to make them matter and you want to make it right. That's a gift, a precious gift. Don't let any one take that away from you, make you all cynical, we have enough of that in the world right now, thank you. It probably feels much easier for you to hate me right now, call me names, like any one else, in your position would, tell yer mates. Please, don't do that Hannah, don't do the obvious. Cos you see, it's people like you, that don't do the obvious. Its people like you who know where the line is drawn, that change things, always has been. You're going to be amazing my girl, whatever it is you do, it's gonna be amazing. I know it. I do love you. And I know you. You'll do what's right for Jamie, and for yourself. You can't help it, despite the chat. It's in you. It's in yer nature. You inspire me, my angel. You make me feel better. You.

Lenny leans forward. Hannah flinches.

Lenny It's alright.

Lenny gently kisses her on the forehead. Hannah and Lenny sit in silence, not saying a word to each other and avoiding eye contact. Hannah has waited long enough, she cannot bear the silence and stands.

Hannah Oh, this is killing me.

Lenny   Where are you going?

Hannah   Find Jamie.

Lenny   Jamie?

Hannah   Yes, Len. Jamie. I'll be there for him. I'll go to court with him, hold his hand.

Lenny   Whatever you decide.

Hannah   But as a friend. That's all I've got to give him, there's nothing more. I best go and get him then, eh?

Lenny   I'm proud of you.

Hannah   Please, don't.

Lenny   We gonna be alright?

Hannah   I dunno Len.

Lenny   I'm not a pervert.

Hannah   I know.

Lenny   I never wanted you to find out, I swear. I'll say no more.

Hannah   Probably best.

Lenny   Yeah.

Lenny lowers his head in shame. His hands are on his head. Hannah tilts his head up. She then leans forward and gently kisses him on the cheek.

4. David Greig

Interview, September 2012

I interviewed David during rehearsals for his play, Glasgow Girls, *a musical based on the true story of a school revolt against the treatment of asylum seekers. Our conversation roamed across many topics but I've organized some of these thoughts into statements.*

San Diego

This was a very conscious attempt to push what I felt I was trying in the form of *Cosmonaut*[48] to its furthest extreme and I wrote it in a retreat in Hawthornden Castle which is just outside Edinburgh and is run by Drue Heinz, the beans millionaire. She invites writers to stay for a month and you get looked after and fed. It's quite monkish; there's a rule of silence during the day and you work in your room and there's a soft knock at the door at lunchtime and a tray is placed outside your door by an invisible person with some soup and a sandwich. And in the evening you gather with your fellow writers, which for me included Zadie Smith, who was writing *The Autograph Man*,[49] and you have dinner with them, and you write again afterwards and again the next day and it's very intense.

I thought I'd go with a project. In fact I went with three projects – it was a very productive month – and one of them was *San Diego*. (The others were the translation/adaptation of *Caligula* and *Dr Korczak's Example*.[50]) What I had was that I wanted to use the form of *Cosmonaut* but take it further: whatever that was, I'd do it *more*. And the other thing was a very specific piece of inspiration, which was that I'd read *Our Town* by Thornton Wilder. I was interested in the way that *Our Town* appears to have the most radical form – you know, it has a stage manager who introduces himself as the stage manager, it's kind of Brechtian – but it's also an emblem of a certain kind of America that's very cosy and safe. So the question that set *San Diego* off was: what would *Our Town* be now? Because there is no 'our town'. There was something that Jo – then John – Clifford said to me; I'd been in South Africa and I came back and talked about seeing townships next to *dorps*, little bourgeois rural white towns with townships right next to them. I hadn't realized that Johannesburg's pairing with Soweto is repeated right through the Transvaal with all of these towns having their own shanty towns attached. And Jo said, 'well of course Edinburgh has that, only we don't know where it is'. And I really liked that thought. And so the question was: what would *Our Town* be in the modern age?

I should also say that I really liked *Our Town*'s form and I liked the opening speech a lot, but I thought it was a real cop-out for Thornton Wilder not to admit that *he* was the Stage Manager; because it is him,

261

he's the orchestrator of events, it's his voice. So I thought I would do that; I'd begin with me introducing the play and take it from there.

And then I followed the *Cosmonaut* process, which was that I said, I will not go back and rewrite a scene; I will just write a scene, and the next day I will write the next scene, but I will not go back. Obviously at the end I would go back and do some rewriting but it meant there was always this forward momentum and a feeling of never quite knowing what might come next because there was no plan. It was required that there was no plan.

And the other thing that's very clear in *San Diego* is that I'm absolutely using – playfully – my own biography. You know, the stories about Paul McCartney coming to record in Nigeria, these are all absolutely mythologies from my childhood in Nigeria. And I don't totally know why I'm doing that. Even now I'm not totally sure what the purpose of doing that was but it felt like it was something to do with being more naked on stage, more honest maybe? Trying not to hide behind things. Because if it's true that any play is always a revelation of one's own psychology, then why not stop pretending and just reveal it? I just remember this very intense time. I was on my own – oh and it snowed that year – and so we were literally stuck in Hawthornden Castle, secluded in a world of writing, and I think it reflects that in its style.

For good or ill, there's a theory behind writing that way. You cannot but tell your story. Everything that's in your head coalesces around a very small number of themes and characters because the brain is an organ of connection and we can't really stop thinking about the things that are bugging us. Even talking to you now, discussing a play that I've sort of consigned to a moment in my career that's passed, I realize, in the context of *Glasgow Girls*, that ten years later I'm still obsessing about some of the same issues. By taking away the conscious layer, what I'm trying to do is let those connections happen that want to happen without my conscious internal police system making it nice or okay or safe or unembarrassing. So it's a twofold thing: when an idea pops into your head it's not only not random but also you might fuck that idea up by trying to think about it.

There's a good example of that from another play, *Pyrenees*.[51] There's a bit of music that Keith hears on the café sound system and he thinks, this is important, it reminds me of something. He's trying to work out who he is and he thinks this song might be a clue. And the song is Toto's 'Africa', which just came into my head. And when it came to rehearsal I thought that was really terrible, really embarrassing. And after the first week of rehearsal I did a set of rewrites and in the rewrites I changed it to a better song – I still can't say this without blushing – a better song, more in keeping with the themes of the play, snow, blankness and so on. I changed the song to 'A Whiter Shade of Pale' . . . And when we did the read-through, the moment someone even *said* it, I think, the whole room's buttocks clenched. It was the stupidest, stupidest idea anyone had ever had. But then I also realized that the other song's called 'Africa' and it's mentioned in the story that Keith has had some time in Africa in the past . . . But the point is, the thing I thought was stupid, that maybe I even thought was me taking the piss, was much much better than the thought-out thing. That's post-*San Diego* but that's the impulse I was exploring.

Everything in my writing process is an attempt to achieve that. I'm now onto a different way of achieving it but that's only because the internal policing system has got used to that method, so I'm not going to get past it now with that. It'll get 'Whiter Shade of Pale' in there somehow, so I have to try another way. I have to not know what I'm doing in order to do it.

One particular episode in the play came from experience. When I was in Nigeria, aged, I don't know, seven or eight, a young black boy was in our garden one day. It was quite a large garden and he just appeared. He'd come to play I suppose. And I was playing with a chemistry set and I was deliberately trying to create poison, so I was mixing everything that was in the chemistry set and anything I could find, like dog shit, and it had this horrible blue colour. And suddenly this boy was there about ten, twenty feet away. And I don't know what happened but I remember there was a bit of a stand-off and we looked at each other and then I threw the contents of the test tube at him, so it went across his face. What interested me was that afterwards I didn't tell anybody about it because I thought I'd blinded him. I was convinced of it; I'd made poison! And what interested me was that I thought I'd get away with it and even at the time I thought I'd get away with it because I was white and he was black. *Copper Sulphate*[52] is a sort of naturalistic retelling of that story but in *San Diego* I brought him back because I wanted to get to know him a bit.

But he objects to every scene I put him in. He won't have it. He responds with violence; he doesn't like me. He kills me. It was interesting to write, a character that doesn't have much time for his author. I saw a documentary recently about the ventriloquist Nina Conti – she was taking these dolls to a ventriloquist doll graveyard in America – and what became clear to me was that the act of ventriloquism and the act of playwriting are very close. She uses the dolls to sort of personify voices that are in her head and I find that very true to the experience of playwriting. It's not just there are multiple yous in your head; it's that other people exist in your head and that's what comes out in your play. So the experience of having a character not cooperate with you and tell you to fuck off and not do scenes, you can imagine that being a ventriloquist doll easily.

And the other thing about writing the way I try to write, is that if you're going to be a writer, you have to be a kind of antenna on the world, but you can't *know* what you're looking for. It's right to use your intellect to work out what's going on in the world, but that's a different job, I think, from being a fiction writer. Your job is to be as . . . true. . . . an antenna as possible. I wrote *San Diego* in the Spring of 2001. I think it's interesting that it's a play about post-colonial rage that expresses itself in uncompromising violence, that will not speak to liberals, is very involved in aircraft. . . . and then, maybe four months later, September 11th happened. Now, there's no question that I was consciously doing that – I'd not claim that – but it's interesting that those anxieties and troubles were present in the world, not just in my psyche.

The play was a kind of high point of 'derring-do' for me. *San Diego* was written for Suspect Culture and we were pretty securely funded, off the back of *Mainstream,* which was a pretty radical show in itself.[53] So I had this feeling that the company for which I was writing required the most avant-garde statement I could make. And I think I felt personally that's what I wanted to achieve, so the whole thing coalesced into this attempt to do something wholly and completely, however absurd and extreme it might be, characters seizing control of the play and so on, I would really commit to that idea.

When it came to it, Graham and I came to think the play needed more resources than Suspect Culture could give it. I did a reading of it at the Traverse; I got Marisa Zanotti in to help and I immediately liked her approach, because we decided to do the reading round a table and I asked her what she thought of the script and Marisa said, 'I'm very interested in the relationship between the performer's head and the table' and I thought it was so brilliant that she didn't ask me what it meant or why I'd done this or that, but instead went with this strange physical thought. And we did this reading and someone from the official Festival came and said, would you do this at the Festival? What they intended that to be – and I think we probably said it *would* be – was just a reading round a table. And then this Portuguese company came in with some money and the Tron and it turned into a much bigger thing.

There was a moment in rehearsal that I've always remembered, when an actor said to Marisa 'I'm not absolutely sure where I am in this scene,' and Marisa said, 'you're on a stage!' I went around after Marisa a lot, trying to smooth things over, because I know that's not very helpful for an actor but I felt it was an important moment: she's right, you're on a stage.

Of course, you have to remember that *San Diego* was on for a very short run. Three nights at the Edinburgh International Festival, and then a longer run at in Glasgow, but you know it wasn't what you'd call a hit. So I never got to live with it that way. It was its own exciting moment. It was only a few years later that I noticed it was getting attention abroad; there were productions in Denmark and the National Theatre there, in France I think, and there was a production in America. But it's never had a lot of full-on major productions so I'm not sure how people respond to it. I don't really know if people found it interesting. I don't know.

There's a thing that *San Diego* doesn't know but the plays thereafter start to know. I tried to push against story as far as I could in *San Diego* and I had the realization that actually story is the source of ambiguity and endless reflexiveness. One of the things that helped me realize that was that the actors did the 'panto' version of *San Diego* at the end of the Tron run, where the Pilot was Baron Hardup, and David the patient was Buttons, Pious and Innocent were the Ugly Sisters . . . and it really worked! The whole thing was surprisingly true to the story. I realized that my subconscious, when it lets go, pretty much just spews out fairytale narratives. That's the moment where I realized you can't fight story. I start being much happier with the idea of narrative from that point. I now feel that story really thrives on taking a bit of a beating; you say, I'm going to tell a story, but I'm going to tell it from 27 different angles, do it all in rhyme, tell it from the point of view of the iPhone or something, story *loves* that, it goes, oh yeah, fantastic, do more of that.

The American Pilot

It was first done on the radio, but that was a sneaky trick. Don't tell the BBC. It was an attempt to double my money. I wrote the play on spec, not to commission. I was sitting in a café reading a Heiner Müller play and it's set on the Russian front in the Second World War and they're imagining the German coming and THE GERMAN is always in capital letters.[54] I read the first paragraph, that's all, and I had the idea for the play, wrote the first speech, knew what it was about. And I was writing *Pyrenees* at the time but I had this visceral feeling that if I didn't complete *The American Pilot* very quickly it would never be written, but I was also anxious that I didn't want to interrupt the writing of *Pyrenees* which also needed to go on. So I think I gave myself something like three days and decided I'll just have to get it out as fast as I can. And I thought, how will I get *paid* for this? So I sent it to the radio. But I always intended that it would be done on stage.

The Afghanistan situation it was responding to wasn't actually the invasion. Rufus Norris, when we were in Palestine, said to me, did I know about this group of people living in a valley in Afghanistan, and the Taliban had closed in completely on them, and the Americans weren't supporting them, and he said 'they must be the most fucked people on earth'. What he was actually talking about was Ahmad Shah Massoud in the Panjshir Valley, who was holding out against the Taliban. So the area I had in my mind was a high, remote central

Asian valley with a warlord fighting against a much more powerful set of enemies who wasn't friendly with the Americans – basically a really complicated geopolitical situation, into which plops the American pilot.

It came out in 2005 at the height of the invasion of Afghanistan, but what I was much more interested in was to ask what is the world like from the point of view of people in Afghanistan? And since they're probably not going to write plays about it that will get on at the RSC in the immediate future, I was trying – in a Brechtian way – to make that imaginative leap. But there was another thing and it's a Scottish thing; I noticed that people often talked about Afghanistan in terms of 'clans', 'warlords', 'mountains' and it's all supposed to be terrible, but I come from a country where we mythologize that as our romantic past. There are stories about how, you know, the Macdonalds were betrayed by the Campbells and the Campbells were in league with the government and so on, that would sit completely within an Afghan context. So I had this feeling that we're very quick to say 'warlord' as if there's no society behind that or complexity or reason for people to behave in certain ways. All I thought was that the alien invader is American and they have to react to it, and if I try to inhabit them as best I can, something interesting will occur that might illuminate why people behave in ways that seem mysterious or savage or bewildering.

Also I'd been doing these workshops in Ramallah when the Israelis first used F16s to bomb the Palestinian territories. So I had been on the other end of a place that was bombed. And I fucking hated it, hated it beyond measure; I can't tell how angry I felt – and I was just *nearby*. And when I was writing this play part of me wanted to express how, if you bomb people, you take people who are possibly complex, sophisticated and even friendly towards you, and turn them into people who will hate you. That's certainly what the ending is about, that feeling when, out of nowhere, you are under assault in the most horrific way.

Ramin [Gray]'s production of the play is one of my favourite productions of any of my plays. He did a very Brechtian production; the violence against the American pilot is very abstracted; he used a lot of music. It was very like *The Caucasian Chalk Circle*, people sitting around, telling a story. And then he used every bit of resource that the

267

RSC had in a sustained, ten-minute barrage at the end, where he got extras who were in the company, who would rope in from the ceiling, there were smoke bombs, guns, shooting, the loudest sounds it was legal to have. And you had come to believe that wasn't the play you thought you were in.

I thought I will make this as true as I can to the upper Panjshir Valley at a particular time but I won't name God – I'll just make people quite religious – I'll give people names that are as recognizable as possible, I'll make them speak in English rather some made-up language . . . and that was Brecht, for me. Brecht was my mode. With *Damascus*, I made the conscious choice to really locate it in Syria; they would be actual people with particular Syrian names and so on. But there's a tremendous anxiety behind both plays, which is the anxiety of authority. I don't know that both plays entirely solve that problem, but perhaps what I'd say is that the problem of authority comes about from the question – and this goes back to *San Diego* – how can you write *Our Town* if our town is also Afghanistan? I don't feel I can write *my* story unless Afghanistan is somewhere in the picture. And if I always only do that from my point of view and don't try to imagine the other point of view, where does that take me? And we understand that question on the individual level: we say, men can write women, and posh people can write poor people, and vice versa, but we haven't worked this out at the level of globalization. And maybe if I hadn't done workshops for ten years across the Middle East/North Africa region getting something like 45 plays from young writers, I might not feel I was entitled to have a go myself at writing some characters from the Middle East. Because I do think that the way to hear stories from the Middle East is to have people from the Middle East write those stories. But it also seems to me there are pressing things to be discussed and they have to be discussed.

Obviously there's a lot of Brecht in it too. It's a kind of *lehrstück*.[55] Of course, I recognize that I'm hanging on to a particular understanding of Brecht that I got at a particular time that I find useful. I wouldn't pretend to be an expert. But what I find useful goes back to Marisa's comment to the *San Diego* actor that you're on a stage, this happens on a stage. I keep coming back to that. I also think it's the best answer to the problem of representation, that if you're clear that you're telling a story on a stage, representation becomes much less of an issue than if you have some pretence that you're showing people something real. I was recently discussing this in relation to the issues around disability in the theatre, because lots of people say we need more parts for disabled people and part of me wants to say there shouldn't be such a thing as a part for disabled people if that means there are parts that are not for disabled people; disabled people should be able to play any part. And you get the response, ah but that won't work, because it's not plausible that this particular character would be disabled, and you go round the houses on that, but surely the answer is don't set it in a house: set it on a stage. You say, here's the troupe of actors and they're going to tell this story and it could be, I don't know, the story of Sinbad the Sailor or the story of Jesse Owens at the 1936 Olympics. And it doesn't mean that at a stroke you've solved every possible political problem, but it does mean you're freed of that terrifying anxiety. That only works if you've committed to it and I'm more and more interested in committing to that.

What I also think about with Brecht is a sort of total theatrical boldness that has no rules, no fear, no sense of the impossible. So he does the flight of Lindbergh across the Atlantic and the sea is played by a choir. Brecht also means music and what I like about putting music on a stage is that it changes the space into a space in which we are performers and you are an audience and we all know we're here and we're going to tell you a story. And I think he has an interesting fight with himself, which I also feel. There's a kind of Good Brecht and there's a Naughty Brecht. Good Brecht wants to be a communist and wants to tell people important things about the world, and Naughty Brecht wants to fuck around and have sex with actresses and be amazing on a stage and fuck up Good Brecht's work. He's Baal, basically. And I like that tension of the writer who is attempting to apply their intellect to think through things and is constantly being sabotaged by their id rampaging across the stage. And then there's politics, which in some ways is the least important aspect for me. But it's more the idea that the theatre is an excellent place to embody political problems and look at them and analyze them and work them out. But Good Brecht thinks he already knows what the answer is, though Naughty Brecht puts paid to a lot of that. Whereas I would go in a more Adorno-y way to say that the theatre is an excellent place to embody insoluble tensions, such that one maybe finds a gap or a moment of insight.[56]

Damascus

Damascus is my most – I hesitate to say this – David Harean play. I mean it's a four-walls, naturalistic . . . okay, it's got God in it, but it's got a central character whose experience of Syria is not dissimilar to mine. But when that play toured through the Middle East, one of the things I was accused of was Orientalism and probably not without foundation.[57]

I first went to the Middle East in 1999, with Rufus Norris (to devise and make a comedy about the intifada in Arabic . . .).[58] This will seem like enormous hindsight but I think I did manage to write it so I feel I can lay claim to this: I kept working with a generation of young people who seemed to me to be open, interesting, willing to talk, but crushed between the Scylla and Charybdis of a West that was determined to see them as hostile and the dead hand of a regime – whether Syria, Egypt, even the Palestinian Authority – dead, autocratic failed regimes that couldn't let them progress. And then, coming up was fundamentalist Islam, which they were also not buying into. During the ten years I was working in the region, things like Facebook developed and they were all on that. These were middle-class kids because that's mainly who would speak English and come to a writing workshop, so I'm not saying they were completely representative of the Arab people, but I was struck by how much I liked them, how interesting they were and how much they had to say about the world we're in. And I was saying all through that decade, I would grab people and say: these are the people that we need to be talking to. I mean my joke is that *Damascus* played in Syria, Egypt, Tunisia and look what happened a year later: the Arab Spring. . . . I'm not saying I knew that would happen, in fact if you'd asked me I'd have said no, that's extremely unlikely, but it turns out that that generation was more than 27 playwrights; they *were* representative of a whole situation in need of release.

So I originally wrote *Damascus* to tell Western audiences about those people and it was never intended to go to the Middle East; but when the British Council said they wanted to tour it, I had a very difficult time in a number of places. We'd have after-show discussions and the audience would be quite hostile; they'd shout things like 'a young Syrian person is proud to be Syrian; they would never kill themselves – this is a non-Arab act!' And I'd think, maybe they're right, maybe I am an Orientalist, but then when the Arab Spring starts after a young Arab man, so trapped by the situation he finds himself in, sets fire to himself in Tunis, well, I won't say I feel vindicated, but I do wish I could replay some of those conversations. Virtually every male playwright I worked with over there, virtually all of their plays ended in suicide. I *knew* that young Arab men were haunted by the idea of suicide as a means of escape from oppression. And of course after the talks I'd get a queue of young people coming up to me and saying 'don't listen to what they said, you got it exactly right but we can't speak, because he's our professor. . . .' So now I feel differently about it but at the time it was horrible.

And I have some sympathy with them. Imagine there was a play called *Edinburgh*, written by an American and funded by the CIA (because the British Council is understood by many in the Arab World to be an arm of the Foreign Office and therefore virtually MI6 . . .), which comes to the biggest theatre in Edinburgh, and has a budget ten times anything you'd ever get in Scotland, and imagine that every actor in it is an American doing a Scottish accent, how do you think people are going to feel? So if the play survived any of that, it's fortunate.

You know, it was censored? When we played it there, it was censored by the Syrian authorities. But then I was invited to read from the play at a dinner for the British Syrian Society at the Syrian Embassy in London. And the Syrian ambassador specifically chose that I read a section that had been censored and as I read it, he kept thumping the table and saying, 'That's *exactly* right, that's *exactly* right'. Fuck knows what was going on there. And we went to America, at the 59East59 Theatre, in the heart of the Upper West Side – which is probably the most pro-Israeli area of the world outside Tel Aviv, I should imagine. Why they chose to put *Damascus* on I don't know, but we got a bit of a pasting. Though I changed the ending. He didn't kill himself, he

271

burned his script. I think I was very affected by being told that an Arab man wouldn't kill himself.

The thing is, without going into too much detail, most of what happens in the play is true. For example, the first time I went to Damascus, I lost my sense of smell and the ammonia in the toilets was the only thing that could cut through that, which just seemed funny to me. And the piano player is real; she was there, in the hotel I stayed in, every day. I'd come back to the hotel at midnight and she'd still be there, this Russian or maybe Lithuanian woman who was probably a concert-standard pianist and having to play fucking Richard Clayderman to the hotel guests. And Zakaria, I've written about meeting him in the Citadel in Aleppo,[59] so when people would tell me Zakaria couldn't exist, he's just one of your Orientalist fantasies, I'd think yeah – except that I met him and he spoke to me and I've pretty much quoted him word-for-word.

Damascus got a very naturalistic production. It could have a much less naturalistic production. It has a 'dream play' quality to it. I have said you could replace the word 'Damascus' with the word 'writing' and it would still make sense. I don't know if that's true; I think that's true. I think it's surprisingly true. I think the play is as much about writing as it is about the Middle East. *Damascus* is all about representation and writing is also about representation. So being worried about being called Orientalist is entirely what that sort of play should be about, because it's a play that's already aware of that; that's what 'Middleton Road' is about, that's what Muna's edits are about. But also, the piano player, that's a bit like David Greig in *San Diego*, or God or something. I kept saying to Philip [Howard, the director], the piano player makes everything happen: that foyer is both a naturalistic foyer of a hotel in Damascus and it's also heaven, a dream world – or it's the stage isn't it? It's the stage on which representation happens. One thing that became clear to me – and this is a very typical *Damascus* problem – when I say to you 'Damascus', until recently, you would probably not have thought of Syria, you'd have thought of Saint Paul and you'd imagine this is a play about someone who undergoes a conversion. And that was absolutely in my mind, but of course in the Middle East it doesn't have that resonance at all. Even for Christians in the Middle East it doesn't have that resonance. To get a sense of how they heard the title in the Middle East, I might as well have called it *Birmingham*.

Damascus Notes, September 2006

This short document, no more than a page, is Greig's first roughing out of what would become his play Damascus. *The final play is still visible from these fragments.*

If You Do Not Stop Flying Your Children Will One Day Indict You For Crimes Against Humanity.

Or Damascus

Paul, a small businessman, goes on a trip to Damascus hoping to seal a deal.

Peter
Leila
Zacharias
Trader
Youthful Girl
Youthful Boy
Wife/
Singer

He does not want to go. He wants to be safe. He tries not to think about things. He tries to put his worries to the back of his mind. Has lost his sense of smell.

Powerful argument and dialogue scenes, real barnstorming
speeches.
Songs and singing from lounge singer in hotel.
He goes through many emotions/big emotions.
Brecht influence.
Some kind of climactic ending of violence. Or beginning of
violence?
A man wants.

Damascus Diary, March 2009

The Traverse Theatre production of Greig's Damascus *went on a short tour to the Middle East. It received many admiring and some angry responses. After several such evenings, Greig wrote emails home.*

(Sorry about the length of this email. I didn't have time to make it shorter.)

Sorry for radio silence. I thought I would have free time on this trip but I don't. I've been scheduled to do press conferences and talks and meeting writers and so on – The moments of silence I manage to get are so precious that even texting seems too wordy and I just sort of sit and stare out into space.

I loved your email the other night by the way . . . the little contacts from you and from a + r are lovely little cool droplets of home in the middle of the noisy souk of here.

The show went well the first night and the audience were with it from the start. They laughed and gasped. I felt extremely proud when I saw groups of women wearing headscarves giggling and tutting at the central romance.

The actors rose to it beautifully and did a great show. But what affected me most was that – seen through this audience's eyes – the play was a better play. Scenes which were a kind of generalised local colour in the UK were, here, very alive and very important debates which – being aired in public like this – created an electric atmosphere. It was as if the audience completed the play for me. All the gaps I felt in the UK were filled in by the knowledge and the feelings the audience brought to it. I felt proud.

Up on stage for the post show and hundreds of people had stayed. Suddenly the whole atmosphere turned. A woman started shouting at me that I portrayed negative stereotypes of Arabs. Another man said 'no Syrian woman would behave like this' . . . someone else called me an 'neo-orientalist'. All of this was filtered through translation and there was no chair or moderator so it quickly descended into a shouting match. I was desperately trying to NVC[60] the comments but I was being drowned out by shouting. Also – I was getting more and more emotional. They were so horrible. They said Zakaria committing suicide was wrong and Arab boys don't do things like that or feel things like that. Effectively saying that what I had seen, I hadn't seen. That I was racist and that they were offended by my traduction of their city. One person interpreted Paul's lost sense of smell being rediscovered in a toilet by the smell of piss as saying 'you think Damascus smells of piss, that's all you're interested in.'

Eventually I sort of burst out in a very passionate speech which, I'm told, my voice was cracking a bit with emotion but I absolutely don't remember anything I said except that I wrote the play with an open heart and I felt sad that people were hearing things I didn't say.

I felt very shaken but then afterwards I was surrounded by a group of twenty or so young women – who all excitedly and passionately told me how much they liked the play. It transpired that the audience was heavily dominated by a party of students and tutors from the Drama Academy. The people shouting at me were the teachers at the Drama Academy and the students – who had been much much more positive about the play – didn't want to speak up publicly and say they had liked it because they were intimidated by their tutors.

The stage management were trying to drag me out to the bus at after midnight and there were two girls still waiting. I said 'I'm sorry I have to go' and one said 'Please I've waited and waited and missed my bus to talk to you . . .' So, of course I stayed and she said that she wanted to tell me how much the story of Zakaria affected her and that she totally disagreed with the shouters. This was how she felt. Then the other girl followed me to the bus and began to cry while she tried to tell me that Zakaria's suicide was not '"false"; – this is what we live with every day' she said. I felt pretty sure she meant 'this is what I live with every day' but I'm not sure.

Afterwards I was so shaky and angry and sad that I was desperate to be with the actors and share some camaraderie and a laugh and a drink. We went to a bar near our hotel and drank till about 4 in the morning.

Yesterday my head was thumping with hangover and nicotine and lack of sleep. Not only had I smoked two fags but also everyone smokes indoors here so I had been bathing in nicotine for hours.

A taxi took me to the press conference and as we drove to the venue I could see hills in the far distance. It was sunny but cool and I felt an almost physical craving to go and run them. Later I asked someone if there were walking trails in the countryside. 'No you cannot walk,' she said. I don't know why.

The Press conference turned out to be lovely. I was able to speak calmly and I answered a lot of the difficult questions well and NVCishly. It turns out there was an enormous amount of misunderstanding happening. Nobody here knows that 'Damascus' to us immediately suggests St Paul and The Road To Damascus. That, in English, their city name is a metaphor. So, for them, my title meant I must be writing directly about their city now. As if I'd called the play 'Cairo' or 'Birmingham'. So once I explained that there was a little relaxation.

One journalist who had disliked the play was a very very beautiful and bright young woman so . . . of course . . . she got a long in-depth interview . . . but bit by bit I got the wall of distrust down and by the end she said she was going to see the play again and she was beginning to think she might like it.

After the conf. I felt incredibly low. Really like the whole thing was a waste of time. I had this awful feeling that if they could be so distrustful of me and this play then what chance of contact or dialogue between people. I felt sad, and worried that the actors would go off on this tour and just face hostility everywhere. I felt sad that Laila's big project to bring east and west together through 'real' dialogue was failing.

The British Council director said, after the night before, 'Maybe we should bring some contemporary dance next year'. She wasn't joking.

So in the end I wandered out into the neighborhood of the theatre and looked for somewhere to eat. Just wandering about and enjoying an ordinary neighbourhood streetlife I felt I was in a lovely bubble away from words. I really do like this city and I really do like Damascenes and it felt reviving to just silently bathe in the café life and people watching.

I found a restaurant where nobody spoke English and I managed to order food and a 7 Up and write the diary.

Walking back to the theatre I felt like I was going to the firing squad. I expected hostile audience and more horrible shouting.

I had this thought going round and round in my head 'this is my punishment, this is my punishment, this is my punishment.'

What's my crime?

Suddenly it was the end and there was long and loud applause. The audience came out and I was told it was a huge hit and that the show had gone brilliantly. Better than the night before.

The post show discussion was beautifully chaired and the questions and comments much nicer. There were criticisms but they were said politely and responded to calmly. Afterwards the same gaggle of young people very keen to talk about how it had affected them.

Redemption

I felt so relieved. Even if there's criticism [in] the post-shows the show speaks to people and the actors out on stage are loving it. My mood, finally, was lifted.

Another night where no bedtime till four but no fags and a happy mood make a big difference.

Today – meetings with my lovely young writers and then a dinner.

* * *

Dear

Words words words everything is words . . . on Saturday at the big day long conference on Damascus and on 'The Idea Of The Other in British and Arab Theatre' . . . a young man came up to me. He told me he'd loved the play and that I ought to ignore anyone who told me that I'd got it wrong. He said – welcome to Damascus – even if it gives you an allergy.

I told him and his friend the story of my dream in which I was carrying a cart full of words, a yoke on my shoulders. They understood it instantly. For Arabs words are physical things – the Koran discourages representation of the human form and so Arab art is often Calligraphy. Making words physical.

They also understand dreams

So when I said about being a slave, under the yoke of words, and that's what the excema was telling me then they were very sympathetic. It also led to another observation – that I do have an allergy to Damascus

277

because – for me – the word 'Damascus' in the play *Damascus* means 'Writing'.

So when characters say 'Damascus is a place of changes' or 'Damascus belongs to us' they are really talking about the power of words.

They do seem to have the power to give me an allergy.

So in the spirit of trying to limit the amounts and since you'd been so lovely about receiving the last long email I decided to combine email and diary and save half my words – . . . I'll do it in headings though because it's harder to structure all these events chronologically – it would take a literary strength I don't think I have after such an intense week.

[*Diary continued March 19th, Train London To Edinburgh*]

So to resume the story.

I met one of my young Syrian writers, Abdullah in the foyer and he led me through the weekend streets to a place called The Art Café. Abdullah's a lovely young man, determined to write and to bring together other writers. After I left Damascus a couple of years ago he was a major catalyst in forming the writers group 'The Street'. There is no support for young writers in Syria and precious little encouragement so they got together and now meet every month to exchange their plays, set writing tasks for each other and they have even organised readings of their work.

Abdullah was happy to see me and told me all about the work they'd been doing as we walked along. He was worried that [I] would have been upset by people's reaction to the play.

At the café half the group were there. They asked questions about the play and I asked them about their responses. They were mostly very positive but not without questions or criticisms. Mostly they didn't like the production which they thought was too naturalistic. The set, they thought, was a cliché.

KM came along later, I had invited her to meet them. She was very good with them and they eventually told us what they had been working on. As each of them told us the outline of the play they were writing I felt immensely proud of them. Regardless of the immediate quality of their work their determination to write new plays and to support the writing of new plays will in the end produce a world where the kids below them will inherit a larger space to write than they had and so on.

Philip was ill. After all the stress of getting the show in he slept for 19 hours. So KM and I went alone to the meeting of speakers – a preliminary to the conference.

We were taken to a very swanky restaurant on a hill looking out over the river Barada which runs through the city. The sun was going down, the moon rising over the mountain and the city looked beautiful.

We were served bittersweet mint lemonade and Turkish coffee.

The meeting wasn't easy. One of the speakers, Osama, a teacher at the Drama School, had greatly disliked the play. He also didn't like the way the panels were organised: one British panel then one Arab panel. There was much talking about talking. Much dismantling of the theme 'representing the other in theatre' . . . Shaza, who was organising the event and had been very close to tears for days now occasionally erupting in sobs when people's criticism got too much . . . looked as if she was about to crack.

I said that every conference I had ever been to began with each speaker explaining how the conference title was wrong and anyway they were the wrong person to speak about it.

Osama kept wanting 'context' and I got a handle on his problem. It's not so much that he disliked the play as he disliked the unfairness of the world that allowed me to swan about writing plays like that and having them staged in his city while he had had to stifle his own creativity and bury himself in a job. He clearly hated teaching students art they would never have a chance to pursue for a living.

He was an angry man

At dinner I wore my suit. All the girls on the show had put on their best dresses. Dolya looked stunning in a little black number with pearls. I sat next to Tash who had scrubbed up rather glamorously as well but was wearing a shawl as she had spotted that every Syrian woman in the restaurant was covered.

KM sat next to Osama and tried to persuade him to like the play.

279

KM told me that Osama had said to her that he was annoyed by my writing workshops. His students had told them they were 'the best thing they had ever done'. I'd screwed with his teaching.

Paul Higgins had a big grin as he wandered around organising us to go up to his new friend's club. He told me about his mate and about the trip to the shrine and about the electricity on stage. I could feel him just relishing the intellectual, acting and physical challenge of it all. He was up for it and it was up for him.

Karim's club was very trendy – a converted bath house – marble floors, rich thirtysomething couples, eighties music – it was eighties night.

Karim told me later that everything's changed in the last eight years. The arrival of satellite channels mean that everyone has complete exposure to ideas outside the regime. Also, Bashir, the son of the old President Assad, is a young western educated man at the head of a young elite who are desperate to open up to globalisation.

Economically they're strong at the moment because they had no credit crunch. Everything feels possible.

He told me the regime use censorship not to control information (everyone has satellite) but as a sort of bargaining chip with the West. When they want to show willing with America they loosen censorship. When they want to play hardball they tighten it up again. 'It's a sign of weakness, they have no other chips to play with'.

I talked a lot to Joyce McMillan about Scotland and Syria and theatre and poetry and all sorts. Her eyes sparkle when she talks about ideas. Someone handed out tequila with oranges and cinnamon coffee grounds which you drink down in one – then suck on the orange and coffee.

I was giddy.

One lot wanted to go back to the hotel. Another lot wanted to stay and dance. I knew I had to talk the next day so I went back.

I was on the first panel and I spoke a little about the play and how it came to be. I then went on to my main point. The play represents a battle of two aspirational political correctnesses – British and Syrian. Each believes that representing the world is a way of changing it. But – and this is what in the end I think the play is exploring – representation is always a failure. Writing can never capture. The only thing it can do, and it can do it brilliantly, is to conjure.

The panels both go well. Osama speaks with some hostility but not in an aggressive way. In the interval I am once more besieged by students telling me to ignore the criticisms. Then finally Dr Minha from Egypt, a chain smoking fiftysomething lady critic who said she was too nervous to speak – delivered a speech about the play. She said she read it imagining it had been written by an Arab writer. Suddenly she could see what it was trying to do. Laughter from the audience as she deconstructed it as an Arab text. Then she told a story about how she had wanted to write a memoir of her childhood but found she had forgotten it. She asked for photographs of her as a child from her family and eventually had seven photos. She said it was her childhood in a bag. She took them to Holland as part of a project and there they were stolen. I wasn't clear how this had happened. She knows how it feels she said to entrust your life to someone and for it to be taken away.

Lastly she spoke about a young Egyptian playwright whose play – which attacked the Saudi regime – had been taken off after complaints by the Saudi. A month later the young man had cut his wrists in the bath.

It happens.

I looked at Philip, he had tears welling up. Me too. I felt like for the first time in Syria and even for the first time ever since writing the play . . . someone had heard me.

Elizabeth White, the BC director sat next to me in the audience and sketched in her beautiful notebook. I noticed that she drew a picture of the forth rail bridge with mountains in the distance and a slim man in a suit leaning over a landrover gazing across the water at the hills . . . she titled it 'the traveller returns'. That set me crying. Quietly. But I needed it.

In the lunchbreak there was more lovely support from various youth. After lunch the discussion continued and was mostly extremely kind towards me and to the play. I tried to end on a positive note by finally hearing Osama and explaining the 'context' of *Damascus*. That the reason I can write *Damascus* in the way I do has only marginally to do with whatever talent I may have. It's the result of a longstanding new writing culture in a well-funded theatre sector and the decision of my powerful western country to fund tours of this type. None of this is available to a Syrian playwright. That must be annoying.

Nods.

In the evening I go with Katherine and Roxanna to meet with Mohammed (Syrian Writer from the Royal Court Group), Abed and Arze (Lebanese), Omar Abu Sadr (Syrian Director). We have some food and some beers. They are all charming to Rox and KM and they tell me about what they're writing and working on. I feel relaxed. No Royal Court line to peddle, no British Council line to peddle.

I explain that – and this is the truth – if it had been up to me I would have toured Damascus as a travelling reading with local actors. Something more low-key.

Later KM, Rox and I join Carole McFadden for drinks in Elizabeth White's house in the old town. It's a proper old Damascene courtyard. She's only just moved in so it's joyfully haphazard and undecorated. She says she's tempted to keep it that way.

So then four hours sleep and off to the airport. KM talks and talks and talks all the way to the airport. Rox and me are desperate for her to shut up.

At the airport café I show them how to read coffee grounds (Liz White taught me). You swirl the dregs in the cup then turn it upside down and let it drain. After a time you look at the patterns and interpret them.

I love this because it seems to me to be a clever way for Arab women to talk to each other and give advice and empathise indirectly – 'oh look Salma, it's a very regular pattern . . . maybe you need a more regular man in your life . . .'

My grounds seem to show a kangaroo raping a racoon.

In the airport KM has me do her grounds.

I swirl, I tip and I turn.

A thick glob of dark sludge slides back down the side of the cup.

'Goodness there's a lot of dark stuff down there.' Says KM.

She says it seems like a Tsunami. But that can't be right she says. No it's a volcano. No it's all wrong. Do it again.

I say, did you notice you used the metaphor of a tidal wave and a volcano when you looked at the grounds?

On the plane I write a short play for the Traverse Wildfire event. I sit down and write – letting the words conjure. It comes joyfully and easily and I'm pleased and intrigued with the play.

Rox and me watch Robin Hood with no sound on the tv and discuss how like *Dunsinane* it is – wenches and knights.

I joke about Shakespeare having to face a post-show discussion in Edinburgh after the Elizabethan Council's tour of *Macbeth* in Scotland.

Damascus, New York ending

As he says in the interview and diary, Greig experienced some hostility during the tour, particularly to the idea that Zakaria would kill himself. In May 2008, the production came to 59E59 Theatre in New York and Greig used the opportunity to rewrite the play, particularly its ending.

9.

[. . .][61]

Zakaria falls asleep.

Paul *(to himself)* Lover never know love never.
Lover never lover never love

Paul is asleep.
A taxi horn sounds.
It sounds again.
Zakaria wakes up.

Zakaria   Mr Paul.

Paul   Mmm.

Zakaria   Taxi is here.

Wake up, Mr Paul.
Wake up,

Paul   Oh great. Thanks Zakaria.

Zakaria Come, I take your luggage.

Paul No – I'll take it.

Zakaria OK.

Paul Zakaria, we understand each other, you and I.

Zakaria Of course.

Paul We have a connection.

Zakaria We connect

Paul We connect. Yes.

Look – Zakaria I hate goodbyes so:

I want you to have this -

Paul offers Zakaria the record player.

Zakaria No.

Paul I insist Zakaria.

It's a gift.

Zakaria Mr Paul.

Paul Please.

It's yours.

It belongs here, in Damascus.

Zakaria No.

Paul I insist.

Zakaria No.

Paul Really.

Zakaria No.

Paul Come on Zakaria.

Beat.

Zakaria takes the record player.

Thank you.

Zakaria Welcome.

Paul embraces Zakaria.

Paul leaves.

Zakaria takes his life out of the record player.

10.

Elena At this time in the morning, I play the notes so far apart you might not notice that it's music. But it is.

Zakaria takes his life out of the bag.

Zakaria puts his life in the fountain.

Zakaria burns his life.

Elena Poor Zakaria.

What else do you want me to say?

Welcome to Damascus.

What else could a transsexual Ukrainian Christian Marxist cocktail pianist possibly say that would make things any better for you?

I know.

I'm here.

I'm always here.

At this time of the morning I play the notes so far apart you might not even notice that it's music, but it is.

5. debbie tucker green

green is well-known for her belief that the work should speak for itself and she prefers not to give interviews and fiercely guards the privacy of her

285

creative process. In this section therefore, we have gathered a small selection of her rare public comments on the work.

Starting to write

I never set out to write plays. I was just messing about, writing stuff down and throwing it away or keeping it if it interested me. Then the writing started to get longer. I didn't know whether it was a poem, the lyrics to a song or a play. It is all much of a muchness to me. It's all words, ain't it?[62]

On dirty butterfly *and* born bad

To start with, both plays are quite mundane. Then they just get darker. I'm interested in normal situations that become dark. I find it intriguing; it's all out there. Somebody who beats on his wife might be the nicest workmate you can have. In *born bad*, I was interested in betrayal, in women betraying women, which is the point of the play.[63]

The psychology of her characters

You sometimes hear in trials of abusers that the mother said she didn't know. And you ask yourself: how come? [. . .] There's a whole heap of psychology going on and I'm not in a position to even go there. The play is about subjective truth. Each character has a version of the truth that is real to them.[64]

Dialogue

That's how people speak [. . .] Listen to a group of kids: just repeat and repeat and repeat [. . .] 'It's hot outside; it's really hot, innit? I bet it's really hot.' Suddenly you've got half a page of dialogue.[65]

Who she writes for

The people who influence me are the people who do their own thing. People who don't look left or right to check if they are doing the right thing, but who write what they think and what they feel. I don't write for critics. It is written for people who will feel it. It's for the people who come out saying 'That's just like my aunty' or 'That's just like me'.[66]

Being a black writer

I'm a black woman. I write black characters. That is part of my landscape. But with *Stoning Mary* I was interested in questioning what we don't see and hear. The stories of people who would be in the headlines every day if what was happening to them was happening to white people. It happens all the time. Look at Rwanda. It just fell out of the news. Or Zimbabwe. We're always hearing what is happening to the white farmers but what about the black political activists who are also being killed? Where are the news stories about them? [. . .] It makes me laugh when I walk into theatres and people are tripping over themselves because I am a black playwright. If you're black and working in a shop nobody trips over themselves.[67]

NOTES

1. Theatre in the 2000s

1. Popular twentieth century saying, attributed to Arnold Toynbee, cited in *The History*, Alan Bennet, Faber, 2004, p. 85.
2. http://beescope.blogspot.de/2007/10/way-upstream-well-known-ache-borne.html
3. *A State Affair* was Soans' second verbatim piece, following a piece inspired by Klaus Pohl's *Wartesaal Deutschland Stimmenreich* (translated as *Waiting Room Germany* – Royal Court, 1995) in 1997.
4. Nicholas de Jongh, *Evening Standard* review quoted: http://microsites.nationaltheatre.org.uk/?lid=7792&dspl=reviews
5. www.nationaltheatre.org.uk/discover-more/platforms/platform-papers/david-hare-on-the-permanent-way
6. www.defense.gov/Transcripts/Transcript.aspx?TranscriptID=2367
7. www.culturewars.org.uk/2005–01/terrorists.htm
8. http://microsites.nationaltheatre.org.uk/13361/watch-this-space-2007/roundtable-rumbles-politics-and-power.html
9. www.culturewars.org.uk/2007–05/account.htm
10. www.nationaltheatrescotland.com/content/default.asp?page=s161
11. One of the most interesting objections came from Chris Goode: 'It has refused the complexity and the contingency of [all of the critical objections that might be raised about it], it has simply populated itself with a bunch of lads who will alternately charm and threaten the objections out of you. But is it the reality of life in the theatre of war that's looming over you in that unarguable way? No, not a bit. It's the play itself. The play, not the men, is the real bully. The play is committed to a kind of partiality that's both awesomely seductive and deeply, erotically in love with the violence it narrates, for all that it might feel pity for its invisible victims or shame about its institutional basis.' http://beescope.blogspot.co.uk/2008/07/scattered-dreams-certain-treats.html

    Charles Spencer of the Daily Telegraph was sceptical: 'Having missed the show at its Edinburgh Festival premiere in 2006, I find myself in the uneasy position of belatedly reviewing a piece that has already been almost universally acclaimed as a masterpiece. Can *Black Watch* really be as good as it's cracked up to be? The short and brutal answer is no, it can't.' www.telegraph.co.uk/culture/theatre/drama/3555126/Black-Watch-searing-insights-into-the-horrors-of-modern-warfare.html
12. www.whatsonstage.com/features/theatre/northeast/E8831257785351/Philip+Ralph+on+the+Controversy+Around+Deep+Cut.html
13. www.whatsonstage.com/reviews/theatre/london/E8821157728073/Trouble+with+Asian+Men+(London+%26+tour).html
14. www.culturewars.org.uk/2007–06/baby.htm

15. www.recordeddelivery.net/ComeOutEliInfoPack.pdf
16. www.cix.co.uk/~shutters/reviews/04016.htm
17. www.guardian.co.uk/stage/2003/sep/09/theatre3
18. Chris Megson. *Modern British Playwriting: The 1970s* (London: Methuen Drama, 2012), pp. 37–8.
19. Unpublished interview with Andy Field, 2012.
20. http://thearcadesproject.blogspot.de/2007/10/rider-spoke-at-or-indeed-around.html
21. www.anthampton.com/romcom.html
22. www.anthampton.com/romcom_frank.html
23. Unpublished interview with Tim Crouch, 2012.
24. www.linkedm11.net/index2.html
25. www.independent.co.uk/arts-entertainment/music/news/city-opera-project-a-walkon-role-427141.html)
26. www.andwhilelondonburns.com/
27. www.melaniewilson.org.uk/projects/mari-me-archie
28. http://carouseloffantasies.blogspot.co.uk/2010/06/review-electric-hotel-sadlers-wells-off.html
29. http://postcardsgods.blogspot.co.uk/2009/10/beyond-frontline-lowry-salford.html
30. www.timeout.com/london/theatre/event/154752/they-only-come-at-night
31. http://postcardsgods.blogspot.de/2010/04/would-like-to-meet-barbican.html
32. www.thestage.co.uk/features/2010/10/in-a-world-thats-wired-for-sound/
33. www.timeout.com/london/theatre/features/6459/Best_theatre_of_2008.html
34. www.guardian.co.uk/stage/theatreblog/2008/feb/06/sitespecifictheatrepleasebe
35. www.shunt.co.uk/archives/reivewsbobfranctimeout2.htm
36. www.shunt.co.uk/archives/reviewsbobfrancguardian.htm
37. www.guardian.co.uk/stage/2000/aug/16/theatre.artsfeatures1
38. www.totaltheatre.org.uk/awards/pastwinners.html
39. Mark Espiner, *Time Out*, 14 February 2001, quoted: www.shunt.co.uk/archives/reviewsbobfranctimeout.htm
40. www.londontheatreblog.co.uk/mischa-twitchin-on-the-history-of-shunt-and-their-new-show-money/
41. Ibid.
42. www.guardian.co.uk/stage/2003/dec/17/theatre2
43. Tom Morris interviewed by Caroline Ansdell and Terri Paddock for *What's On Stage* www.whatsonstage.com/news/theatre/london/E8821153323003/NT+Supports+Punchdrunk's+New+Promenade+Faust.html
44. www.guardian.co.uk/stage/theatreblog/2007/oct/04/themasqueofthereddeathle
45. Andrew Haydon (ed.), *Raw Talent: 50 Years of the National Student Drama Festival* (London: Oberon, 2005).
46. www.guardian.co.uk/stage/2005/feb/24/theatre1
47. *Paper Stages* (Edinburgh: Forest Fringe, 2012).
48. www.guardian.co.uk/stage/theatreblog/2008/apr/03/foreditors9
49. http://encoretheatremagazine.blogspot.de/Polemics.html#Court
50. Unpublished interview with Duncan Macmillan, 2007.
51. Interview with anonymous Royal Court source and www.whatsonstage.com/news/theatre/london/E8821132739336/Caryl+Churchill+Pulls+Play+from+Royal+Court+50th.html
52. www.culturewars.org.uk/2006–01/drunkenough.htm
53. There is some dispute whether, thanks to the re-routing of some National Lottery money, this really amounted to as large an increase as was claimed – www.

publications.parliament.uk/pa/cm199900/cmhansrd/vo991126/debtext/91126–04.htm

54. www.guardian.co.uk/stage/theatreblog/2007/may/03/tonyblairbritishtheatresac

55. Bradwell, Mike, *The Reluctant Escapologist*, Nick Hern Books, London, 2010, p. 261.

56. The best study of this period is Jacqueline Bolton's as yet unpublished PhD thesis.

57. http://postcardsgods.blogspot.de/2011/03/rewriting-nation-aleks-sierz-methuen.html

58. Dan Rebellato, 'Review: State of the Nation by Michael Billington', *Contemporary Theatre Review*, 18 (2008), 528–30.

59. www.royalcourttheatre.com/playwriting/the-studio/unheard-voices/

60. www.guardian.co.uk/stage/theatreblog/2007/nov/04/shinetheatresspotlightonevery shadeofblack

61. An amusing example from a *Guardian* feature where they sent a writer to Russia to interview a new Royal Court playwright: '"That kind of contemporary dirty realism has been done before and much better by others," huffed one indignant colleague. "You should interview Bogaev or Leontchuk; those are the writers that we respect out here"' from www.guardian.co.uk/stage/2003/feb/03/theatre.artsfeatures

62. www.standard.co.uk/arts/theatre/courting-controversy-7195936.html

63. www.independent.co.uk/arts-entertainment/theatre-dance/news/royal-court-discovers-the-middleclass-hero-435336.html

64. www.guardian.co.uk/uk/2007/feb/07/theatrenews.theatre

65. www.telegraph.co.uk/news/uknews/1541825/Les-miserables-at-the-Royal-Court-throw-out-kitchen-sink-drama.html

66. Ramin Gray, personal interview. 12 October 2012.

67. www.culturewars.org.uk/2007–05/mychild.htm

68. www.culturewars.org.uk/2007–05/thatface.htm

69. www.nachtkritik.de/index.php?option=com_content&view=article&id=5616%3Askydiving-blindfolded-impulsreferat-des-britischen-dramatikers-simon-stephens-zur-eroeffnung-des-stueckemarkts-beim-theatertreffen-2011&catid=101%3Adebatte&Itemid=84

70. www.telegraph.co.uk/culture/theatre/drama/3604681/Magnificent-Moor.html

71. Goold had already directed Frank McGuinness' newly commissioned *Speaking Like Magpies* for the previous year's Gunpowder Season.

72. As Chris Goode puts it: 'this is emphatically not "director's theatre" of the kind our Eurosceptic parents warned us about, nor the creeping "auteurism" that so many middle-of-the-road playwrights like to use, to such little effect, as a piñata when they feel like giving something – anything, but preferably something inexistent which cannot then speak up for itself – an aggrieved thwack'. http://beescope.blogspot.de/2009/02/all-face.html

73. www.culturewars.org.uk/2006–01/faustus.htm

74. http://postcardsgods.blogspot.co.uk/2007/09/macbeth-gielgud-theatre.html

75. http://postcardsgods.blogspot.de/2008/09/six-characters-in-search-of-author.html

76. www.guardian.co.uk/stage/2008/oct/08/pinter

77. http://headlong.co.uk/productions/production_details.php?Title=King_Lear&production_id=9

78. www.guardian.co.uk/culture/2008/nov/07/pete-postlethwaite-king-lear

79. Dan Rebellato, 'Katie Mitchell: Learning from Europe', in *Contemporary European Theatre Directors*, ed. Maria M. Delgado and Dan Rebellato (Abingdon: Routledge, 2010), pp. 317–38.

80. www.cix.co.uk/~shutters/reviews/02092.htm
81. www.ft.com/cms/s/0/089cbec6–12e4–11dd-8d91–0000779fd2ac.html
82. www.guardian.co.uk/stage/2007/may/25/theatre1
83. http://beescope.blogspot.de/2007/10/way-upstream-well-known-ache-borne.html
84. http://encoretheatremagazine.blogspot.de/Polemics.html#Nunn
85. www.guardian.co.uk/stage/2002/sep/16/theatre.artsfeatures
86. www.telegraph.co.uk/culture/theatre/drama/3593690/Hooray-for-Springers-trail-of-trash.html
87. www.culturewars.org.uk/2007–06/philistines.htm
88. www.guardian.co.uk/stage/2005/jun/27/theatre
89. http://theater.nytimes.com/2010/09/29/theater/reviews/29brief.html?_r=0&adxnnl =1&pagewanted=all&adxnnlx=1354208738-egWNWlHeiI1rNmhM+walQw
90. www.guardian.co.uk/stage/2007/dec/21/theatre
91. *Times* 14 May 2007
92. www.guardian.co.uk/stage/theatreblog/2007/jun/03/whatireallythinkaboutthea
93. *Prompt Corner*, www.cix.co.uk/~shutters/reviews/07123.htm
94. Ian Shuttleworth in his *Prompt Corner* column for *Theatre Record* two years earlier, for example: 'The number-ones have been around now for a fair old time. In his recent public lecture on the history of *Theatre Record*, my esteemed colleague and predecessor Ian Herbert pointed out that our very first issue in 1981 contained reviews by Michael Billington, Michael Coveney, Nicholas de Jongh, Sheridan Morley and Benedict Nightingale. While Michael B. is the only one still writing for the same publication, the point stands: room is simply not being made for the next generation to come through, in a way that did happen more often for our predecessors.' www.compulink.co.uk/~shutters/reviews/05141.htm
95. Michael Billington. *State of the Nation: British Theatre since 1945* (London: Faber & Faber, 2007), p. 409.
96. www.guardian.co.uk/stage/2007/may/11/theatre2
97. http://beescope.blogspot.co.uk/
98. http://onewriterandhisdog.blogspot.co.uk/
99. http://onewriterandhisdog.blogspot.co.uk/
100. www.superfluitiesredux.com/
101. http://theatrenotes.blogspot.co.uk/
102. www.guardian.co.uk/stage/theatreblog/2007/oct/09/fromthetheatreblogs
103. 'We would not normally list bloggers, but this duo brought the blogosphere into repute with their 'Paint Never Dries" tag for Lloyd Webber's *Love Never Dies*.' – www.thetimes.co.uk/tto/arts/stage/theatre/article2844309.ece
104. www.guardian.co.uk/stage/theatreblog/2007/oct/04/themasqueofthereddeathle
105. www.guardian.co.uk/stage/theatreblog/2006/dec/04/wavessetsahighwatermarkfo
106. www.guardian.co.uk/commentisfree/2007/oct/02/comment.art
107. www.guardian.co.uk/stage/theatreblog/2007/sep/17/whoneedsreviews

2. Playwrights and Plays

1. Simon Stephens, *Plays: 3* (London: Methuen Drama, 2011), p. 322.

Playwrights and Plays: Simon Stephens

* I am grateful to Simon Stephens for making available unpublished material.

1. Simon Stephens, *Bluebird*, in *Plays: 1* (London: Methuen, 2005), pp. 26–7.

2. Stephens, *Plays: 1*, p. viii.

3. Eastbrook School in Dagenham is where the protagonist of *Motortown*, Danny, claims he went to school. See Simon Stephens, *Motortown*, in *Plays: 2* (London: Methuen, 2009), p. 173. all further quotations from *Motortown* taken from this source.

4. Simon Stephens, unpublished interview with Jacqueline Bolton, 18 May 2010.

5. Simon Stephens, qtd. Aleks Sierz, 'Breaking In', *The Stage* (2004) www.thestage.co.uk/features/feature.php/3373/breaking-in-simon-stephens (Accessed 3 August 2010).

6. Compare with Robbie's speech in Mark Ravenhill's *Shopping and Fucking* (1996): 'I think . . . I think we all need stories, we make up stories so that we can get by. And I think a long time ago there were big stories. Stories so big you could live your whole life in them. The Powerful Hands of the Gods and Fate. The Journey to Enlightenments [sic.]. The March of Socialism. But they all died or the world grew up or grew senile or forgot them, so now we're all making up our own stories. Little stories. It comes out in different ways. But we've each got one'. *Modern Drama: Plays of the 80s and 90s* (London: Methuen, 2001), p. 335).

7. Aleks Sierz, *In-Yer-Face Theatre: British Drama Today* (London: Faber & Faber, 2001), p. 4.

8. Sierz, *In-Yer-Face Theatre*, pp. 4, 6.

9. Ibid., p. 4.

10. Aleks Sierz, 'Still In-Yer-Face? Towards a Critique and a Summation', *New Theatre Quarterly*, 18.1 (2002), pp. 17–24 (p. 20).

11. Sierz, 'Still In-Yer-Face?' p. 21.

12. Ken Urban, 'Cruel Britannia', in *Cool Britannia? British Political Drama in the 1990s*, ed. Rebecca D'Monté and Graham Saunders (Basingstoke: Palgrave Macmillan, 2008), pp. 38–55 (p. 38).

13. All references to these plays in the text are taken from Simon Stephens, *Plays: 2* (London: Methuen, 2009).

14. Anderson also directed *Bluebird* (1998) and *Country Music* (2004), both at the Royal Court.

15. Stephens, 18 May 2010.

16. Amanda (Milly) Dowler was 13 years old when she was abducted on her way home from school in Walton-on-Thames, Surrey, on the 21 March 2002. Her body was discovered in Minley Woods near Yateley Heath, Hampshire, on 18 September 2002. In March 2010, eight years after her disappearance, Levi Bellfield, a 41-year-old former doorman, was charged with her kidnap and murder.

17. Lyn Gardner, *One Minute* review, *Guardian*, 9 June 2003. Reprinted in *Theatre Record*, 21 May–17 June 2003, p. 770.

18. Stephens, 18 May 2010.

19. Dan Rebellato, 'New Theatre Writing: Simon Stephens', *Contemporary Theatre Review* 15.1 (2005), pp. 174–8, (p. 175).

20. Jeremy Kingston, *One Minute* review, *The Times*, 10 June 2003. Reprinted in *Theatre Record*, 21 May–17 June 2003, p. 770.

21. Fiona Mountford, *One Minute* review, *Evening Standard*, 9 February 2004. Reprinted in *Theatre Record*, 29 January–11 February 2004, p. 150.

22. Ibid.; Patrick Marmion, *One Minute* review, *Time Out* 11 February, 2004. Reprinted in *Theatre Record*, 29 January–11 February 2004, p. 150.

23. Charles Spencer, *One Minute* review, *Daily Telegraph*, 10 February 2004. Reprinted in *Theatre Record* 29 January–11 February 2004, p. 151.

24. Ibid., p. 231.

25. Stephens was in fact father to two boys, Oscar and Stanley, at the time of writing *One Minute*. His daughter, Scarlett, was born in 2007.

26. Spencer, *One Minute* review, p. 151.

27. Rebellato, 'New Theatre Writing: Simon Stephens', p. 175.

28. Ian Shuttleworth, *One Minute* review, *Financial Times*, 11 February 2004. Reprinted in *Theatre Record* 29 January–17 February 2004, p. 151.

29. Gordon Anderson, unpublished interview with Jacqueline Bolton, 5 May 2010.

30. 'At the time [of the workshops for *One Minute*], although I was aware of the disconnect between people, I also became aware of the power of tiny connections and their capacity to heal. And this didn't only become part of the content of the play, it was also part of the process of putting it on – what happened with the actress who improvised a lot of Marie Louise's stuff was one of these "connects". This actress wasn't free when we came to do the production because she was going to drama school. I ran into her some years later and she said that she had decided after *One Minute* that she wanted to be an actress properly and had gone to drama school partly because of those workshops. So, out of what was quite a bleak beginning for me, something happened which was an inspiration to someone else – a connection! And it was a two-way street; she was inspired to go to drama school and we were inspired by her imagination and we used it in the play. I showed her the script and said "look, there's your speech!" She was really, really touched by that'. Anderson, 5 May 2010.

31. Sarah Frankcom, unpublished interview with Jacqueline Bolton, 28 June 2010.

32. Paul asks this of Danny in *Motortown*, p. 167. I am grateful to Ramin Gray for these thoughts.

33. Stephens, 18 May 2010.

34. Stephens, *Plays: 2*, p. xi.

35. The hijackers crashed a third plane into the Pentagon in Arlington, Virginia. The fourth plane crashed into a field near Shanksville in rural Pennsylvania after some of its passengers and flight crew attempted to retake control of the plane, which the hijackers had redirected towards Washington, DC. The invasion of Afghanistan was launched in order to depose the Taliban, a political regime suspected of harbouring al-Qaeda terrorists.

36. The Second Gulf War began in March 2003 with the stated intention of removing from power the Iraqi dictator, Saddam Hussein. The regime of Saddam Hussein was toppled within three weeks of combat operations.

37. Live 8 was a series of benefit concerts held on the 2 July 2005 in the G8 states and South Africa. They were timed to coincide with the G8 conference in Scotland from 6–8 July and the twentieth anniversary of Live Aid. The success of London's Olympic bid was announced by the International Olympic Committee in Singapore on the 6 July 2005.

38. Stephens, 18 May 2010.

39. Stephens, *Plays: 2*, p. xvii.

40. Ramin Gray, unpublished interview with Jacqueline Bolton, 24 May 2010.

41. Simon Stephens, 'Why I Wrote *Motortown*', education pack produced by the Royal Court Theatre, 2006. p. 4. Provided by Simon Stephens.

42. Simon Stephens, qtd. Nadia Abrahams, 'Simon Stephens: Interview', *Time Out*, 19 April 2006. www.timeout.com/london/theatre/features/244/Simon_Stephens-Interview.html (Accessed 30 August 2010).

43. Gray, 24 May 2010.

44. Dan Rebellato, 'When We Talk of Horses; Or, what do we see when we see a play?', *Performance Research*, 14.1 (2009), pp. 17–28 (p. 18).

45. Rebellato, 'When We Talk of Horses', p. 25.

46. Interestingly, the character of Paul tacitly summarizes this condition of theatre and performance in one of his pseudo-philosophical spiels: 'There is no solidity. Only a perception of solidity. There is no substance. Only the perception of substance. There is no space. Only the perception of space. This is a freeing thing, in many ways, Danny. It means I can be anywhere. At any time. I can do anything. I just need to really try' (164). Stephens, *Motortown*, p. 164.

47. Stephens, 18 May 2010.

48. See Stephens, *Plays: 2*, p. xvii; Simon Stephens, *Motortown*, unpublished draft dated 20 July 2005, p. 2. Apart from Marley and Jade, all the names in *Motortown* are the first names of the actors for whom Stephens initially wrote the character: Lee Ross, Tom Brooke, Helen Schlesinger, Justin Salinger and Paul Ritte. Stephens, 18 May 2010.

49. Stephens attests to a number of audience members asking afterwards whether there was petrol or water in the canister. Informal conversation with Jacqueline Bolton, 7 September 2010.

50. Matt Wolf, *Rainbow Kiss/Motortown* review, *International Herald Tribune*, 24 May 2006. Reprinted in *Theatre Record* 7–20 May 2006, p. 603.

51. Dan Rebellato, 'New Theatre Writing: Dennis Kelly', *Contemporary Theatre Review*, 17.4 (2007), pp. 603–8 (p. 606).

52. Simon Stephens, qtd. Steve Cramer, 'Pornography – Simon Stephens Interview: Shock Values', *The List*, 17 July 2008. www.list.co.uk/article/10159-pornography-simon-stephens-interview/ (Accessed 16 September 2010).

53. Stephens, *Plays 2*, p. xviii.

54. http://news.bbc.co.uk/1/shared/spl/hi/uk/05/london_blasts/victims/default.stm> (Accessed 16 September 2010).

55. Stephens, *Plays 2*, p. xviii.

56. See Sarah Grochala, 'Shaping the Political: The Politics of Dramatic Structure in Contemporary British Playwriting', unpublished PhD thesis, Queen Mary University, pp. 70–87.

57. See Stephens, *Plays 2*, p. 221, p. 230, p. 265.

58. Stephens, *Plays 2*, p. xxi.

59. Sean Holmes, unpublished interview with Jacqueline Bolton, 21 June 2010.

60. Ibid.

61. Nübling had previously directed Stephens' *Herons* at the Staatsschauspiel Stuttgart, in conjunction with the Junges Theater, Basel, in 2003.

62. Stephens, 18 May 2010.

63. Stephens, *Plays 2*, p. xix.

64. Stephens, 18 May 2010.

65. Ibid.

66. The list of characters in this draft reads: Jason, Sarah, Mark, Marie Louise, Bryony, Rebecca, Kane, Richard, David. The file is saved as 'Pornography draft chronological english'.

67. Simon Stephens, *Pornography*, unpublished draft dated 8 December 2006, p. 2.
68. Holmes, 21 June 2010.
69. Stephens, 18 May 2010.
70. Gray, 24 May 2010.
71. Stephens, 18 May 2010.
72. Ibid.
73. Ibid.

Playwrights and Plays: Tim Crouch

1. Tim Crouch, quoted in Stephen Bottoms, 'Authorising the Audience: the Conceptual Drama of Tim Crouch', *Performance Research*, 14.1 (2009), p. 67.
2. Tim Crouch, *An Oak Tree* in *Plays One* (London: Oberon, 2011), p. 101. All page numbers in the body of the essay refer to this volume.
3. A couple of them are published in Tim Crouch, '*The Author*: Response and Responsibility', *Contemporary Theatre Review*, 21.4 (2011), pp. 416–22.
4. Foyles bookshop in London organized a 'Play of the Decade' promotion in 2010, asking a number of playwrights to suggest their play of the 2000s. Churchill's text is quoted from an email from the event's organizer Seanan McDonnell, 27 April 2012.
5. Quoted in Patrick O'Kane (ed.), *Actors' Voices: The People Behind the Performances* (London: Oberon, 2012), p. 88.
6. See Stephen Bottoms, 'Authorising the Audience', for a sophisticated account of Crouch's affinities with debates around performance art.
7. Quoted in O'Kane, *Actors' Voices*, p. 89.
8. Actioning is a rehearsal technique associated with the British director Max Stafford-Clark and involves assigning an active, transitive verb to every line (e.g. 'persuades', 'seduces', 'threatens') to explain what the dialogue is *doing* rather than merely what it *means*. Hot-seating involves improvizing answers to questions while in character: there is a complex example of this in Crouch's *The Author*: Tim Crouch, *Plays One* pp. 185–8.
9. Tim Crouch. 'Darling You Were Marvellous' in *Out of the Silence*, ed. Caridad Svich (Roskilde: Eyecorner, 2012), p. 105. See also O'Kane, pp. 89–95.
10. It is worth noting the more recent tendency for theatre programmes to list separately 'Cast' and 'Creatives', as if the former cannot be part of the latter.
11. 'Interview: Tim Crouch – Theatre Director', *The Scotsman* (21 June 2010). www.scotsman.com/news/interview-tim-crouch-theatre-director-1-820005 (Accessed 2 December 2011).
12. 'a smith' is the deliberately elusive name that performance artist Andy Smith uses for his theatre work.
13. O'Kane, p. 109.
14. Tim Crouch, *My Arm* (London: Faber & Faber, 2003), p. 9.
15. The text of *Shopping for Shoes* was published in Tim Crouch, *My Arm*, ibid., pp. 57–75.
16. Seda Ilter, '"A Process of Transformation": Tim Crouch on *My Arm*', *Contemporary Theatre Review*, 21. 4 (2011), p. 398.

17. Indeed, insofar as intention is involved, Crouch has said 'I make a point of not selecting the objects to type, you know, I don't find a feminine object to represent a mother; I don't find a masculine object to present a father', Louise LePage and Dan Rebellato, 'Tim Crouch and Dan Rebellato in Conversation', *Platform: Postgraduate eJournal of Theatre & Performing Arts*, 6 (2012), pp. 16–17.

18. In Tim Crouch's original production, there were also home movies played against the rear wall, showing images like a slow-motion shot of a boy running through a field. The production never precisely indicated that these were intended to represent the protagonist of the story, but it was an easy conclusion to draw; but even this is complicated since its clash with the performance's dominant mode of address posed the question, what does it mean to possess film footage of a fictional character?

19. Stephen Bottoms, 'Introduction: Tim Crouch, the Author, and the Audience', *Contemporary Theatre Review*, 21.4 (2011), p. 392.

20. Tim Crouch, 'Darling You Were Marvellous', p. 106.

21. Tim Crouch, quoted in Helen Freshwater, 'The Author: Tim Crouch in Conversation with Helen Freshwater', *Performing Ethos*, 1.2 (2010), p. 184.

22. Tim Crouch, *My Arm*, p. 9. At one moment in his story, the protagonist recalls wanting to return home and remarks, in a very matter-of-fact tone, 'Not having cried for as long as I could remember, I had now taken to crying like a new-born lamb looking for its mother in the rain', *Plays One*, p. 41. The line is jarringly sad though the emotion is not underlined by the actor.

23. Tim Crouch, quoted in Seda Ilter, p. 400.

24. Michel Sanouillet and Elmer Peterson (eds), *Salt Seller: The Writings of Marcel Duchamp* (New York: Oxford University Press, 1973), p. 136.

25. In my essay, 'When We Talk of Horses: or, what do we see when we see a play?', *Performance Research*, 14.1 (2009), pp. 17–28, I try to demonstrate the inadequacy of thinking that we 'see' fictional worlds in the stage picture before suggesting that the relationship between stage and fiction should be thought of as metaphorical.

26. Tim Crouch, in Seda Ilter, p. 402, and 'Interview: Tim Crouch – Theatre Director'.

27. Tim Crouch, quoted in Caridad Svich, 'Tim Crouch's Theatrical Transformations', in *HotReview.org: Hunter on-line theater review* (New York: Hunter College Theatre Department, 2006). www.hotreview.org/articles/timcrouchinterv.htm (Accessed 19 January 2012).

28. Tim Crouch, Interview with Dan Rebellato, Royal Holloway University of London, 25 November 2009. http://rhul.mediacore.tv/media/tim-crouch-interview-with-dan-rebellato

29. Michael Craig-Martin. *An Oak Tree, 1973*. Tate Britain, London.

30. O'Kane, p. 103.

31. Bottoms, 'Authorising the Audience', p. 66.

32. Colin Radford, 'How Can We Be Moved by the Fate of Anna Karenina?', *Proceedings of the Aristotelian Society, Supplementary Volumes*, 49 (1975), p. 78.

33. Stephen Bottoms, 'Materialising the Audience: Tim Crouch's Sight Specifics in *ENGLAND* and *The Author*', *Contemporary Theatre Review*, 21.4 (2011), p. 447.

34. Different galleries had different effects. Crouch describes it being performed 'at the Andy Warhol museum in Pittsburgh where the theme of Warhol just screamed, you know, just hit the theme of that play with huge force. We performed that play in the Yale Center for British Art in New Haven where there were Constables and Turners and the themes of those pieces of Empire and history and Englishness hit the play

with huge force, but completely differently', Louise LePage and Dan Rebellato, 'Tim Crouch and Dan Rebellato in Conversation', pp. 24–5.

35. Crouch, '*The Author*', p. 421.
36. Freshwater, 'The Author', p. 185.
37. The title is not given. Vic says 'I played the part of Pavol [. . .] the abuser of the title' (p. 172) and Adrian recalls that 'the title of the play referred to the girl in it, I suppose' (p. 179). *Abused* seems a guess that satisfies both statements and sounds like a plausible Sarah Kane pastiche.
38. Kane, from an interview with Clare Bayley in *The Independent* (23 January 1995), quoted in Graham Saunders, *'Love Me or Kill Me': Sarah Kane and the Theatre of Extremes* (Manchester: Manchester University Press, 2002), p. 24.
39. Aleks Sierz, *In-Yer-Face Theatre: British Drama Today* (London: Faber & Faber, 2001), pp. 4–5.
40. Helen Freshwater, '"You Say Something": Audience Participation and *The Author*', *Contemporary Theatre Review*, 21.4 (2011), p. 409.
41. 'A Conversation About Dialogue', *Contemporary Theatre Review*, 21.4 (2011), p. 429.
42. Freshwater, 'The Author', p. 185.
43. Crouch, '*The Author*', p. 422.

Playwrights and Plays: Roy Williams

1. *The No Boys Cricket Club* (1996) was nominated for the Writers' Guild Best New Writer Award and the TAPS Writer of the Year Award. *Starstruck* (1997) won the thirty-first John Whiting Award, the 1997 Alfred Fagon Award and the 1998 EMMA Award. *Lift Off* (1999) received The George Devine Award in 2000. *Clubland* (2001) earned Williams the Evening Standard Charles Wintour Award for Most Promising Playwright. In 2004 Williams received the South Bank Show Arts Council England decibel Award for his contribution to the black and Asian arts sector. In 2008 Williams was awarded an OBE for his services to Drama. Credits for work other than theatre include a BAFTA for television drama *Offside* (2002) and a Screen Nation Award (2008) for his adaptation of *Fallout* for Channel Four.
2. As Hall notes, representation plays a '*constitutive* and not merely a reflexive, after-the-event, role' and thus has 'a formative and not merely an expressive place in the constitution of social and political life'. In 'New Ethnicities', in *Black British Cultural Studies: A Reader*, ed. Houston A. Baker, Manthia Diawara and Ruth H. Lindeborg (Chicago and London: The University of Chicago Press, 1996), p. 165.
3. Aleks Sierz, *In-Yer-Face Theatre: British Drama Today* (London: Faber and Faber, 2001).
4. Suzanne Scafe, 'Displacing the Centre: Home and Belonging in the Drama of Roy Williams', in *I Am Black/White/Yellow: An Introduction to the Black Body in Europe*, ed. Joan Anim-Addo and Suzanne Scafe (London: Mango, 2007), p. 72.
5. Amelia Howe Kritzer, *Political Theatre in Post-Thatcher Britain: New Writing, 1995–2005* (Basingstoke: Palgrave Macmillan, 2008), p. 78.
6. See Peacock's chapter 'Black Theatre in Britain' in *Thatcher's Theatre: British Theatre and Drama in the Eighties*, D. Keith Peacock (London: Greenwood Press, 1999), pp. 171–86.

7. For a contemporary example of such usage see Kwame Kwei-Armah's *Elmina's Kitchen* (2003), *Fix Up* (2004) *and Statement of Regret* (2007).

8. See Brah's concept of 'diaspora space' as a space in which 'multiple subject positions are juxtaposed, contested, proclaimed or disavowed; where the permitted and the prohibited perpetually interrogate; and where the accepted and the transgressive imperceptibly mingle even while these syncretic forms may be disclaimed in the name of purity and tradition' in Avtar Brah, *Cartographies of Diaspora: Contesting Identities* (London: Routledge, 1996), p. 208.

9. D. Keith Peacock, 'The Question of Multiculturalism: The Plays of Roy Williams' in *Companion to Modern British and Irish Drama: 1880–2005*, ed. Mary Luckhurst (Oxford: Blackwell, 2006), p. 531.

10. Ibid.

11. Ibid. p. 540.

12. Harry Derbyshire, 'Roy Williams: Representing Multicultural Britain in Fallout', *Modern Drama*, 50.3 (2007), p. 417.

13. Paul Gilroy, 'Cruciality and the Frog's Perspective: An Agenda of Difficulties for the Black Arts Movement in Britain' (1988), in *Writing Black Britain, 1948–1998: An Interdisciplinary Anthology*, ed. James Procter (Manchester: Manchester University Press, 2000), p. 310.

14. Roy Williams, 'Shades of Black', www.guardian.co.uk. 29 April 2004. www.guardian. co.uk/stage/2004/apr/29/theatre.race. (Accessed 30 September 2010).

15. See Scafe's critique of 'increasingly vibrant and self-affirming' discourses of cultural hybridity in relation to Williams' work which she sees instead as characterized by 'models of 'social antagonism', exclusion and unbelonging' in 'Displacing the Centre', pp. 71–87.

16. All quotations from the play are taken from: Roy Williams, *Plays: 2. The Gift, Clubland and Sing Yer Heart Out for the Lads* (London: Methuen Drama, 2004).

17. The play was also successfully produced by Pilot Theatre Company and toured to regional theatres in York, Nottingham, Birmingham and Manchester in 2006/7. A filmed version of the 2004 NT production can be viewed at the NT Archives, 83–101, The Cut, London.

18. Roy Williams, 'Foreword' in Roy Williams, *Plays: 2*, p. x.

19. Unlike Williams' previous plays such as *The Gift* (2000) and *Clubland* (2001) which portrayed the fraught nature of cultural slippages, *Sing Yer Heart Out* functions along much starker lines.

20. Paul Gilroy, *There Ain't No Black in the Union Jack: The Cultural Politics of Race and Nation* (London: Routledge, 1987), p. 61.

21. Ibid., p. 55.

22. Benedict Anderson, *Imagined Communities: Reflections on the Origin and Spread of Nationalism* (London: Verso, 1991).

23. Notably, in the 2004 NT version the Cottesloe space was transformed into a replica traditional English pub with the audience positioned at tables placed around the central area of performance. Through their proximity the audience become implicated not just as witnesses but as punters/regulars themselves in this culturally familiar space.

24. Gilroy, *There Ain't No Black in the Union Jack*, p. 43.

25. Errol Lawrence, 'Just Plain Common Sense: The Roots of Racism' in the Centre for Contemporary Cultural Studies, University of Birmingham, *The Empire Strikes Back: Race and Racism in 70s Britain* (London: Hutchinson, 1982), p. 47.

26. Enoch Powell 16.11.68 qtd in Gilroy, *There Ain't No Black in the Union Jack*, p. 46.
27. See Anderson, *Imagined Communities*, pp. 6–7.
28. E. J. Hobsbawm, *Nations and Nationalism since 1780: Programme, Myth, Reality* (Cambridge: Cambridge University Press, 1990), p. 143.
29. Anderson, *Imagined Communities*, pp. 6–7.
30. All quotations from the play are taken from: Roy Williams, *Plays: 3. Fallout, Slow Time, Days of Significance and Absolute Beginners* (London: Methuen Drama, 2008).
31. In 2008, Williams adapted the play for Channel 4 television, which earned him a Screen Nation Award.
32. For an analysis of the problematic investigation and trial of the case see: 'The Damilola Taylor Murder Investigation: The Report of the Oversight Panel'. www. guardian.co.uk. December 2002. http://image.guardian.co.uk/sys-files/Guardian/ documents/2002/12/09/damilola.pdf (Accessed 30 September 2010). Since *Fallout* was written the Taylor trial was re-opened and two brothers, Danny and Ricky Preddie, were convicted of manslaughter in 2006.
33. In 1993 a black British 18-year-old Stephen Lawrence was murdered. Despite five suspects being arrested nobody was convicted for the crime. The crime was seen as racially motivated and the inability of the police to find the criminals and their handling of the case was also linked to racial prejudice. In 1999 the Macpherson Report was published which criticized the Metropolitan Police of institutional racism. Ten years after the report was published a new report found that although improvements had been made within the Metropolitan Police, '[b]lack communities . . . are disproportionately represented in stop and search statistics and on the National DNA Database' a gap which has increased since 1999. The report goes on to highlight that 'This perpetuates black people's over-representation in the criminal justice system' and 'that any gains made by the use of stop and search may be offset by its potentially negative impact on community relations'. See: House of Commons Home Affairs Committee, 'The Macpherson Report – Ten Years On', www.statewatch.org. 22 July 2009. www.statewatch.org/news/2009/jul/uk-hasc-macpherson.pdf (Accessed 30 September 2010).
34. See 'How Violent is Britain?', www.news.bbc.co.uk. 10 December 2000. http://news. bbc.co.uk/1/hi/talking_point/1048339.stm (Accessed 29 September 2010).
35. Williams' plot follows the Damilola case fairly closely. In his play Ronnie is based on the key witness in the Damilola case under the pseudonym 'Bromley' whose questionable evidence and motivation to testify led to the trial's dissolution.
36. Rhoda Koenig, 'Fallout, Royal Court, London' in *The Independent*, 23 June 2003. www.independent.co.uk/arts-entertainment/theatre-dance/reviews/fallout-royal-cour t-london-541589.html (Accessed 30 September 2010).
37. See Deirdre Osborne, 'The State of the Nation: Contemporary Black British Theatre and the Staging of the UK' in *Alternatives within the Mainstream: British Black and Asian Theatres*, ed. Dimple Godiwala (Newcastle: Cambridge Scholars Press, 2006), pp. 82–100.
38. Pat Cumper, the artistic director of black British theatre company Talawa, has refused to 'put another dead young black man on stage' again for precisely these reasons. See: Patricia Cumper, 'I will not put another dead young black man on stage' www. guardian.co.uk. 4 March 2009 www.guardian.co.uk/stage/theatreblog/2009/mar/03/ dead-young-black-man-stage (Accessed 30 September 2010). The responses to

Cumper's blog posting provide further interesting opinions from the general public on the matter.

39. Kobena Mercer, *Welcome to the Jungle: New Positions in Black Cultural Studies* (London: Routledge, 1994), pp. 233–58.

40. Roy Williams, 'Black theatre's big breakout', 27 September 2009. www.guardian. co.uk. www.guardian.co.uk/stage/2009/sep/27/black-theatre-roy-williams (Accessed 30 September 2010). See Cumper's response to this article where she continues the debate about the violent representation of young black men on stage.

41. Aleks Sierz, 'theartsdesk Q&A: Playwright Roy Williams' in *The Arts Desk*, 24 October 2009. www.theartsdesk.com/theatre/theartsdesk-qa-playwright-roy-williams (Accessed 30 September 2010).

42. Elizabeth Barry and William Boles, 'Beyond Victimhood: Agency and Identity in the Theatre of Roy Williams' in *Alternatives within the Mainstream: British Black and Asian Theatres*, ed. Dimple Godiwala (Newcastle: Cambridge Scholars Press, 2006), p. 299.

43. Derbyshire, 'Roy Williams', p. 424.

44. Derbyshire bases his reading on Stuart Hall and Tony Jefferson, *Resistance through Rituals: Youth Subcultures in Post-War Britain* (London: Hutchinson [for] the Centre for Contemporary Cultural Studies, University of Birmingham, 1976).

45. Rupa Huq, *Beyond Subculture: Pop, Youth and Identity in a Postcolonial World* (London: Routledge, 2006), p. 16.

46. Ibid.

47. David Wilson, *Inventing Black-on-Black Violence: Discourse, Space, and Representation* (Syracuse, NY: Syracuse University Press, 2005), p. 159.

48. Spencer, Charles, 'Estate of the Nation' in *Telegraph.co.uk*, 19 June 2003. www. telegraph.co.uk/culture/theatre/drama/3596889/Estate-of-the-nation.html (Accessed: 30 September 2010); Michael Billington, 'Fallout', *The Guardian*, 18 June 2003, www.guardian.co.uk/stage/2003/jun/19/theatre.artsfeatures (Accessed 30 September 2010).

49. The set design added another layer to Williams' method of undermining stereotypical representations. The set, designed by Ultz, was placed in the middle of the stalls and surrounded by wire with the audience looking down on the performance space from their vantage point in the circle. The design drew attention to the way in which black youth have come to embody the displaced fears of white society. The tension created between the content and performance of the piece with the audience's positioning created an uncomfortable situation whereby the audience were made to feel complicit in the youth's objectification. This sense of discomfort is characteristic of Williams' style that uses stereotypes to create a deliberate tension between mainstream assumptions and a radical re-positioning of the black (and white) subject. For an alternative perspective see: Osborne, 'The State of the Nation', p. 89.

50. Stuart Hall, 'New Ethnicities', in *Black British Cultural Studies: A Reader*, ed. Houston A. Baker, Manthia Diawara and Ruth H. Lindeborg (Chicago and London: The University of Chicago Press, 1996), p. 166.

51. Ibid., pp. 165–6.

52. All quotations from the play are taken from: Roy Williams, *Plays: 3. Fallout, Slow Time, Days of Significance and Absolute Beginners* (London: Methuen Drama, 2008).

53. The last act of the play was modified for its London performance. In the Stratford-Upon-Avon version the final scene provided an externalization of Hannah's inner conflict over whether to support Jamie or not and involved Hannah's step-father

Lenny trying to take sexual advantage of her. In the Tricycle version which was published and is used in this chapter, Williams asserted a more realist style in the third act and inverted the sexual propositioning so that it is Hannah who attempts to seduce Lenny. Extracts of the original third act are published in this volume (pp. 254–60). For another account of the original version see: Janelle Reinelt, 'Selective Affinities: British Playwrights at Work', *Modern Drama*, 50.3 (2007), p. 319.

54. Williams states: 'This year I had a crack at creating drama about soldiers with my play *Days of Significance*. My soldiers were white. I did this because I wanted to, not because I had to, and because I am as angry about a white kid getting killed in Iraq as I am about a black youth being stabbed on the streets of London' in Roy Williams, 'Will black people's lives ever be as interesting as white people's?', in *Guardian Film Blog*. 25 May 2008. www.guardian.co.uk/film/filmblog/2008/may/25/whenigotothe (Accessed 30 September 2010).

55. As in *Sing Yer Heart for the Lads* Williams uses two spaces to indicate the them/us binary at the core of national discourses.

56. In line with *Much Ado*, before the first act ends, Jamie and Hannah's first spark of love is almost extinguished by the anti-war Dan (Don John), who tells Jamie that Hannah has been ridiculing him behind his back for being scared to fight in Iraq. When Jamie breaks up with Hannah, Trish insists that Ben avenge her cousin. However, nothing serious comes of it, Dan's lie is exposed and Ben and Trish, Jamie and Hannah are united.

57. Even when the venues such as the Tricycle could not accommodate a promenade configuration the actors broke the fourth wall and intermingled with the audience members.

58. Qtd in Barry and Boles, 'Beyond Victimhood: Agency and Identity in the Theatre of Roy Williams', p. 298.

59. Susannah Clapp, 'Army Dreamers', *The Observer*, 21 January 2007. www.guardian.co.uk/stage/2007/jan/21/theatre1 (Accessed 30 September 2010).

60. William Shakespeare, *Much Ado About Nothing*, ed. Sheldon P. Zitner (Oxford, Oxford University Press, 1993).

61. Cavendish, Dominic, 'Days of Significance: A nation's soul', *Daily Telegraph*, 20 March 2008. www.telegraph.co.uk/culture/theatre/drama/3671963/Days-of-Significance-A-nations-soul.html (Accessed 30 September 2010).

62. Reinelt, 'Selective Affinities', p. 317.

63. Charles Spencer called the play 'an anthem for doomed youth, and an appalled meditation on dumbed-down, boozed-up modern Britain', qtd in Reinelt, 'Selective Affinities', p. 317.

64. Jamie's inability to express himself is demonstrated from the start of the play when he is unable to tell Hannah he loves her and must express his emotions through the lyrics of Frankie Goes to Hollywood's 'The Power of Love' (completely miscomprehending the explicit anti-war nature of the band, especially their singles 'Two Tribes' and 'War').

65. As Osborne states of *Fallout*, he treads 'a fine line between perpetuating negative typing of black people and staging aspects of black British working class experience to spark debate', 'The State of the Nation', p. 93.

66. As Williams states: 'Many pieces of drama (stage or screen) that address racial issues lose their bottle and drown themselves with wishy-washy liberal platitudes', in 'Foreword', *Roy Williams Plays: 2*, p. x.

67. Sierz, 'theartsdesk Q&A'.

68. Williams, Roy, Interview with Michael Pearce, 15 September 2010.

Notes

Playwrights and Plays: David Greig

1. See Graham Eatough and Dan Rebellato (eds), *The Suspect Culture Book* (London: Oberon, 2013).

2. See Margaret Rose and Emanuela Rossini, 'Playwriting in Scotland Today', in *A Theatre that Matters: Twentieth-Century Scottish Drama and Theatre*, ed. Valentina Poggi and Margaret Rose (Milan: Edizioni Unicopli, 2000), pp. 244–8.

3. See Nadine Holdsworth, 'The Landscape of Contemporary Scottish Drama' and Adrienne Scullion 'Devolution and Drama', in *A Concise Companion to Contemporary British and Irish Drama*, ed. Nadine Holdsworth and Mary Luckhurst (Oxford: Blackwell, 2008), pp. 125–45.

4. Cited in Peter Billingham, *At the Sharp End: Uncovering the work of five leading dramatists* (London: Methuen, 2007), p. 81. For a discussion on the importance of change see David Greig, 'Plays on Politics', in *State of Play: Playwrights on Playwriting*, ed. David Edgar (London: Faber & Faber, 1999), p. 66.

5. Dominic Cavendish, 'The Coy Wonder', *Daily Telegraph* (6 August 2003), p. 19.

6. David Greig, 'Rough Theatre', in *Cool Britannia? British Political Drama in the 1990s*, ed. Rebecca D'Monte and Graham Saunders (Basingstoke: Palgrave, 2008), pp. 219, 213, 212.

7. See Greig, 'Rough Theatre', pp. 213–19.

8. Joyce McMillan, 'Finding the Shadow City', *The Scotsman* (28 August 2003), p. 15.

9. Hilary Whitney, 'The Arts Desk Q & A: Playwright David Greig' (6 February 2010).

10. McMillan, 'Finding the Shadow City', p. 15.

11. Neil Cooper, 'San Diego', *Herald* (20 October 2003), p. 19.

12. Dan Rebellato, 'Introduction', in David Greig, *Plays: 1* (London: Methuen, 2002), p. xx and Adrienne Scullion, 'Devolution and Drama: Imagining the Possible', in *The Edinburgh Companion to Contemporary Scottish Literature*, ed. Berthold Schoene (Edinburgh: Edinburgh University Press, 2007), p. 69.

13. Page references are to David Greig, *San Diego* (London: Faber & Faber, 2003).

14. Neil Campbell and Alasdair Kean, *American Cultural Studies: An Introduction to American Culture*, 2nd edn (London: Routledge, 2006), p. 176.

15. See Marc Augé, *Non-Places: Introduction to an Anthropology of Supermodernity*, trans. John Howe (London: Verso, 1995).

16. John Hartley, 'Introduction: "Cultural Exceptionalism" Freedom, Imperialism, Power, America', in *American Cultural Studies*, ed. John Hartley and Roberta Pearson (Oxford: Oxford University Press, 2000), p. 3.

17. Ian Shuttleworth, 'San Diego', *Financial Times* (19 August 2003), p. 13.

18. Heiner Müller, *Theatremachine* (London: Faber & Faber, 1995), p. 141.

19. Peter Billingham, *At the Sharp End*, p. 90.

20. Michael Billington 'Dark Lessons from a Lost Pilot', *Guardian* (7 May 2005), p. 19.

21. Hemming, Sarah, 'The View from All Sides: An Interview with David Greig', *Financial Times* (25 April 2005), p. 17.

22. John Hartley, 'Introduction "Cultural Exceptionalism"', pp. 4–5.

23. Page references are to David Greig, *The American Pilot* (London: Faber and Faber, 2005).

24. Andrew Hammond, *What the Arabs think of America* (Westport, CT: Greenwood World Publishing, 2007), p. ix.

25. Benedict Nightingale 'A World Flying into Trouble', *The Times* (7 May 2005), p. 24.

26. Rohan Preston, 'American Pilot Navigates Dramatic Turbulence', *Star Tribune* (6 May 2008), p. 8 and Joe Adcock, 'American Pilot is a Brash Look at Politics in the Third World', *Seattle Post* (2 May 2008), p. 27.

27. Charles Isherwood, 'A Soldier's Plane Crashes, and Then the Real Danger Begins', *The New York Times* (22 November 2006), p. 5.

28. David Greig, 'Author's Note' *Damascus* (London: Faber & Faber, 2007), n.p.

29. Qtd in Joyce McMillan, 'Our Society is Still in Danger', *The Scotsman* (8 August 2007), p. 4.

30. Dominic Cavendish, Interview with David Greig, TheatreVoice (30 July 2007), www.theatrevoice.com/2192/david-greig-on-his-latest-play-damascus/ (Accessed 1 February 2011).

31. Page references are to David Greig, *Damascus* (London: Faber & Faber, 2007).

32. Ibid.

33. Neil Cooper, 'Damascus', *Herald* (7 August 2007), p. 14.

34. Adrian Turpin, 'The Pain and the Pleasure; Edinburgh Festival', *The Sunday Times*, Culture section (12 August 2007), p. 18.

35. Dominic Cavendish, Interview.

36. Lyn Gardner, 'Arab-western Relations get Lost in Translation', *Guardian* (11 February 2009), p. 36.

37. Jim Quilty, 'Scottish Theater and Pedagogy Clash in 'Damascus', *Daily Star*, Lebanon (19 March 2009), n.p.

38. Joyce McMillan, 'Traversing the Divide', *The Scotsman* (19 March 2009), p. 47.

39. Joyce McMillan, 'To Damascus: David Greig's Damascus in Syria and Lebanon', *Scotsman Arts* (19 March 2009). http://joycemcmillan.wordpress.com/2009/03/19/damascus-to-damascus-and-beirut-on-tour-with-david-greigs-2007-traverse-hit/ (Accessed 29 November 2010).

40. Quoted in ibid.

41. Billingham, *At the Sharp End*, p. 17.

Playwrights and Plays: debbie tucker green

1. All review citations are taken from reprints of the original newspaper articles in the relevant issue of *Theatre Record*. Full citations are placed under play titles in the bibliography.

2. debbie tucker green's short play *Two Women* (2000) was produced as part of Paines Plough's *Wild Lunch IV* season at the Soho Theatre in 2000.

3. tucker green has also written a number of radio plays, including *freefall* (BBC Radio 3, 2002), *to swallow* (BBC Radio 4, 2003), *handprint* (BBC Radio 3, 2006) and *gone* (BBC Radio 3, 2010).

4. See Ken Urban's 'Cruel Britannia' (2008), which examines traits of in-yer-face theatre in tucker green's *stoning mary.*

5. Ken Urban, 'Cruel Britannia', in *Cool Britannia: British Political Theatre in the 1990s*, ed. Rebecca D'Monte and Graham Saunders (Basingstoke: Palgrave, 2008), pp. 52–3.

6. Lyn Gardner, 'I Was Messing About', *guardian,* 30 March 2005. www.guardian.co.uk/stage/2005/mar/30/theatre (Accessed 2 May 2012).

7. Ibid.

8. The Eclipse Conference was held at the Nottingham Playhouse in June 2001, and the subsequent *Eclipse Report* (Arts Council, 2002) recommended a review of equal opportunities policies and the setting of targets for employing Afro-Asian artists in regional arts venues. Sustained Theatre aims to foreground issues of black and Asian artists within a national arts framework. Decibel is an annual showcase of culturally diverse black and Asian theatre. See http://sustainedtheatre.org.uk/Home

9. See, for example, plays by Levi David Addai, Bola Agbaje, Michael Bhim, Lennie James, Mark Norfolk, Kwame Kwei-Armah and Roy Williams. Deirdre Osborne's introduction to *Hidden Gems* (Oberon, 2008) presents a comprehensive list of productions of plays by black British writers produced between 2003 and 2008.

10. Aleks Sierz, 'If you hate the show, at least you have passion', *Independent on Sunday* (27 April 2003), available, with a subscription, at www.questia.com/library/1P2-1762255/if-you-hate-the-show-at-least-you-have-passion

11. Elaine Aston's 'A Fair Trade: Staging Female Sex Tourism in *Sugar Mummies* and *Trade*' (2008) presents an in-depth analysis of the how feminist discourses function in tucker green's play.

12. Aleks Sierz, 'If you hate the show . . .'

13. Wares directed *trade*, *generations* and *random*.

14. Quoted in Helen Cadbury, *random: Background Pack* (London: Royal Court, 2008), p. 6.

15. debbie tucker green, *dirty butterfly* (London: Nick Hern, 2003), p. 2.

16. Ibid., p. 9.

17. Ibid., pp. 12–14.

18. Ibid., p. 34.

19. Ibid., p. 2.

20. D. Keith Peacock, 'Black British Drama and the Politics of Identity', in *A Concise Companion to Contemporary British and Irish Drama*, ed. Nadine Holdsworth and Mary Luckhurst (Oxford: Blackwell, 2008), p. 61.

21. debbie tucker green, *dirty butterfly*, pp. 40–1.

22. Aleks Sierz, *In-Yer-Face Theatre: British Drama Today* (London: Faber & Faber, 2001), p. 4.

23. Deirdre Osborne, 'Not "In-Yer-Face" But What Lies Beneath: Experiential and Aesthetic Inroads in the Drama of debbie tucker green and Dona Daley', in '*Black*' *British Aesthetics Today*, ed. R. Victoria Arana (Newcastle upon Tyne: Cambridge Scholars Press, 2007), p. 231.

24. Osborne, 'Not "In-Yer-Face" But What Lies Beneath', p. 231.

25. debbie tucker green, *stoning mary* (London: Nick Hern, 2005), p. 2.

26. Emily McLaughlin, *stoning mary: Education Resource* (London: Royal Court, 2005), p. 4.

27. D. Keith Peacock, 'Black British Drama and the Politics of Identity', p. 60.

28. green, *stoning mary*, p. 4.

29. Ibid., p. 21.

30. Ibid., p. 63.

31. Ibid., pp. 61–3.

32. Ibid., p. 73.

33. Twenty-seven teenagers were murdered in 2007 and 28 in 2008; 40 of these 55 deaths were stabbings and about three-quarters of those killed were black males.

34. For example, Roy Williams' *Fallout* (2003), *Little Sweet Thing* (2005), Kwame Kwei-Armah's *Elmina's Kitchen* (2003) and Bola Agbaje's *Gone Too Far!* (2007) and *Off Da Endz* (2010).

35. debbie tucker green, *random* (London: Nick Hern, 2008), p. 18.
36. A front room feel was heightened in the 2010 revival of the play as front row audience members were seated on leather sofas to listen to Sister's account.
37. green, *random*, p. 3.
38. Ibid., p. 4.
39. Ibid., p. 7.
40. Ibid., p. 26.
41. Ibid., p. 41.
42. Ibid., p. 45.
43. Marissia Fragkou, 'Intercultural Encounters in debbie tucker green's *random*', in *Contemporary Drama in English: Staging Interculturality*, ed. Werner Huber and Margaret Rubik, 17 (2010), p. 83.
44. green, *random*, p. 36.
45. Joe Kelleher, *Theatre & Politics*, Theatre& (Basingstoke: Palgrave, 2009), p. 22.
46. Patrick Wintour and Vikram Dodd, 'Blair Blames Spate of Murders on Black Culture', *Guardian* (12 April 2007), p. 4. www.guardian.co.uk/politics/2007/apr/12/ukcrime. race (Accessed 18 December 2010).
47. Tony Blair, Press Notice, 'The Callaghan Memorial Lecture' (10 Downing Street, 11 April 2007), p. 10. http://image.guardian.co.uk/sys-files/Politics/documents/2007/04/11/blairlecture.pdf
48. green, *random*, p. 42.
49. Ibid., p. 41.
50. Ibid., p. 41–2.
51. Ibid., p. 49.
52. Ibid., pp. 49–50.

3. Documents

1. I must record my thanks to Jacqueline Bolton for her assistance with sourcing and contextualizing the unpublished materials by Simon Stephens.
2. Simon Stephens, unpublished interview with Jacqueline Bolton, 18 May 2010.
3. Simon Stephens, e-mail to Jacqueline Bolton, 18 April 2012.
4. Stephens, unpublished interview.
5. Peter Brook, *The Shifting Point: Forty Years of Theatrical Exploration 1946–1987* (London: Methuen, 1988), p. 3.
6. Arts Council England.
7. The Arte Povera ['poor art'] movement emerged in Italy in the 1960s and was characterized by the use of cheap, everyday materials and their political opposition to mass industrialization. In *Untitled* (1969), Arte Povera artist Jannis Kounellis caused a sensation by exhibiting 12 horses at the Galleria L'Attico in Rome.
8. David Knight is a 'comedy hypnotist', whose act involves placing 'hypnotised audience members in embarrassing situations'. Tim Crouch and the company watched two of his shows on video while making *An Oak Tree* and he was an important influence on creating the shabby hypnotist act in the first half of the play.
9. Long-running BBC radio soap opera, set among country folk.

10. Susan Broadhurst, and Josephine Machon, *Sensualities/Textualities and Technologies: Writings of the Body in 21st Century Performance* (Basingstoke: Palgrave Macmillan, 2009), p. 72.
11. Jasper Johns, *Writings, Sketch Notes, Interviews*, ed. Kirk Varnedoe (New York: Museum of Modern Art, 1996), p. 54.
12. Kozlowski is a Polish conceptual artist, born in 1945. This quotation would appear to be a summary of one of his key ideas rather than a direct quotation.
13. From Blake's 'Auguries of Innocence' (c. 1803) see William Blake, *The Complete Poems* (Harmondsworth: Penguin, 1977), p. 506
14. Rene Daumal, *Mount Analogue: A Novel of Symbolically Authentic Non-Euclidean Adventures in Mountain Climbing* (London: Duckworth, 2005), p. 8.
15. See p. 133.
16. Bruce Nauman, *Please Pay Attention Please – Bruce Nauman's Words: Writing and Interviews*, ed. Janet Kraynak (Cambridge, MA: MIT Press, 2002), p. 62.
17. The source of this quotation has been difficult to track down but may be from an article by US 'hypnotherapy expert' Edward J. Longo entitled 'Words: The Most Powerful Element of Guided Imagery'.
18. Actually Act 3, Scene 4, lines 93–8 in most modern editions, though the act/scene divisions in *King John* are notoriously confused.
19. The sources of these quotations – if they are quotations – are unknown.
20. Charlie Walton, *When There Are No Words: Finding Your Way To Cope With Loss and Grief* (Ventura, CA: Pathfinder, 1996), p. 31.
21. Martin Jacques, 'The death of intimacy', guardian.co.uk 18 September 2004, www.guardian.co.uk/uk/2004/sep/18/britishidentity.comment (visited 27 September 2012).
22. This is a line from T. S. Eliot's poem *The Waste Land* (1922).
23. *Violent Incident* (1986) is a video depicting a staged fight apparently between two party guests. It is performed in four versions: by a man and a woman, by the same two but in reversed roles, by two men, and by two women. These videos – and other images gathered during the recording of the fight – are played on a bank of 12 television screens in a 3×4 configuration. Nauman's large-scale sound installation for the Turbine Hall at Tate Modern in October 2004 was called *Raw Materials*.
24. From Janet Kraynak's introduction to Bruce Nauman, *Please Pay Attention Please*, p. 17.
25. Ibid., p. 18.
26. Ibid., p. 76.
27. Ibid., p. 32.
28. Ibid., pp. 50, 61.
29. Valerie Austin, *Self Hypnosis* (London: HarperCollins, 1992), pp. 50–1.
30. Tim Crouch, e-mail to Dan Rebellato, 13 April 2012.
31. Rose Bruford College is a drama school in Kent.
32. *King Lear* opened at the Royal Court Theatre in January 1993.
33. Polly Stenham's *That Face* opened at the Royal Court when she was only 19 to widespread acclaim. The production transferred the following year to the West End.
34. The Transformation season ran from April to September 2002 and featured 17 premieres – including new plays by Gary Owen, Owen McCafferty, Simon Bowen, Richard Bean and Tanika Gupta – in a redesigned Lyttelton theatre and a new temporary 100-seat theatre called the Loft built into the Lyttelton circle foyer. *Sing*

Yer Heart Out for the Lads opened in the Loft in May 2002 and was revived in the Cottesloe two years later.

35. England played Germany at Wembley on 7 October 2000. Germany won 0–1 thanks to a Dietmar Hamann goal in the fourteenth minute.

36. The Monsterists were a group of writers fed up with being 'ghettoised' in small studio theatres and wanted access to the largest spaces. They published a manifesto in 2005 and, after many of their demands were championed by Nick Hytner when he took over the National Theatre, they faded away in triumph. See Colin Teevan, 'Free the Playwrights! A brief introduction to Monsterism', *Contemporary Theatre Review*, 16.2 (May 2006), pp. 239–45.

37. All four of these plays were given their premieres on the Olivier stage, the largest stage of the National Theatre's four stages. *Market Boy* opened in June 2006, *Her Naked Skin* in July 2008, *England People Very Nice* in February 2009, *Welcome to Thebes* in June 2010.

38. *Earthquakes in London*, a vastly ambitious large-cast play by Mike Bartlett, opened in the Cottesloe at the National Theatre in August 2010.

39. Ian Rickson was artistic director of the Royal Court from 1998 to 2006 and directed the premiere of *Fallout*.

40. For *Fallout*, the designer, Ultz, extended the Royal Court's stage area out across the stalls, part-enclosed by a chain-link fence, with the audience watching from above and through the fence.

41. In November 2000, Damilola Taylor, a bright ten-year-old Nigerian boy living in Peckham, South London, was killed on his way home. There was evidence that he'd been bullied at school, though the Metropolitan Police insisted that his death was accidental. During a first trial, the case against two suspects collapsed when it became apparent that a police witness was unreliable. Eventually, in October 2006, two brothers were found guilty of manslaughter and sentenced to eight years in youth custody.

42. Williams adapted *Fallout* for television and it was broadcast on Channel 4 in July 2008, also directed by Ian Rickson.

43. Then literary manager of the Royal Shakespeare Company.

44. The RSC's Complete Works Season ran from April 2006 to May 2007 and featured performances of all Shakespeare's works by an international network of theatre companies.

45. Branagh's film of *Much Ado About Nothing* was originally released in 1993.

46. *The Deer Hunter* (1978) was directed by Michael Cimino and follows a group of friends in Pennsylvania as they go off to fight in the Vietnam War. The three parts of the film show them preparing to go, the horrors of war and the aftermath when they return.

47. Hannah, revolted, scorns him by mock-offering him sex; Lenny is appalled. The dialogue is very similar to that in the final version, see Roy Williams, *Plays: 3, Contemporary Dramatists* (London: Methuen Drama, 2008), pp. 275–6.

48. David Greig's *The Cosmonaut's Last Message to the Woman He Once Loved in the Former Soviet Union* was first performed by Paines Plough in April 1999.

49. *The Autograph Man* was published by Hamish Hamilton in 2002.

50. *Dr Korczak's Example* was first performed by TAG in 2001. Greig's version of Albert Camus's *Caligula* was produced by the Donmar Warehouse, London, in April 2003.

51. *Pyrenees* was produced by Paines Plough on a tour starting at the Tron in Glasgow, in March 2005.

52. *Copper Sulphate* is a radio play by Greig that uses the same story. It was broadcast on BBC Radio 3 in November 1996.

53. *Mainstream* was first performed in February 1999.

54. The play is *The Road of Tanks*, published in Heiner Müller, *Theatremachine* (London: Faber and Faber, 1995).

55. In the 1930s, Brecht wrote a series of lehrstücke (learning plays) that were designed to offer audiences ethical and political problems that the form would allow actors and audience to develop collective answers. They are collected in Bertolt Brecht, *Collected Plays: Three*, trans. and ed. John Willett (London: Methuen, 1997).

56. I have written about the relation between Adorno and Greig's theatre in 'Suspect Culture: Reaching Out' in *The Suspect Culture Book*, ed. Graham Eatough and Dan Rebellato (London: Oberon, 2013), pp. 299–329.

57. In March 2009, the Traverse production of *Damascus* toured to Damascus, Beirut, Amman, Cairo, Tunis and Ramallah, sponsored by the British Council.

58. This was *Mish Alla Ruman (Not About Pomegranates)* directed by Rufus Norris at the Al-Kasabah Theatre in Ramallah in 2001.

59. David Greig, 'Doing a Geographical', *Contemporary Theatre Review*, 16.1 (2006), pp. 160–4.

60. NVC refers to Nonviolent Communication, an attitude to dialogue that aims to resolve conflicts through empathy and honesty.

61. The point where this diverges from the published text can be seen at David Greig, *Damascus* (London: Faber & Faber, 2007), p. 113.

62. Lyn Gardner, 'I Was Messing About', guardian.co.uk, 30 March 2005 www.guardian.co.uk/stage/2005/mar/30/theatre (visited 9 July 2012).

63. Aleks Sierz, 'Interview with debbie tucker green', inyerface-theatre.com (visited 9 July 2012).

64. Ibid.

65. Ibid.

66. Lyn Gardner, 'I Was Messing About'.

67. Ibid.

SELECT BIBLIOGRAPHY

1. Books on the 2000s

Angelaki, Vicky, (ed.), *Contemporary British Theatre: Breaking New Ground* (Basingstoke: Palgrave Macmillan, 2013). A collection of essays covering a range of work from the 2000s.

Burke, Jason, *The 9/11 Wars* (London: Penguin, 2012). A very substantial account of the 'war on terror' from many points of view, written by a respected journalist.

Campbell, Alastair, *The Blair Years*. ed. Alastair Campbell and Richard Stott (London: Hutchinson, 2007). The inside story of the Blair governments through Number 10's Director of Communications.

Footman, Tim, *The Noughties: A Decade That Changed the World 2000–2009* (Richmond: Crimson, 2009). A journalist's survey of the decade, organized by various themes, including environment, technology, politics, music and surveillance.

Lanchester, John, *Whoops! Why Everyone Owes Everyone and No One Can Pay* (London: Penguin, 2010). A witty and admirably comprehensible account of the global credit crunch and subsequent downturn, written by a novelist.

Rawnsley, Andrew, *The End of the Party: The Rise and Fall of New Labour* (London: Viking, 2010). An enjoyably gossipy account of the Blair and Brown era in British politics.

Seldon, Anthony, (ed.), *Blair's Britain, 1997–2007* (Cambridge: Cambridge University Press, 2007). A compendious collection of academic essays surveying all aspects of Blair's decade – social, political, economic and cultural.

Seldon, Anthony and Guy Lodge, *Brown at 10* (London: Biteback, 2010). A substantial account of Gordon Brown's brief tenure of Number 10, both critical and sympathetic.

Seldon, Anthony, with Peter Snowdon and Peter Collings, *Blair Unbound* (London: Simon & Schuster, 2007). The second volume of Anthony Seldon's biography begins with 9/11 and takes the story right up to Blair's resignation in 2007.

2. Books on theatre in the 2000s

The other books in this series, all published in 2012, covering the 1950s (David Pattie), the 1960s (Steve Nicholson), the 1970s (Chris Megson), the 1980s (Jane Milling) and the 1990s (Aleks Sierz) are excellent introductions to those key debates and writers of those decades.

Billingham, Peter, *At the Sharp End* (London: Methuen Drama, 2007). A portmanteau volume, in which David Edgar, Tim Etchells, David Greig, Tanika Gupta and Mark Ravenhill are bundled together rather awkwardly for analysis and interview.

Brown, Ian, (ed.), *The Edinburgh Companion to Scottish Drama* (Edinburgh: Edinburgh University Press, 2011). A collection of essays spanning the history of Scottish theatre from the fifteenth century to the present. The last four chapters consider theatres and playwrights of the 2000s.

Chambers, Colin, *Black and Asian Theatre in Britain: A History* (Abingdon: Routledge, 2011). A substantial history stretching back to the early renaissance but offering some substantial analysis of Black and Asian theatre in the contemporary period.

Devine, Harriet, (ed.), *Looking Back: Playwrights at the Royal Court, 1956–2006* (London: Faber and Faber, 2006). A collection of interviews with Royal Court writers of the last 50 years. The 2000s are represented by Richard Bean, Leo Butler, Lucy Prebble, Simon Farquhar, Simon Stephens, Roy Williams, Conor McPherson and several writers from earlier generations whose work continued to be produced at the Court in the decade.

Hingorani, Dominic, *British Asian Theatre: Dramaturgy, Process and Performance* (Basingstoke: Palgrave Macmillan, 2010). The first substantial survey of British Asian theatre since the 1970s. The second half of the book focuses on writers and companies of the 2000s.

Kritzer, Amelia Howe, *Political Theatre in Post-Thatcher Britain – New Writing: 1995–2005, Performance Interventions* (Basingstoke: Palgrave Macmillan, 2008). A discussion of British playwriting that occasionally strays into the 2000s and attempts to argue for the political astuteness of this work.

Lane, David, *Contemporary British Drama, Edinburgh Critical Guides* (Edinburgh: Edinburgh University Press, 2010). An outline of contemporary British theatre which privileges the playwright less than most volumes. There are specific sections on verbatim theatre, devising, theatre for young people and adaptation, as well as analyses of Black and Asian playwriting and discussions of Simon Stephens, Gregory Burke, Caryl Churchill, Martin Crimp, debbie tucker green and others.

Middeke, Martin, Peter Paul Schnierer and Aleks Sierz, (eds), *The Methuen Drama Guide to Contemporary British Playwrights* (London: Methuen Drama, 2011). Essays on 25 playwrights, most of whom have been active and writing in the 2000s; it also contains a general introduction.

Sierz, Aleks, *Rewriting the Nation: British Theatre Today* (London: Methuen Drama, 2011). The first book-length study of British theatre in the 2000s has a particular focus on 'New Writing'. After an initial analysis of what this latter term means, it considers a huge number of plays under various headings, covering global conflict, economics, inequality, relationships and alternative realities.

3. Recommended books on post-war British theatre

Ansorge, Peter, *Disrupting the Spectacle: Five Years of Experimental and Fringe Theatre in Britain* (London: Pitman, 1975). A quick response to the first wave of counter-cultural and fringe work since the late 1960s.

Barker, Howard, *Arguments for a Theatre*, 3rd edn. (Manchester: Manchester University Press, 1997). A key collection of provocative statements from one of the most important playwrights in post-war Britain.

Billington, Michael, *State of the Nation: British Theatre since 1945* (London: Faber & Faber, 2007). A survey of 60 years of theatre going by the *Guardian's* chief theatre critic, showing a persistent interest in the theatre's ability to address the political world.

Bond, Edward, *The Hidden Plot: Notes on Theatre and the State* (London: Methuen, 2000). Searching and complex essays on the role of theatre from one of the key playwrights of post-war Britain.

Bull, John, *New British Political Dramatists* (London: Macmillan, 1984). Analysis of the generation of left-wing playwrights that came to prominence in the 1970s.

— *Stage Right: Crisis and Recovery in British Mainstream Theatre* (London: Macmillan, 1994). Discussing the state of commercial theatre through playwrights like Frayn, Ayckbourn, Stoppard, Bennett and Gray.

Craig, Sandy, (ed.), *Dreams and Deconstructions: Alternative Theatre in Britain* (Ambergate: Amber Lane, 1980). A broad survey of alternative theatre in the 1970s, looking helpfully beyond playwriting.

Doty, Gresdna A. and Billy J. Harbin, *Inside the Royal Court Theatre, 1956–1981: Artists Talk* (Baton Rouge and London: Louisiana State University Press, 1990).

Etchells, Tim, *Certain Fragments: Contemporary Performance and Forced Entertainment* (London: Routledge, 1999). An incisive collection of essays and performance texts by a leading figure in the British performance art group Forced Entertainment.

Forsyth, Alison and Chris Megson (eds), *Get Real: Documentary Theatre Past and Present* (London: Palgrave, 2009). A key collection of essays on documentary theatre across the world, including verbatim theatre.

Gooch, Steve, *All Together Now: An Alternative View of Theatre and the Community* (London: Methuen, 1984). A vivid, hands-on account of the complexities of working in alternative theatre.

Griffiths, Trevor R. and Margaret Llewellyn-Jones, (eds), *British and Irish Women Dramatists since 1958: A Critical Handbook* (Buckingham: Open University Press, 1993).

Hare, David, *Obedience, Struggle & Revolt: Lectures on Theatre* (London: Faber and Faber, 2005).

Harvie, Jen, *Staging the UK* (Manchester: Manchester University Press, 2005). Discussing various ways that performance has addressed and engaged with the notion of national identity.

Holdsworth, Nadine, *Joan Littlewood's Theatre* (Cambridge: Cambridge University Press, 2011). Key discussion of the work of an important post-war director.

Holdsworth, Nadine and Mary Luckhurst (eds), *A Concise Companion to Contemporary British and Irish Drama* (Oxford: Blackwell, 2007).

Innes, Christopher, *Modern British Drama: The Twentieth Century* (London: Cambridge University Press, 2002).

Itzin, Catherine, *Stages in the Revolution: Political Theatre in Britain since 1968* (London: Methuen, 1980).

Kerensky, Oleg, *The New British Drama: Fourteen Playwrights since Osborne and Pinter* (London: Hamish Hamilton, 1977).

Lacey, Stephen, *British Realist Theatre: The New Wave in Its Context 1956–1965* (London: Routledge, 1995).

Luckhurst, Mary, (ed.), *A Companion to Modern British and Irish Drama 1880–2005* (Oxford: Blackwell, 2006).

Marowitz, Charles, Tom Milne and Owen Hale, *New Theatre Voices of the Fifties and Sixties: Selections from Encore Magazine 1956–1963*. Revised edn (London: Methuen, 1981).

McGrath, John, *A Good Night Out: Popular Theatre – Audience, Class and Form* (London: Methuen, 1981). An influential statement about the political value of the popular theatre tradition.

Motton, Gregory, *Helping Themselves: The Left-Wing Middle Classes in Theatre and the Arts* (Deal: Levellers, 2009). A pugnacious attack on mainstream theatre for ignoring the working class.

Peacock, D. Keith, *Thatcher's Theatre: British Theatre and Drama in the Eighties* (London and New York: Greenwood, 1999).

Rabey, David Ian, *English Drama since 1940* (London: Longman, 2003).

Rebellato, Dan, *1956 and All That: The Making of Modern British Drama* (London: Routledge, 1999). A revisionist discussion of the 'rebirth' of British playwriting in the 1950s.

Rees, Roland, *Fringe First: Pioneers of Fringe Theatre on Record* (London: Oberon, 1992). Interviews with fringe theatre makers.

Reinelt, Janelle , *After Brecht: British Epic Theatre* (Ann Arbor: University of Michigan Press, 1994). A discussion of British political writers such as Brenton, Hare, Churchill and Griffiths, assessing their Brechtian elements.

Roberts, Philip, *The Royal Court Theatre and the Modern Stage* (Cambridge: Cambridge University Press, 1999).

Shellard, Dominic, *British Theatre since the War* (London: Yale University Press, 1999).

Shepherd, Simon, *Cambridge Introduction to Modern British Theatre* (Cambridge: Cambridge University Press, 2009).

Sierz, Aleks, *In-Yer-Face Theatre: British Drama Today* (London: Faber and Faber, 2001). Like John Russell Taylor's and Peter Ansorge's books, this is a rapid-response, vivid encapsulation of a period of theatre.

Stephenson, Heidi and Natasha Langridge, *Rage and Reason: Women Playwrights on Playwriting* (London: Methuen, 1997). Interviews with women playwrights.

Stevenson, Randall and Gavin Wallace (eds), *Scottish Theatre since the Seventies* (Edinburgh: Edinburgh University Press, 1996).

Taylor, John Russell, *Anger and After: A Guide to the New British Drama*. Revised edn. (Harmondsworth: Penguin, 1963).

Trussler, Simon, *New Theatre Voices of the Seventies: Sixteen Interviews from Theatre Quarterly 1970–1980* (London: Methuen, 1981).

Wallace, Clare, *Suspect Cultures: Narrative, Identity & Citation in 1990s New Drama* (Prague: Litteraria Pragensia, 2006). A discussion of the title's themes in the work of playwrights Ravenhill, McDonagh, Kane, Carr and Greig.

Wandor, Michelene, *Post-War British Drama: Looking Back in Gender* (London: Routledge, 2001).

Wyllie, Andrew, *Sex on Stage: Gender and Sexuality in Post-War British Drama* (Bristol: Intellect, 2009). This and the previous title are surveys of post-war theatre with a particular eye to the representation of sex and gender.

4. The playwrights

The editions of the plays discussed in the respective chapters are given here, along with a key critical text and other useful recommended reading.

Simon Stephens
Plays

Stephens, Simon, *Plays: 1* (London: Methuen Drama, 2005).
— *Plays: 2* (London: Methuen Drama, 2009).
— *Plays: 3* (London: Methuen Drama, 2011).

Key book

Innes, Christopher, 'Simon Stephens', in *The Methuen Drama Guide to Contemporary British Playwrights*, ed. Martin Middeke, Peter Paul Schnierer and Aleks Sierz (London: Methuen Drama, 2011), pp. 445–65.

Recommended books and articles

Bolton, Jacqueline, Introduction and editorial material, in Simon Stephens, *Pornography: Student Edition* (London: Methuen Drama, 2013).
Rebellato, Dan, 'New Theatre Writing: Simon Stephens', *Contemporary Theatre Review*, 15 (2005), 174–8.
Sierz, Aleks, *Rewriting the Nation: British Theatre Today* (London: Methuen Drama, 2011).
Stephens, Simon, Interview, in *Looking Back: Playwrights at the Royal Court, 1956–2006*, ed. Harriet Devine (London: Faber and Faber, 2006), pp. 255–64.
— 'Keynote Address: Writing Black People', in *Staging Interculturality*, ed. Werner Huber, Julia Novak and Margarete Rubik (Trier: Wissenschafticher, 2010), pp. 19–36.
— 'Skydiving Blindfolded: or, Five Things I Learned From Sebastian Nübling' *Theatertreffenblog* 9 May 2011, www.theatertreffen-blog.de/tt11/tag/simon-stephens/

Tim Crouch
Plays

Crouch, Tim, *My Arm, I Caliban, Shopping for Shoes* (London: Faber & Faber, 2003).
— *I, Shakespeare: Four of Shakespeare's Better-Known Plays Re-Told for Young Audiences by Their Lesser-Known Characters* (London: Oberon, 2011).
— *Plays One* (London: Oberon, 2011).

Key article

Bottoms, Stephen, 'Authorising the Audience: The Conceptual Drama of Tim Crouch', *Performance Research*, 14.1 (2009), 67.

Recommended books and articles

Bottoms, Stephen, 'Introduction: Tim Crouch, the Author, and the Audience', *Contemporary Theatre Review*, 21 (2011), 390–3.

— 'A Conversation About Dialogue', *Contemporary Theatre Review*, 21 (2011), 423–30.

— 'Materialising the Audience: Tim Crouch's Sight Specifics in *England* and *The Author*', *Contemporary Theatre Review*, 21 (2011), 445–63.

Crouch, Tim, '*The Author* - Response and Responsibility', *Contemporary Theatre Review*, 21 (2011), 416–22.

Freshwater, Helen, 'The Author: Tim Crouch in Conversation with Helen Freshwater', *Performing Ethos*, 1 (2010), 181–95.

— '"You Say Something": Audience Participation and *The Author*', *Contemporary Theatre Review*, 21 (2011), 405–9.

Goode, Chris, 'The Audience Is Listening', *Contemporary Theatre Review*, 21 (2011), 464–71.

Iball, Helen, 'A Mouth to Feed Me: Reflections Inspired by the Poster for Tim Crouch's *The Author*', *Contemporary Theatre Review*, 21 (2011), 431–44.

Ilter, Seda, '"A Process of Transformation": Tim Crouch on *My Arm*', *Contemporary Theatre Review*, 21 (2011), 394–404.

'Interview: Tim Crouch – Theatre Director', in the *Scotsman* (Edinburgh, 2010).

LePage, Louise and Dan Rebellato, 'Tim Crouch and Dan Rebellato in Conversation', *Platform: Postgraduate eJournal of Theatre & Performing Arts*, 6 (2012), 13–27.

O'Kane, Patrick, (ed.), *Actors' Voices: The People Behind the Performances* (London: Oberon, 2012), pp. 88–115.

smith, a, 'Gentle Acts of Removal, Replacement and Reduction: Considering the Audience in Co-Directing the Work of Tim Crouch', *Contemporary Theatre Review*, 21 (2011), 410–15.

Roy Williams

Plays

Williams, Roy, *Plays: 2* (London: Methuen, 2004).

— *Plays: 3* (London: Methuen Drama, 2008).

Key book

Osborne, Dierdre, 'Roy Williams', in *The Methuen Drama Guide to Contemporary British Playwrights*, ed. Martin Middeke, Peter Paul Schnierer and Aleks Sierz (London: Methuen Drama, 2011), pp. 487–509.

Recommended books and articles

Barry, Elizabeth and William Boles, 'Beyond Victimhood: Agency and Identity in the Theatre of Roy Williams', in *Alternatives within the Mainstream: British Black and Asian Theatre*, ed. Dimple Godiwala (Newcastle: Cambridge Scholars, 2006), pp. 297–313.

Derbyshire, Harry, 'Roy Williams: Representing Multicultural Britain in *Fallout*', *Modern Drama*, 50 (2007), 414–34.

Dorney, Kate, *The Changing Language of Modern English Drama 1945–2005* (Basingstoke: Palgrave Macmillan, 2009), pp. 215–19.

Goddard, Lynette, Introduction, *The Methuen Drama Book of Plays by Black British Writers* (London: Methuen Drama, 2011), pp. vii–xxvi.

Kritzer, Amelia Howe, *Political Theatre in Post-Thatcher Britain – New Writing: 1995–2005, Performance Interventions* (Basingstoke: Palgrave Macmillan, 2008).

Osborne, Dierdre, 'The State of the Nation: Contemporary Black British Theatre and the Staging of the UK', in *Staging Displacement, Exile and Diaspora*, ed. Christoph Houswitschka and Anja Müller (Trier: Wissenschafticher, 2005), pp. 129–49.

— '"I Ain't British Though / Yes You Are. You're as English as I Am": Staging Belonging and Unbelonging in Black British Drama Today', in *Hybrid Cultures – Nervous States: Britain and Germany in a (Post)Colonial World*, ed. Ulrike Lindner, Maren Möhring, Mark Stein and Silke Stroh (Amsterdam: Rodopi, 2010), pp. 203–27.

Peacock, D. Keith, 'The Question of Multiculturalism: The Plays of Roy Williams', in *A Companion to Modern British and Irish Drama 1880–2005*, ed. Mary Luckhurst (Oxford: Blackwell, 2006), pp. 530–40.

— 'Black British Drama and the Politics of Identity', in *A Concise Companion to Contemporary British and Irish Drama*, ed. Nadine Holdsworth and Mary Luckhurst (Oxford: Blackwell, 2008), pp. 48–65.

Reinelt, Janelle, 'Selective Affinities: British Playwrights at Work', *Modern Drama*, 50 (2007), 305–45.

Williams, Roy, 'In Conversation with Aleks Sierz', *New Theatre Quarterly*, 22 (2006), 113–21.

David Greig

Plays

David Greig, *San Diego* (London: Faber and Faber, 2003).

— *The American Pilot* (London: Faber and Faber, 2005).

— *Damascus* (London: Faber & Faber, 2007).

Key book

Wallace, Clare, *The Theatre of David Greig* (London: Methuen Drama, 2013).

Recommended books and articles

Billingham, Peter, *At the Sharp End* (London: Methuen Drama, 2007), pp. 72–123.

Eatough, Graham and Dan Rebellato, (eds), *The Suspect Culture Book* (London: Oberon, 2013).

Greig, David, 'Plays on Politics', in *State of Plays*, ed. David Edgar (London: Faber & Faber, 1999), pp. 66–70.

— 'Doing a Geographical', *Contemporary Theatre Review*, 16 (2006), 160–4.

— 'Rough Theatre', in *Cool Britannia? British Political Drama in the 1990s*, ed. Rebecca D'Monté and Graham Saunders (Basingstoke: Palgrave, 2008), pp. 208–21.

Holdsworth, Nadine, 'Travelling across Borders: Re-Imagining the Nation and Nationalism in Contemporary Scottish Theatre', *Contemporary Theatre Review* 13.2 (2003), pp. 25–39.

— 'The Landscape of Contemporary Scottish Identity: Place, Politics and Identity', in *A Concise Companion to British and Irish Drama*, ed. Nadine Holdsworth and Mary Luckhurst (Oxford: Blackwell, 2008), pp. 125–45.

Müller, Anja. '"We are also Europe": Staging Displacement in David Greig's Plays', *Staging Displacement, Exile and Diaspora*, ed. Christoph Houswitschka and Anja Müller (Trier: Wissenschafticher, 2005), pp. 151–68.

Müller, Anja and Clare Wallace, (eds), *Cosmotopia: Transnational Identities in David Greig's Theatre* (Prague: Litteraria Pragensia, 2011).

Nesteruk, Peter, 'Ritual, Sacrifice, and Identity in Recent Political Drama – with Reference to the Plays of David Greig', *Journal of Dramatic Theory and Criticism*, xv (2000), 21–42.

Rebellato, Dan, '"And I Will Reach out My Hand with a Kind of Infinite Slowness and Say the Perfect Thing": The Utopian Theatre of Suspect Culture', *Contemporary Theatre Review*, xiii (2003), 61–80.

— 'Introduction', in: David Greig, *Plays One* (London: Methuen Drama, 2002), pp. ix–xxiii.

— 'Gestes d'Utopie: Le Théâtre De David Greig', in *Dramaturgies Britanniques (1980–2000)*, ed. Jean-Marc Lanteri (Paris-Caen: Lettres Modernes Minard, 2002), pp. 125–48.

Reid, Trish, 'Post-Devolutionary Drama', in *The Edinburgh Companion to Scottish Drama*, ed. Ian Brown (Edinburgh: Edinburgh University Press, 2011), pp. 188–99.

Reinelt, Janelle, 'Performing Europe: Identity Formation for a "New" Europe', *Theatre Journal*, liii (2001), 365–87.

— 'David Greig', in *The Methuen Drama Guide to Contemporary British Playwrights*, ed. Martin Middeke, Peter Paul Schnierer and Aleks Sierz (London: Methuen Drama, 2011), pp. 203–22.

Scullion, Adrienne, 'Devolution and Drama: Imagining the Possible', in *The Edinburgh Companion to Contemporary Scottish Literature*, ed. Berthold Schoene (Edinburgh: Edinburgh University Press, 2007), pp. 68–77.

Wright, Isabel, 'Working in Partnership: David Greig in Conversation with Isabel Wright', in *Trans-Global Readings: Crossing Theatrical Boundaries*, ed. Caridad Svich (Manchester: Manchester University Press, 2003), pp. 157–67.

debbie tucker green

Plays

green, debbie tucker, *dirty butterfly* (London: Nick Hern, 2003).

— *stoning mary* (London: Nick Hern, 2005).

— *random* (London: Nick Hern, 2008).

Key book

Aston, Elaine, 'debbie tucker green', in *The Methuen Drama Guide to Contemporary British Playwrights*, ed. Martin Middeke, Peter Paul Schnierer and Aleks Sierz (London: Methuen Drama, 2011), pp. 183–202.

Recommended books and articles

Aston, Elaine, 'A Fair Trade? Staging Female Sex Tourism in *Sugar Mummies* and *Trade*', *Contemporary Theatre Review*, 18 (2008), 180–92.

— 'Feeling the Loss of Feminism: Sarah Kane's *Blasted* and an Experiential Genealogy of Contemporary Women's Playwriting', *Theatre Journal*, 62 (2010), 575–91.

Dierdre Osborne, 'Not "In-Yer-Face" but What Lies Beneath: Experiential and Aesthetic Inroads in the Drama of Debbie Tucker Green and Dona Daley', in *'Black' British Aesthetics Today*, ed. R. Victoria Arana (Cambridge Scholars: Newcastle, 2007), pp. 222–42.

Gardner, Lyn, '"I Was Messing About"', in *guardian.co.uk*, the *Guardian*, 2005.

Goddard, Lynette, 'New Theatre Writing: Debbie Tucker Green', *Contemporary Theatre Review*, 15 (2005), 376–81.

— *Staging Black Feminisms: Identity, Politics, Performances* (Basingstoke: Palgrave, 2007), pp. 181–97.

— '"Death Never Used to Be for the Young": Grieving Teenage Murder in Debbie Tucker Green's *Random*', *Women: A Cultural Review*, 20 (2009), 299–309.

5. Web resources

TheatreVOICE www.theatrevoice.com
A collection of exclusive interviews with playwrights, directors, critics and more about all aspects of British theatre, set up by Dominic Cavendish in April 2003. The site now has well over 1,000 interviews available to stream or download.

Guardian stage www.guardian.co.uk/stage
Updated every day, the Guardian's stage website has been an engaging, infuriating, eccentric and sometimes essential forum for debating developments in theatre. The site has been active right through the decade.

The 2000s was, in some ways, the decade of the blog, and some of the key discussions happened on blogs. Blogs came and went and more will have come and gone by the time you read this but the following were always engaging:

Carousel of fantasies http://carouseloffantasies.blogspot.co.uk/
Critic Matt Trueman's blog, collecting reviews and comments on theatre.

Encore theatre magazine http://encoretheatremagazine.blogspot.co.uk/
Punchy and opinionated blog by a group of anonymous theatremakers.

In yer face theatre www.inyerface-theatre.com/
Pirate dog www.sierz.blogspot.co.uk/
Two websites both run by Aleks Sierz gathering reviews, articles and other resources.

Interval drinks www.intervaldrinks.blogspot.co.uk/
Natasha Tripney's blog collecting reviews and comments on theatre.

Postcards from the Gods http://postcardsgods.blogspot.co.uk/
Reviews and thoughts on theatre by Andrew Haydon.

Shenton's view. http://blogs.thestage.co.uk/shenton/
Opinion pieces by the *Stage*'s indefatigable chief critic, Mark Shenton.

Thompson's bank of communicable desire http://beescope.blogspot.co.uk/
Never less than astonishing thoughts on theatre, poetry and art by Chris Goode.

View from the stalls www.viewfromthestalls.co.uk/
Reviews of Scottish theatre.

West End Whingers http://westendwhingers.wordpress.com/
Candid, catty and comic reviews by avid London theatregoers.

A younger theatre www.ayoungertheatre.com/
A reviewing website with a conscious desire to get a younger generational perspective.

NOTES ON CONTRIBUTORS

Jacqueline Bolton is Lecturer in Drama and Theatre at the University of Lincoln. Her research interests include dramaturgy, new writing and British fringe theatre of the 1970s and 1980s. She has written for the journal *Studies in Theatre and Performance*, is the editor of the Methuen Drama Student Edition of *Pornography* by Simon Stephens and author of 'Joint Stock' in *British Theatre Companies: From Fringe to Mainstream Volume II*, ed. John Bull and Graham Saunders (London: Bloomsbury Methuen Drama, forthcoming).

Lynette Goddard is Senior Lecturer in the Department of Drama and Theatre, Royal Holloway, University of London. Her research focuses on contemporary black British theatre, looking in particular at new writing by black playwrights and black productions and adaptations of Shakespeare and other canonical plays. Her publications include journal articles and chapters in *Contemporary Theatre Review*, and *Women: A Cultural Review*, and the monograph *Staging Black Feminisms: Identity, Politics, Performance* (Hampshire: Palgrave, 2007).

Andrew Haydon is a theatre critic and blogger who divides his time between London and Germany. He previously worked as a freelance UK theatre critic (*FT, Guardian, Time Out*) and was the editor of the CultureWars theatre section between 2000 and 2010. He is the editor of *Raw Talent: Fifty Years of the National Student Drama Festival* (London: Oberon Books, 2005). His blog can be found at http://postcardsgods.blogspot.co.uk/

Nadine Holdsworth is Professor of Theatre and Performance Studies at the University of Warwick. She has published widely on twentieth- and twenty-first-century British theatre and is the author of *Joan Littlewood's Theatre, Theatre & Nation* and *Joan Littlewood*. She also edited John McGrath's collected writings on theatre, *Naked Thoughts That Roam About* and his *Plays for England*.

Michael Pearce is a PhD student at the University of Exeter. His PhD research examines black British theatre since the 1950s through a transnational lens, paying particular attention to the reciprocal relationship between British and African American, Caribbean and African theatrical contexts for these writers' work. He is currently working with the National Theatre on their 'Black Plays Archive' project, and is also a theatre producer and director who works between the United Kingdom and his native Zimbabwe.

INDEX